IT'S TURNED OUT NICE AGAIN!

The authorized biography of the two
George Formbys, father and son

Sue Smart and

Richard Bothway Howard

Published by

MELROSE BOOKS

An Imprint of Melrose Press Limited
St Thomas Place, Ely
Cambridgeshire
CB7 4GG, UK
www.melrosebooks.com

SECOND EDITION, 2011
First published by Melrose Books, 2011

Cover designed by Tanya Fukes

ISBN 978 1 908645 12 8

Printed and bound in Great Britain by:
CPI Group (UK) Ltd, Croydon, CR0 4YY

FSC
www.fsc.org
MIX
Paper from
responsible sources
FSC® C013604

For Edward ('Teddy for short') and Winifred Formby Booth,
Alan, David and Jacqueline,
and all the Formby family

CONTENTS

ACKNOWLEDGEMENTS AND SOURCES

This book would not have been possible without the generosity of the late Edward Formby in sharing the Formby family archive with us. He gave us hours of his time, explaining the significance of the material he had and giving us a vivid picture of his early family life and of his famous brother. It is a great sadness that he did not live to see in print the story he enabled us to tell. We have benefited enormously from the hospitality of Ted and his wife Win, and from their openness in sharing their memories of George and Beryl, Eliza, Frank and the Formby sisters. We are also most grateful to Win, who gave us permission to publish, and to her elder son Alan for his enthusiastic belief in the project and for making it happen.

We have also drawn on several private collections, most notably the Norman Collection. These have yielded a wealth of contemporary newspaper and magazine reports, photographs, posters, records, playbills, recordings of interviews and other memorabilia. George's films and newsreel footage have also proved invaluable sources.

A great debt of thanks is due to members of the George Formby Society, past and present, who have helped us with material, spent time discussing issues with us and corrected our mistakes where they could. Back copies of The Vellum were indispensable in providing information. We acknowledge our debt to the work of Eleanor Knowles Dugan in her series of articles on George's Leading Ladies published in that magazine. Andy Eastwood, Stan Evans, Neil Forshaw, Graham Greenfield, Gerry Mawdsley, Peter Pollard, Reg Thacker and John Walley have all shared their knowledge and wisdom and saved us from some gaffes.

At the eleventh hour Michael Daly tracked us down in the wake of the launch of his brilliant website, www.georgeformby.org in March. He could have been a rival, but from the beginning he was a friend. In the interests of making this book as comprehensive and insightful as possible he has trusted us with transcripts of tape recordings made by his late father Kevin, a Decca record producer and George Formby aficionado, and Rex Blaker in the 1960s. We recognize the great compliment he has paid us in sharing this material and his ideas about it. Kevin and Rex spent hours searching out relatives, friends and colleagues of the Formby family and interviewing them. Had they written their projected biography this one would probably never have appeared, as their research was meticulous. Michael's generosity has allowed us to bring Eliza Booth's unique contribution to the book and enriched it immeasurably. To see her story in her own words was for us the last piece of the jigsaw, though not the last piece of the puzzle. Mysteries still remain. We feel enormously privileged to have been able to use this source – with no strings attached – and thank Michael for permission to use information on his website. He has also saved us from a number of errors. The mistakes and omissions that remain are, of course, our own.

In the chapters about George's films we acknowledge a considerable debt to Professor Jeffrey Richards of the University of Lancaster. We have leaned heavily on his definitive work. We have also quoted briefly from John Fisher's excellent biography George Formby (1975).

We thank the following people from Norfolk who spared time to share their memories: Geoff Allen, June and Julian Barclay, Margaret Bird, Mr and Mrs David Boag, Maurice Bunting, Jamie Campbell, Peter Canfor, Arthur Castle, Beryl Clark, Sam Cooke, Pooh Curtis, James Hipwell, Anthony Ives, Peter Jay, the late Clive Manson, Michael McKee, James Oxley-Brennan, Joan Ray, Angela Sims, Peter Suckling and Roger Talbot. Roys of Wroxham and Herbert Woods also helped. We are very grateful to Hazel Dormer for her great cartoons of Potter Heigham. R. H. Banger and Audrey Pawson have contributed in a similar way.

Dick Meadows has been a constant source of encouragement and support; in particular writing an article in the Eastern Daily Press about George junior in Norfolk. The Prioress of the Carmelite Nunnery of Up Holland kindly wrote to tell us about Patricia Howson and her legacy. Sue Clayton was most helpful about Myles Hildyard. Daniel Wiles, the television producer, and

Martyn Randall, son of the late Alan Randall, who took up the Formby mantle in the 1970s and 1980s and kept George's name in the public domain, also played their part.

We are grateful for the help of Jack Bamford, Mr and Mrs Edward Evans, David Kenten and Matthew Sutton.

For information about George's boats we gratefully acknowledge the help of John Crevald, Mrs A. Mackintosh, Eunice Ryan and Kevin Shadbolt.

We were also greatly helped by the staff of the Houghton Library, Harvard University, Cambridge, Massachusetts, where the booking records of the Argyle Theatre, Birkenhead, are kept, and the archivists in the Norfolk, Lancashire and Tameside Record Offices where we researched George's boats, the Preston Calendar of Prisoners and the *Ashton Reporter* respectively. We also consulted the Royal Archive, Windsor, the Great Yarmouth *Mercury*, the *King's Lynn News*, the East Anglian Film Archive, the ITN Archive and the Great Yarmouth Library. We thank Joy Wright at the *Eastern Daily Press*, Simon Temlett of *The Gramophone*, Paul Damen Photography, Glen Carr of Jetprint, Erpingham, Norfolk, R. S. Orr Sound Services and Paul Lilley of the EMI Archive for their time and expertise.

Christopher Schofield, and his colleagues at *Achievements*, Canterbury, provided us with vital evidence. We also acknowledge the help of the Horse Racing Museum, Newmarket, Caroline Jarrold at Jarrold's Archive, Jim Bacon of Weatherquest and The Veteran Car Club of Great Britain.

Our publishers, Melrose Books, Ely, have been both supportive and patient in dealing with last-minute amendments and additions. Our thanks go to them.

Lastly we thank our partners and families for their forbearance and support over the book's long gestation.

Sue Smart
Richard Bothway Howard
May 2011

ADDITIONAL SOURCES

Aldgate, Anthony, and Richards, Jeffrey, *Britain Can Take It: British Films and the Second World War* (1994)

Bailey, A., & Foss, P., eds., *George Formby Complete* (1972)

Bret, David, *George Formby: A Troubled Genius* (2001)

Dean, Basil, *Mind's Eye: An autobiography 1927–1972* (1973)

Dean, Basil, *The Theatre at War* (1956)

Fawkes, Richard, *Fighting for a Laugh* (1978)

Fisher, John, *Funny Way to be a Hero* (1973)

Fisher, John, *George Formby* (1975)

Lee, C. P., *Frank Randle and Mancunian Films* (1996)

Leigh, Spencer, *This Record Is Not to Be Broadcast* (2008)

Miller, Russell, Lowe, Jacques, & Boar, Roger, *The Incredible Music Machine* (1982)

Randall, Alan, and Seaton, Ray, *George Formby: A Biography* (1974)

Richards, Jeffrey, and Sheridan, Dorothy, eds., *Mass Observation at the Movies* (1987)

Richards, Jeffrey, *Films and British National Identity* (1997)

Ryan, Brendan, *George Formby: A Catalogue of His Work* (1986)

Waterworth, Alan, *Going to the Flicks* (1990)

Williams, Ned, *Cinemas of Aldridge and Brownhills* (1984)

Williams, Philip and David, *Hooray for Jollywood* (2001)

ancestry.co.uk

findmypast.co.uk

georgeformby.co.uk

itsahotun.com/Frankrandle.html (accessed 30 March 2011)

NOTES

We thought it useful to give an indication of modern money values in key places. They are shown in brackets. This is a complicated matter, but we have relied on the website measuringworth.com and used its Retail Price Index figures.

For the capitalisation of words in song titles and films we have followed the guidance in the *Oxford Manual of Style* (2002).

★ ★ ★

Every effort has been made to trace copyright holders of the photographs printed in this book in order to seek permission to print. The authors would nevertheless be very happy to hear from any copyright holders they were unable to contact.

CHAPTER ONE

The Road to Wigan Pier

A crowd of thousands, controlled by police, thronged the pavements of Knutsford Road, Bridge Street and Buttermarket Street in Warrington, the men standing respectfully bareheaded as the cortège passed by. Six funeral coaches bore the chief mourners to Our Lady's Church, Latchford, where the body had lain since Thursday evening, and two open landaus carried dozens of wreaths. On Shrove Tuesday, 8 February 1921 James Booth, otherwise known as George Formby, 'Lancashire's Own Comedian', had died, aged forty-five. The chief mourners were his widow, Eliza, and three of his children, George, only sixteen years old, Louisa fourteen, and Frank aged eight.

Above: George Formby senior, 1913
Right: Eliza

1

The funeral service was a Solemn Gregorian Requiem Mass, following the rite of James's adopted faith, Roman Catholicism. A male voice choir, two soloists and three clergymen were in attendance, and Handel's Dead March from *Saul* was played as the cortège left the church. Afterwards, according to the custom of the time, a group of the men followed the coffin to the Manchester Road Catholic cemetery. Eliza, Louisa and Mrs Hoy, Eliza's mother, stayed behind, but a crowd of over one thousand saw the coffin, bearing its cross of white lilies from the family, lowered into the ground. The family flowers carried the message: 'To our most precious darling who is sadly missed.' The music hall stars Sir Harry Lauder and Florrie Forde sent telegrams. Lauder's, accompanied by red roses, read: 'Accept my deepest sympathy. A good clean star has ceased to twinkle in our firmament.' Florrie Forde wrote: 'Accept my deepest sympathy. Am very grieved but God knows best. Cheer up and God bless you.' Both messages were matter-of-fact, clipped, in the usual style of telegrams, for which each word was charged. Fred 'Jester' Barnes, principal boy in many pantomimes, wrote from Glasgow: 'God bless you all in your trouble, my old pal at peace now.' John Tiller, in whose pantomime George was appearing just before he died, wrote to Eliza: 'I cannot tell you how I feel about poor George leaving us. I really did not think he would go so suddenly although I felt he was very ill. I cannot realise it even now. It seems a shame – there were thousands of others that could have been better spared. He harmed no-one.' The overwhelming number of wreaths – almost 200 – letters and telegrams sent to his widow reveal a man admired for his bravery, his talent and his devotion to his home and family. One friend, Mark Abrahams, a jeweller of Newcastle-on-Tyne, wrote: 'The "Paper Boys" are shouting the sad news of poor George. It's just a week today since I was with you both in the dressing room – How sad. I cannot find words to express my sympathy after all our years of friendship; one consolation you have. He was loved and respected by everyone & a name of Gold.'

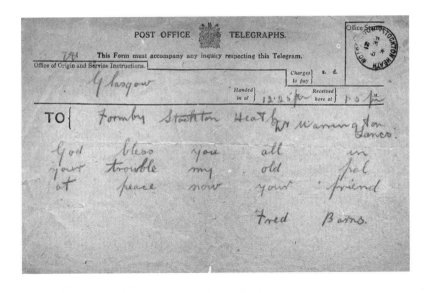

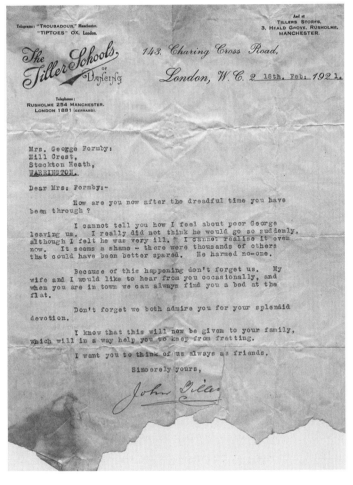

Above: Telegram
from Formby
senior's colleague,
Fred Barnes

Left: Letter
from John Tiller,
founder of the
Tiller School of
Dance

James Booth's life was a story of rags to riches, but myth and truth have always been deeply entangled. His beginnings were undoubtedly hard and bleak. As an adult he commented that his 'childhood was the most miserable as ever fell to the lot of a human creature', though apparently he enjoyed telling the saga of his early life. He cast himself as the hero and victorious survivor. He was born on 4 October 1875 at 26 Hodgson Street, Ashton under Lyne, near Manchester, the illegitimate son and only child of eighteen-year-old Sarah Jane Booth, a cotton weaver. His birth was registered by Sarah herself, and she did not name his father. Previous biographers have said that this was a man who 'passed in the night' and that James scarcely knew him. They have described him as an 'occasional foster father' named Frank Lawler, a collier, who married Sarah Jane when James was six months old. Many years later James told his daughter Ella that Sarah was 'a happy person who loved to sing'. Said to be only four feet one inch tall, Sarah did most of her singing in the evenings at her local pub in return for drinks, until all too often she became drunk and disorderly. The police would be called, she would be carted off to the local police station and locked up overnight to sleep it off. It has been claimed that she had over one hundred convictions for drunkenness, prostitution and a range of other misdemeanours. James, meanwhile, finding himself locked out of the house, had to doss down at a neighbour's house or in the outside privy – or so he told his children George and Ella. James's childhood was certainly comfortless. Perhaps his chest complaints, variously described as bronchitis, asthma and tuberculosis, arose from this period of neglect.

Many years later, James, or George as he was known by then, told a newspaper reporter: 'Unfortunately my parents allowed me to go my own way. When I could be "kidded" to go to school I showed no sign of brilliance, and at the age of eight or nine left altogether, having reached that high position of bottom boy in the second standard. I joined a gang of young bandits whom we styled "the lads" and I became their ringleader.' He claimed that he had run away from home for good at the age of nine, in 1884, and that possessed of his mother's ability to sing, he scraped out an existence by singing on the streets, though he told a reporter, in an article in *The Recorder* published after his death, that his first job was selling newspapers, at a street corner. At that time a penny would buy a bloater, so he could get by, though he said he was often hungry. One of his companions augmented his income by singing. 'As his business improved he urged me to join him occasionally to do what we called the knobbing (or knocking at the doors for money).' Sometimes they were given bread or a 'dish of tea' or even a pair of old boots. He was at pains to stress that he 'never descended to pilfering of even the pettiest description'. As they went on their singing began to harmonise better, and on a fair day they could take as much as five shillings. From the streets, he said, they graduated to performing in the backs of rough alehouses, pubs and 'free and easies', which had developed out of sing-songs in eighteenth-century taverns. This seems to be his version of his time with the Brothers Glenray.

Another was that as a young teenager he joined Cyrus Bell's Minstrel Troupe who worked on the Blackpool sands. Shortly afterwards he met Barney Parsons and acted as his feed in the act – not only duettists but also dancers – known as the Songbirds of the Music Halls. The two boys were managed by a Mr Brown, who reputedly paid James, the soprano, only half what he paid the other boy – the princely sum of threepence. 'My partner had a pretty good voice. I did my best in sentimental songs,' James recalled years later. 'One was "Remember I'm His Mother", a real tear drawer.' When he was seventeen his voice broke and, 'I was compelled to return to work.' As a boy he said he had at times travelled far from home. His first regular work had been in a West Yorkshire cotton mill in Todmorden, nineteen miles away from Ashton. At the age of twelve, he said, he was apprenticed as a blacksmith's striker in a Manchester firm of iron founders, but the sulphur fumes further affected his already fragile health and he had to leave. At this time, he described himself as 'very miserable to all accounts', as he was alone in the world. After the Brothers Glenray folded he had to knuckle down. 'I didn't like it but I managed to get a job in a loom factory at first and then in a bakehouse where I had to turn up at four o'clock in the morning in order to get dough ready for the other men who came on at six. That was at Nelson, and as I was living in Burnley I did the three miles' tramp every morning. My wages were eighteen shillings a week.'

Some parts of this story are true, but others are not. Certainly Sarah Jane and Frank Lawler married, on Sunday (their only day of rest), 23 April 1876, in their local parish church, St Peter's. Frank was only nineteen,

Sarah about the same age. She made her mark rather than signing the register, although Frank wrote his name. The marriage was witnessed by William Booth, Sarah's older brother. Frank's father, named on the certificate, was a watchman in an ironworks and Sarah's, named James, was a weaver. Frank and Sarah had both been cotton mill workers in their early teens and lived only a few streets apart. It seems likely that they had been boy- and girlfriend and that they married as soon as they could, supported by their families. There was no reason for Frank to marry Sarah unless he believed James was his son. Nor did he desert her. By 1881 the census shows the young family of three living together at 106 Hill Street under the name of Lawler, the only family at that address, James by now aged five and a half. But this was a far from happy outcome: he told his wife Eliza that 'his father and mother used to fight', and that:

> When he was a boy four years old, his father was drunk, his mother was drunk. They lived in a small house – they'd only a kitchen and a pantry and two bedrooms – and he was that frightened, he heard them carolling and grumbling to one another, that he got in the top of one of the old kitchen cupboards they had and slept there the night, till morning, and they never missed him.

James spoke in 1910 about his parents and his schooling, but little is known about the period between 1884 and 1892, after the time when he said he had run away from home. The record, however, does reveal one or two important details. Sarah did not have 'over a hundred convictions', but she was certainly not law-abiding. In February 1889 she got a prison sentence of three months' hard labour at Manchester Assizes for housebreaking and stealing a blanket and a sheet from her neighbour. The *Ashton Reporter* gave more details. 'James Lawler, 13, said the prisoner was his mother, and she sent him to pawn the blanket at Gee's and the sheet at Sutcliffe's.' If he had run away it was not for ever. By this time Sarah's husband must have been very ill and possibly no longer working. Frank was still living near at hand, though, in Hill Street, at number 94, and, while he could, working as an iron dresser. This was the address given when he died on 22 October 1890, aged only thirty-three, of pulmonary tuberculosis. The fact that James had shared a small terraced house with a man whose tuberculosis was so severe that he died in his early thirties might explain a great deal about his own illness. James certainly knew some of his relatives, and there were a number of them. His mother Sarah had three older siblings, and Frank had three sisters and three brothers. Eliza described their early marriage. 'In the evenings we would sit in our armchairs and he would relate his young life.' He told her he had stayed at the house of two cousins, Sarah and Clara, when they went off in the mornings to work in the factory. His father's death was registered by an older brother, another James.

The 1891 census, taken on 5 April, shows that the widowed Sarah Jane was struggling. By this time she was living with about forty others in a 'common lodging house' at 104 Crickets Lane. This sort of cheap accommodation for the very poor was attracting national attention at that time as the victims of Jack the Ripper between 1888 and 1891 inhabited similar dosshouses in Whitechapel. Sarah Jane's occupation was given as 'domestic servant, general'. The name following hers on the list is that of her fifteen-year-old son, still with his mother. 'James Lawler' had no occupation written next to his name. Presumably he was singing for pennies. Both their ages are inaccurate: James was recorded as having been fourteen last birthday although he had been fifteen, and Sarah Jane thirty, although she was thirty-two or -three. They must have been desperate for money, however it was come by. By 1895 Sarah was stealing again, and there began a depressing list of petty thefts followed by a month or two of hard labour. The account of the Ashton Borough Police Court in November 1896 shows that Sarah was living in 'furnished rooms' and pinching the quilt off her bed to pawn. She was lent one shilling on it. But amid the gloom Sarah Jane could make the magistrates and the court laugh. 'Prisoner told the magistrates she did "nothing" for a living. [Laughter] Mr Boulton – It seems to agree with you very well. – More laughter… Committed to gaol for a month of hard labour. Prisoner: Thank you.' Sarah was never one for brawling or resisting arrest, and she always pleaded guilty.

Between 1901 and 1904 Sarah was imprisoned four times for larceny. In 1901 she had also thirteen charges of drunkenness and 'importuning passengers' on her record. Matters were becoming serious as the authorities tired of her persistent lawbreaking. By now in her early forties and described in the Calendars of Prisoners as a 'hawker', she was receiving sentences of six and twelve months' hard labour for the pettiest of thefts. She usually stole from a woman or women then took her pathetic loot to a pawnbroker. Only alcoholism or extreme poverty could have motivated her. It was prison or the workhouse. By 1908 she had eleven charges of theft against her, and a greater number of misdemeanours on her record. The local police told magistrates that she had made thirty appearances before them and there were one or two more outside Ashton, but she simply did not have enough time at liberty to clock up another sixty. The record as it stood was bad enough. Few recidivists in Ashton were as determined as Sarah. The court report of November 1906 shows the sad predicament she was in.

> LAWLESS LAWLER PUNISHED. Sarah Lawler completed her thirtieth appearance in the dock on a charge of being drunk and disorderly in Coalpit-lane on 28 October. Constable Harris said she was using very filthy language. She was bound over for six months in sureties of £20 in herself and two other sureties of £20 each. In default, six months imprisonment.

As the sureties were nonsensical for a person in her situation, it was, of course, to prison that she eventually went.

Sarah Jane died in 1912 aged fifty-five (her age given as fifty-two), in the hospital attached to the Union workhouse. Although an address for her was given, 39 York Street, the 1911 census taken in April lists her as a patient at that time, over eighteen months before she died. She must have been in and out of hospital and her occupation, 'cotton frame tenter', surely by now a fiction. A new infirmary had been built in 1906, so the conditions might have been a little better and the care more professional than the grim words 'workhouse hospital' suggest. George junior's sister Ella recalled that, 'My mother met her once. My father got a letter to say his mother was dying. He didn't want to go and see her but my mother insisted. She was a small woman with long straight blonde hair. She looked like Louie

[Ella's elder sister]. She was in a hospital for people who don't have anything.' Eliza's account gives much more moving detail. She described a man who made several attempts to meet her.

When we were at the Ardwick Empire, he came round to the stage door to see me. George was very busy that night, he couldn't see George, but he made arrangements for me to meet him the following week. He didn't give me his business or anything about him, and I said I would, if I was home the following week, which was very likely, due to the negotiations about the house. [They were thinking of moving to Hindley House at the time.]

So I met this gentleman. Went to the Continental [restaurant] and over a cup of tea he said, 'I don't know if you've ever met George's mother?'

I said, 'I have never actually met her, but when we were away and lived in Dicconson Street she once came, and my mother was home and met her. And naturally as us not being home [sic] my mother didn't ask her in, not knowing who she was. She didn't say she was George's mother.'

'Well,' he said, 'she's a very sick woman, Mrs Formby, and I know she won't give away who her son is, but I've heard from Ashton under Lyne that it is George Formby. I wanted to know if that was the truth.' Some of George's relatives must have told him.

[He told Eliza that she had] 'A cancer and isn't long to be with us at all.'

I said, 'I will make all attempts to meet her, but on condition, until things pan out, you don't tell her who I am. Give me your number and I will ring up to make an appointment to meet you. But I shall not tell my husband that I am doing it. I shall do it when I'm at home on my own.'

So the opportunity came... I had a nice little grey costume on, nice little smart hat, scarlet with a blue feather at the side.

So I went down and he arranged to meet me, at the gates of Ashton under Lyne Workhouse! I met him and he told me more about her condition. 'Could she be moved?' I said.

'It's an impossibility,' he said.

It was agreed that Eliza would pose as an official workhouse visitor, and in this role she approached the bed. Sarah was, she said:

> Only about five foot high, a little thin person, so I got up to the bed, sat down and said, 'Good afternoon, I've come to see you.'
>
> She said, 'Oh! That's very nice.'
>
> And we shook hands, and I bent over her to look at her and talk to her and said, 'You're very poorly. Have you been here long?'
>
> 'Off and on, but this time about three months.'
>
> 'Where do you live?'
>
> 'Well,' she said, 'unfortunately I've got to live in the best place I can, I've got no stated home.' I asked if she had a family. She said, 'Yes, I have one, a son.'
>
> 'Has he been to see you?'
>
> 'No,' she said. 'He doesn't know me, he doesn't come here.'
>
> I said… 'Would you like him to come to see you?'
>
> 'Oh,' she said, 'he's a big man; he wouldn't come to see me.'
>
> I said, 'You don't know, you never know.'

Eliza offered to give the institution £2 (£147) a week, for some delicacies for the sick woman, and told Sarah:

> 'I will promise you faithfully at the first opportunity I will come and see you again.'
>
> She said, 'That's very nice of you.' And I bent over to her and I put my arms around her and I kissed her, and she was very, very undone. She looked me up and down and her hand trembled.

A month later Eliza visited again.

I took Louie and naturally I knew which was her bed. I said, 'I've brought my little daughter to see you.' And she looked at her, because she's the image of her father. She had lovely light hair, and had the uniform of Notre Dame [a private Catholic school], Wigan.

Louie said, 'I have brought you a nice parcel.' She took her sweets, chocolate biscuits and she put a half-crown in her purse which lay on top of the cubby-hole next to the bed. She said, 'That's my pocket-money, and Mother said I must give it to you.'

'Oh no!' she said.

'Yes, I want to give it to you.' And she shook hands with her. We weren't there long, she kept looking at Louie and asking her about her schooling, and different things like that.

We had to go, and I said to her, 'I don't know when I'll be able to come again, and I have not forgotten your request – as soon as I can I will do it for you.'

She said, 'He won't come.'

'Then I will do my best – I am sure he will come.' Anyway, I said to Louie, 'Shake hands with the lady and kiss her.' I did the same, and we came home.

As I was coming down the stairs, child's curiosity all over, she said, 'Who is that, Mother?'

I said, 'That is your grandmother.'

'No! My grandmother's at home.'

I said, 'This is your father's mother, Louie, but I want you to tell nobody that we have seen her.'

In October Eliza asked George to come with her to see his mother.

And he agreed to come; he put his best suit on to look nice. 'I don't want to go you know, I'm going to suit you.' And poor George was feeling very, very sad; it had upset him dreadfully

11

to oblige me. He got up and went to the side of the bed, and with the other men being with him, she thought he was a young doctor. And she just looked at him and then turned over on her side, and closed her eyes.

But George sat down on the chair… and he said it took him all the courage under the sun to speak. And all he said to her was, 'Mother.' And that was the finish.

She was broken up, naturally, and George was very cut up and she turned round to him, and she said, 'Jim.'

'Yes, Mother,' he said, 'it's Jim.'

She said, 'Have you seen that lady?'

'Yes,' he said.

'Who is she, and who is that lovely little girl?'

'She is mine.'

'I thought there was something like that. Your wife is a lovely woman, Jim. She's been very kind to me.'

'I know, Mother.' And he held his mother's hand all the time, he never left her, he spent a solid hour with her.

And I patiently waited, and when we were coming out whatever he said to his mother, I never asked him; but he was very cut up, very undone, really, the tears were there, and the pair of them were very touched. And he bent down and kissed her, and hugged her. He never saw her no more. And I went in and she just said, 'Thank you – very much.'

Sarah died on Christmas Eve of cervical cancer, her name registered as Sarah Jane Lawler, though her husband had been dead for twenty-two years. Her body was brought to George's house in Wigan and placed in an undertaker's 'exhibition' coffin, festooned with lace and satin, as the season made arrangements difficult. George's engagement diary shows that he took two nights off from the Tivoli, and Sarah was buried, as she had asked to be, alongside her son's three little daughters.

George's professional engagement diary shows that only once between 1905 and 1912 did he play Ashton under Lyne, in December 1907, in pantomime at the Hippodrome. But Sarah knew that the bill-topping George Formby was her son. Many years later, Ella, a granddaughter she never met, discussed the possibility of writing a play about her father and her brother. 'If I did,' she said, 'I would start it with a young blonde girl singing in a pub.'

CHAPTER TWO

The Man from Lancashire

During the 1890s James began to develop a stage act based on comic songs and a clownish appearance, working the free and easies on Fridays and Saturdays. These were described by Dan Leno, 'the archetype of the modern stand-up comedian', who had also performed in them. The audiences, he recalled, were drunk by six o'clock, and, if they didn't like the act, 'pitiless'. The performer could expect an assortment of missiles, from vegetables to dead rats, to be hurled at him. Not so 'free and easy'. Presumably James, as Leno had done in London, slept at a lodging house or wherever he could.

In 1896 his Assignments Book, with all the agreement letters for songs he had bought pasted into it, scrapbook fashion, shows that he was already, at the age of twenty, buying and collecting songs. Between April and November he bought half-singing rights to five songs – two of them in deals conducted in the Painter's Arms in Old-street, Ashton under Lyne, and another in the Dog and Partridge in nearby Stockport. The first in the book, dated 31 August 1896, is written on the back of a printed 'Memorandum', the letterhead proclaiming that it came from: 'Orrell and Formby, Eccentric Comedians and Burlesque Dancers.' Its subtitle was: 'The Original Madmen. Success everywhere.' He was investing in his stage career and running it as a business.

Already he had taken 'George Formby' as his stage name. 'George' seems to have been a tribute to George Robey, the great music hall comedian and star, who had shown interest in him when he was in the Brothers Glenray. For his surname, the usual story is that he chose the Lancashire place name he had seen on the side of a railway truck, because no one else in the business was called Formby and it would identify him immediately. If that was the case, it worked. Eliza said he chose the name because it 'flowed', and because he bore in mind 'the shorter the name the bigger the letters' on the posters. But Orrell is also a local place name, suggesting that the two men wanted from the beginning to publicise their Lancastrian roots. This distinctive 'northernness' became George's 'unique selling point'.

The following year, 1897, Denis J. (Denny) Clarke, proprietor of the Argyle Theatre, Birkenhead, found George performing in the singing room of the Hen and Chickens, Manchester. That year the young singer acquired rights to another nine songs – one by Ernest Dukinfield, his sometime pianist – and composed another, 'Boogie Boys', himself. His new 'Memo' letter-head, complete with a portrait photograph of him in wing-collared evening dress (and with no mention of Orrell), described him as: 'The Universal Favourite. Eccentric Character Singer comedian. Extra Special.' The image of urbane elegance and sophistication he projected was completely at odds with his beaten-up stage persona and a striking forerunner of his son's equally immaculate theatre appearance three decades later. Clarke offered him £2 a week to sing at his hall, and the two became lifelong friends. Some say that Clarke chose his stage name because at this time the young singer was illiterate. However, several assignment letters are written in a distinctive, artistic, even flowery, hand remarkably similar to the one appearing in his professional engagement diary. His spelling was sometimes inaccurate but his writing hand was mature. Eliza proudly described it as, 'Plain and distinct. Self-taught entirely.'

Who was Orrell?

George Formby senior's writing paper, 1897

The name George Formby first appeared on a playbill in Birkenhead in 1897. Around this time Walford Bodie, 'The Electrical Wizard of the North' and highly successful music hall star, signed George as a comedian in his Royal Magnets show at the Lyceum Theatre, Blackburn, with a forty-week tour to follow. He was offered 30s. a week plus expenses, and this, he said later, 'was my first rise in life'. It was when he was playing the Wigan Empire during that tour in 1898 that George met nineteen-year-old Eliza Ann Hoy. Her mother was employed there as a cashier. It was a tiny place, according to Eliza, with its entrance off the Market Square. She also worked at the Empire as a dressmaker and took the tickets for the dress circle – 'pennies for the gallery', as her son Ted later described it. Formby asked her if she knew where he could find digs. Attracted to him, she gave the address of her parents, who were at that time taking in music hall artists, though her father's main occupation, having been a jockey in earlier life, was as an undertaker's horse breaker. When Formby arrived at 8 Marsh Lane, only a five-minute walk from the Empire, he was met, to his surprise, by Eliza, sporting smudges and a moustache from black-leading the grate. She let him in, put him in the best room and made him a cup of tea. She told him, 'You had better wait and see my father.' George told her, 'I like you. You look smashing. But I don't like your black moustache!' Wiping her face, she replied, 'I like you too. But I don't care much for your flat cap!' George recalled, 'That week I was on a "perhaps" two pounds which turned out to be ten shillings, with the result that Liza's father took pity on me and gave me my Sunday's dinner.' He took the room and married Eliza a few months later in the local register office, on 11 August 1899. On the marriage certificate he gave his occupation as 'actor' and she was described as a dressmaker. George named Frank as his father, interestingly, and wrongly, referring to him as 'Frank Booth', cotton mill mechanic, deceased. Eliza must have known about this time that she was pregnant.

In their early married life the young couple lived with Eliza's family at 8 Marsh Lane. Their first years together were marred by the deaths of their first three daughters as babies. Louisa, born in January 1900, died on 10 April, after suffering convulsions for three days. Edith Lily (or Lilian), born in

Marriage certificate of James Booth and Eliza Hoy, 1899

March 1901, died on 4 August of the same year. According to the death certificate, she died of 'zymotic enteritis', inflammation of the small intestine caused by infection, after being ill for seven days. Eliza and baby Edith spent census night, 31 March 1901, far from home in the Infirmary at Chichester in Sussex. The explanation seems to be that Eliza had been staying with her uncle James and his family, as that was where her widowed mother Louisa was at the time. The third daughter, Beatrice Hoy, just one year old, died of diphtheria in early August 1903.

George had to supplement his irregular wages from the halls and ran a 'small wares' business. He was buying the rights to perform new songs at the same time. In 1898 he bought four from Fred Elton, who later wrote for Sir Harry Lauder. He also had a regular weekly engagement at the People's Palace, St Helen's. Such 'turns' paid only about 30s. a week, and George described to a journalist for *The Sound Wave and Talking Machine Record* in 1910 the atmosphere of singing rooms at the turn of the twentieth century. 'The names of those engaged generally appear on the large mirror that usually adorns these places, written with the end of a wax candle.' He said 'he was never so proud in his life as when he saw his name appear in the premier position on the mirror of the public house where he got his first engagement'. It was at this time that he met Oswald Stoll, the vastly influential theatre manager, in Dublin. In 1898 Stoll had merged his business with that of Edward Moss and by 1905 there was an 'Empire' or 'Coliseum' theatre in most large towns.

> I was singing at the Tivoli Music Hall (then known as the Lyceum) on my third engagement. I was giving the audience exactly the same repertoire that I did on the first, and you can imagine my surprise when I got a message that Mr Stoll wanted to see me. As all know, this gentleman is possibly the controlling force of the music hall world, and when he made me an offer of £5 a week I thought I was made. That was ten years ago…

This was the beginning of big money and fame for the 'Wigan Nightingale'.

Many years later in an article in *The Times* about the painter L. S. Lowry, a northern industrial town of George's time was described.

Mr Lowry's skies may be unvaryingly grey and wintry, the streets and squares he represents may be lacking the least architectural distinction, and the open spaces muddy and squalid, but his colour schemes of black, brown and grey, lit with occasional touches of red, are pleasantly harmonious, and the small figures with which he crowds his scenes are skilfully grouped and full of life and of a gently melancholy humour. His is an art which seems equally descended from Breughel and from the elder George Formby.

At this early stage in his career George's stage persona was the living embodiment of Lowry's matchstalk man, in shabby clothes, with pale face and gloomy expression and a hunched stance.

Formby senior in clown character

Early photographs show that his act also owed something to the traditions of the clown. In one taken in 1901 he is shown with heavily painted face and elaborate costume as 'The Derby Winner'. Wearing heavy boots at the end of spindly legs, with pockets hanging out of his too-tight jacket and a hat jammed down on his head, he was gormlessness personified. He habitually powdered his eyebrows and painted two black spots on his forehead. This was helpful in playing to the gods (upper balcony) and apparently helped him rest his eyes by closing them for short periods, necessary because of the damaging glare of the limelight. Limelight was produced by the burning of hydrogen and oxygen in specially designed lamps. Some theatres had

The Derby Winner

Note the black spots on the forehead

their own gas production plants, but in others the gas was taken in large gas bags carried on men's backs. The hydrogen in particular was very unstable, especially in enclosed areas such as theatres, lit by candles or gas lamps and with cigarettes and pipes smoked freely in the auditorium. The lump of lime was in the focus of the gas and as the heat increased a very bright light was produced. The supply had constantly to be tweaked to keep the lamps bright. Heated limestone is an irritant to eyes and chest, damaging the eyes of George junior as well as those of his father.

Even before he appeared on stage George senior got a laugh from his audience. The orchestra would play him in, repeatedly, but he did not emerge. Eventually the music stopped and a voice called weakly from the wings 'I'm ready!' The laugh was gained, the music struck up again and he arrived. Standing alone on the stage, without a microphone of course, he would sing his songs, characteristically simple, some with tunes derived from Methodist hymns, and with catchy choruses. He would then move to the front and produce his 'patter', chatting in a gentle husky voice to the conductor and front-stalls audience as if conducting a private conversation. He would ask the conductor in confidential tones if 'he had his men well under control, as there was a woman in the second verse'. Gracie Fields recollected that he 'had her in stitches. In those days the theatres were deadly quiet – well, they had to be for him'. His 'coughing better tonight' was a regular part of the act. 'I'll cough you for five shillings and give you five coughs up,' he challenged the audience. On other occasions he would praise his favourite patent medicine Zambuk, a herbal embrocation, and was the originator of the saying 'It's not the coughin' that carries you off it's the coffin they carry you off in'. All sorts of asides and comments amused the audience: 'I might dance yet, but I might not' or 'they're playing the chorus a second time, and I've not asked them to – very willing lads'.

Soon Eliza began to make George's stage clothes and to stand in the wings while her husband performed. Once he lifted the drop cloth, revealing her legs and feet. 'Aren't I a lucky chap?' he asked the audience. 'These belong to me.'

She was, he said, his 'Guardian Angel', and at other times called her his 'dear wife and pal', adding, 'She is worth her weight in gold and a million doctors. Only Eliza knows how to get me right.' Over the years his act was refined and developed more and more, often with Eliza's help and advice. She herself said, 'Offstage, I did half the work for him.' A central invention was the character John Willie, the archetypal Lancashire lad. It may be true that George was the first stage artist to exploit the use of dialect, and in the north this was massively popular. The song 'John Willie, Come On!' – words uttered by his wife when John Willie's eyes strayed towards the ladies – produced a catchphrase, familiar to a wide audience, including those who had never seen a live performance by Formby. The slow delivery was deliberate, though his son Ted said many years later that as he drew his breath with difficulty he *had* to speak slowly. It was most likely George who coined the joke about 'Wigan Pier'. The real Wigan Pier was a coal gantry on the Leeds and Liverpool Canal. It was used to load coal from railway wagons into the canal barges below, about a mile from George's home, but George spoke of it as if it were one of the fashionable pleasure piers at seaside resorts. 'It's aw right you lot laughin'. It's very nice is Wigan Pier. Ah've been there many a time in my bathing costume and dived off t' high board into t' water.' Not only George Orwell took '*The Road to Wigan Pier*'; many others flocked to enjoy the delights of the seaside and found instead a dirty industrial site.

George was 'discovered', as far as the London market was concerned, by E. H. (Ted) Granville in Leeds in 1902. Eliza remembered the circumstances of the introduction, through Belle Elmore, the wife, and in 1910 the murder victim, of Dr Crippen.

And Belle Elmore, who had come up from London, was impressed by George, she said, 'You're a good turn. You're very good.' (He wore slacks then, baggy slacks and big black shoes like Little Tich.) 'I know two good agents in London and I will write to them to come up and see you. You are worthy of a Moss Empire Tour, you really are!'

'Well, Miss Elmore,' he said, 'I'll be delighted.'

So Ted Granville came down. He wore a beard.

Granville booked him to appear at the Royal Albert Music Hall, Canning Town, in October that year at a salary of £3 a week, and became his London agent. Formby was reluctant to try his luck in London, feeling that his act depended on the culture of northern humour and working-class life. However, with Eliza's encouragement he gave it a try, his songs and routines portraying him as the naïve boy trying to fit in with the sophisticated south. The contrast between his northern accent and metropolitan bravado was humorous, and the more urbane and sophisticated his audience the more George exaggerated his provincial gormlessness. 'Good evening, I'm Formby fra' Wigan... I've not been in England long...' Several of his most famous songs were written and performed for his London audiences – 'Did You See the Crowd in Piccadilly', for example, and 'Looking for Mugs in the Strand'. In 'Playing the Game in the West' he boasted of what was supposed to be a great, but was obviously a dreadful, evening, ending with the lines:

> And I'm not going home until quarter to ten,
> Cos it's My Night Out!

The title of one of his most famous songs curiously recalled his newspaper-selling past and foreshadowed a similar success for his son – 'Standing at the Corner of the Street'. The sheet music reveals that Hunt and Formby wrote it, George sensibly, and increasingly, having a hand in his own material. Sometimes he combined the London songs with the Wigan material, opening at the Tivoli with 'One of the Boys' and 'The Wigan Sprinter'. He also developed themes. A sequel to 'Playing the Game in the West' was 'Playing the Game Out West', exploiting a cowboy routine – another nonsensical notion considering his physical state. The great music hall star Marie Lloyd quickly became a fan and put in a good word for him, securing him a ten-week booking at the Tivoli, Oxford Circus.

On 26 May 1904 George Hoy Booth, George and Eliza's first son and eldest surviving child, was born at home, 3 Westminster Street, Wigan, in a terraced house much like those in the familiar opening shots of the roofs of *Coronation Street*. At this point George senior still gave his occupation as

'Small ware dealer (Master)' on the boy's birth certificate although he was playing the Argyle Theatre, Birkenhead, the evening the baby was born. Even this child's arrival was blighted – he was blind. The often-repeated family story was that George was born with a caul, traditionally thought to be lucky. But this one apparently obstructed his eyes. As so often in the Formby stories, the facts are hard to establish and there are a number of versions of the extraordinary moment when the baby first gained his sight. It's obvious that his mother was in the best possible position to know what happened, and Eliza's account is intriguing.

He never opened his eyes when he was born, and although he didn't open his eyes, he knew me. I used to feel his hand, and we had a dog called Nettle, she was a bitch and she loved Georgie and I made a little pram, like a cradle in the corner when I was doing my dressmaking. The little cot was next to the fireplace and I used to say: 'Now, Nettle, when Georgie cries, you be very careful how you jump on that cot.' And he knew it was a dog. He put his little hand out, and she would lick it. And she would take one jump into that cradle and she wouldn't harm that child at all. It was quite high, but she would jump that high. Nettle – we had her from a puppy, and with her licking his hand he would be contented and would go to sleep with the dog lying at his feet at the bottom...

People said sea air would do his eyes good, so I thought I would go over to New Brighton one day and take him. Of course in those days you could [get a] two shillings return from Wigan to Liverpool on an excursion. So I went down, got off at Lime Street station and got the tram down to the pier head. When I got there, there was no boat in for New Brighton, but they said there's one in for Hoylake – that's a nice place. I said, 'All right then, I'll go to Hoylake'... I had made a cover that I put round my shoulders to take the weight off to hold him. I looked under the cover and stroked his face two or three times and all of a sudden as I was riding in the tram – he opened his eyes! That was the first time he had opened them from being born, he was three months old, and he smiled at me. I said, 'Oh God bless you, Georgie – you can see!' And I held his hand and I took him over on the boat... He had like a varicose vein on the top of his head when he was born, and he told me to be very careful, and just as he opened his eyes and I took him on the top of that boat, his little nose started to bleed. It was right on top of his head, where the opening is. Of course I was concerned, I was only young, but I wiped it off, it wasn't long, and that disappeared and his eyes opened. And when we got to Hoylake, there was an old-fashioned iron bandstand, and the band was playing 'Walker Walked Away', one of my husband's songs. Sent my husband a wire, 'George opened his eyes – write home.'

In Australia in 1947 George described himself as being born blind 'like a kitten', not opening his eyes for three months, though in a *Daily Mirror* article in 1939 he had said that his wife had his caul and that it was likely to become a family heirloom. It seems impossible that it could cause blindness at all, and certainly not for any length of time. Importantly, Eliza, whose mother was a midwife, makes no mention of it.

Her account is very clear, but a diagnosis of the baby's condition is difficult. She seems to think that the 'varicose vein' and the nosebleed were significant. Was George suffering from mild hydrocephalus, with pressure on the cranial nerve, which suddenly resolved itself? If so, why were his eyes closed?

CHAPTER THREE

Standing at the Corner of the Street

The year 1904 was a very important one for George senior, professionally as well as personally, as he bought the singing rights to a huge number of new songs. Until this point he had been buying about ten to twenty a year but in 1904 he had assignment letters for fifty-seven, about a third of the total for the whole ten years between 1896–1905. Considering that the most usual price for the sole singing rights was a guinea (£1.05), (£84), this was a serious investment. In May and June alone he bought fifteen songs. He established a writing partnership with another music hall performer Alec Kendal, who, according to his own publicity, was a 'naturally funny comedian and dancer'. While he made a point of naturalness, George at this stage in his career used 'odd', 'eccentric' and 'droll' to describe his act. This was an era when 'variety' meant just that, and 'oddity' must have been difficult to pitch amongst the legmania, upside-down sand dancing and 'Ice Skate Dancing on the Back of a Plate'. Of seven 'Press Opinions' of George in 1905, four referred to him as 'the odd fellow from Lancashire', while the critic of *The Entr'acte* commented: 'He strikes quite an original note in make-up. His walk up and down the stage is extremely funny too. He has a capital song in "Walker Walked Away".' Together George and Alec Kendal wrote four songs and Kendal wrote another twelve at least for Formby on his own. His most famous song was, perhaps, 'I'm Twenty-one Today!' written in 1912 and made famous by the Yorkshire comedian Jack Pleasants. Another of George's songwriters was the young Worton David who is remembered in Florrie Forde's 'Hello, Hello, Who's Your Lady Friend?'. Some song titles emphasise the change in popular slang in a hundred years. 'I Smote Him on the Boko with My Wangee' would leave most of an early twenty-first-century audience baffled!

At about this time, 1905, George Robey recommended George to the management of a Newcastle pantomime and a new phase of his career began. This contract earned him his first big salary of £35 a week, and it was with those entries in December 1905 that he started his professional engagement diary. Even outside the pantomime season he could make £15 or £20 a week. In the year 1906, according to his own reckoning, he earned £556 (£44,300). This was a vast salary by the standards of working men at the turn of the twentieth century. The Fabian Maud Pember Reeves, in a survey of working-class families in Lambeth between 1909 and 1913, called the book which emerged from her research *Round about a Pound a Week*. George was earning more than ten times that amount, and his children knew nothing of the extreme poverty which had blighted his own childhood.

George Formby senior's professional engagement diary

'Gone are the once-nightly bills of fifteen or twenty turns, when – say, about 1912 – no connoisseur of such things would have dreamed of going to the Tivoli unless there were at least half a dozen good single-turn comedians appearing… Comic singing, once the mainstay of the whole evening's enjoyment, scarcely survives… The old performers dealt in character-drawing, in jovial good nature, in the cheerfully absurd.' George was part of the golden age of music hall comedy, an era recalled with nostalgia almost half a century later, in *The Times* in 1951, in an article describing London music halls. At this time there were 500 of them in London alone, some of them pretty rough. The legendary Morris Abrahams, from 1906 the manager of the Queen's Theatre, Poplar, had enough control of his East End audience to have little problem with rowdyism, but it was not unknown elsewhere in London to have vegetables, pease pudding and pigs' trotters raining down from the gallery. In Glasgow and Newcastle they threw steel rivets. On the other hand, some, like the Metropolitan Theatre (The Met.) had gilt everywhere, with fauteuils (easy chairs) for hire – or footles as the London audiences called them – and while the bar for the pit was low-roofed and decorated in pale yellow tiles, the stalls bar enabled the more affluent to watch the show, albeit at an oblique angle, while 'lounging'. The same feature was offered by the Queen's, Poplar, built in 1873, where the stalls consisted of chairs and tables as well as a chairman's table in the old tradition. Given that many of the audience would be drinking, smoking and some even eating, performers had to have something special to grab their attention.

YATES'S "WINE LODGE," (OPPOSIT[E]

HOOPER STRUVE'S MINERAL WATERS LONDON & BRIGHTON

◆ PROGRAMME. ◆

Saturday Matinee at 2.15. Reduced Prices

MONDAY, Decr. 30th, 1912, & Every Evening

The Programme is subject to alteration. The Management disclaim responsibility for the unavoidable absence of any Artiste.

1 Overture ... "Rag-time Revue" *Pether*
2 Ed. E. Ford ... Australian Sundowner
3 Dora Lyric ... ... Comedienne
4 Ernest Shand ... ... Comedian
5 Tom Clare ... ... At the Piano
6 Bert Coote & Co. present
" A Lamb on Wall Street "
An Episode of the New York Stock Exchange
by BERT COOTE
Harold Tapsley Framingham ... BERT COOTE
Randolph Horton (partner) ... J. C. AUBREY
Eleanor Belding ... ... ADA RUSSELL
Scene : Office of Framingham & Horton,
Stockbrokers, New York
Time : The present.
7 The Two Bobs (Adams & Alden) . Original
Ragtime Entertainers
8 Haidee de Rance ... Girl Violiniste
9 Alfred Lester ... In " THE SCENE-SHIFTER'S
LAMENT." Assisted by Miss BUENA BENT.
10 Selection "Songs without words" *Mendelssohn*
11 Sam Stern ... ... Character Comedian
12 Cinquevalli ... Incomparable Juggler
13 Neil Kenyon ... Popular Scottish Comedian
14 George Formby ... Lancashire Comedian
in his Latest Successes
15 Carl Muller ... ... Dancer
16 Ruffell's Bioscope With Latest Pictures

Turns at the Tivoli, 1912

George had just that quality. By 1906 he was achieving great popular and national success. The *Glasgow News* in November of that year gave him a rave review when he played in 'an all-round excellent' company at the Coliseum. Calling him 'the pretty boy from Lancashire', the reviewer wrote: 'This comedian has established himself a firm favourite with the Glasgow music-hall public, and last night his comical ditties, rendered in his own peculiar and inimitable style, practically took the house by storm.' The following month, this time at the Zoo Hippodrome in the same city, his performance was reviewed with equal enthusiasm. Described as 'the quaintest of comedians', the writer commented that 'he is an artist who believes in submitting new business, and this he is doing with much acceptance here this week. Never a smile crosses his face while on the stage, and his peculiar and unique ways provide no end of amusement. Formby has to respond at every performance and in fact the audience can hardly get enough of him'. Astonishing, as Glasgow was notorious as a graveyard for English comedians.

George's originality, use of the Lancashire dialect, new songs and engaging patter were evolving into a very special stage act. He seems to have had the gift of being able to convey total naturalness through very carefully wrought business. This is not to say that he was not a genuine character – he was revered for being the same man offstage as well as on – without pretension and with a directness which impressed those who met him. But he was at the same time a consummate professional with a highly creative instinct when in front of an audience. In 1907 at the Royal, Oldham, for example, he introduced into his act a donkey, which was wildly popular. One evening he had the notion of placing a child on its back. The young Harold Fallows, whose uncle was a stagehand, was the lucky child.

While his career was thriving, he and Eliza had to suffer the loss of another, probably stillborn, baby in 1905 before Louisa was born, at 27 Turner Street, a two-bedroomed terrace house, in May 1906. She was named for the first child who had died and after her maternal grandmother. The family had moved from Westminster Street because of a smallpox scare. Despite George's popularity he was anxious to provide as much as possible for his children. This house had a shopfront which enabled Eliza to set up a small business cooking chips on a gas stove for the lunchtime trade. She also kept up her work as a seamstress, making and selling dresses. For three years she ran a lock-up toffee shop. In August, George, feeling at last that he had material wealth to leave, made his will, naming Eliza as the sole executrix and heiress to his estate. The family then moved further from the centre of Wigan to the suburbs of Dicconson Street, into a substantial late-Victorian terraced house with a front-room bow window and small front garden.

In 1906 George also made his first records for Louis Sterling's cylinder company. Having to speak or sing into a large funnel put some artists off and they completely 'dried' without an audience – Dan Leno was one of them. But George did not need any such stimulus. He gave just as much to his performance as he did in the halls, using his confidential manner now to talk to the recording machine. His ad-libbing was endearing. 'I'm just talking to fill t' time in,' he'd say after he had recorded the song. And at the end, 'That's champion, I'm going, I'm gone.' He liked the new technology, and the following year signed a record contract with the Zonophone Company, with the result that he left about 190 recordings still in existence today.

But music hall was his bread and butter. Booking records carefully kept by Denny Clarke over many years show how hard the life could be. A bill-topping artist at the Argyle could hope to make £70 a week in 1907, a beginner £5. But proprietors were unsparing of their criticism in a tough business. The 'Remarks' alongside the other details in Clarke's record pulled no punches. 'Useless' described the Three Rio Tintos in 1907, while Lawrence Barclay was dismissed as 'Vulgar'. John Lawson and Co. got a fuller comment. 'Good show but Mrs Lawson very disagreeable & under the influence of drink. Kept stage waiting over 5 mins. on 2 nights.' Alec Kendal was 'good – blue', and quickly re-engaged. George appeared there in November, top of the bill at £20 a week, at a time when an established favourite, Harry Lauder, could command £60. The booking records show how some performers earned a good and steady income from the halls without hitting the heights. Ella Shields and Daisy Wood were two such. Others like George gradually joined an élite of perhaps twenty or so artists who could regularly earn a three-figure sum even in the provinces, a group which included not only Lauder but Vesta Tilley and Little Tich.

It was probably in the spring of 1908 that a momentous meeting occurred. The booking record for 30 March that year shows Fred Karno's Company topping the bill at the Argyle with George on second. Charlie Chaplin, aged about nineteen, had just begun working with Karno's theatre troupe and was employed 'at thirty bob a week'. He saw Formby's routine and met him backstage. One of George's costumes was a too-tight jacket, baggy trousers, large shoes and a cane. Chaplin asked to borrow the outfit, bowler hat and cane and for permission to sing 'One of the Boys' for an audition. George was happy to oblige but never used the character or the song again. He had so many it did not really matter. Louie, his daughter, maintained that he actually gave Chaplin his knotted curly cane. The distinctive twirl and the 'little duck walk', which had been George's, gained international fame in the career of the younger man, fame on a scale that George himself never managed.

George senior in Chaplinesque character

But his popularity in London was a huge breakthrough for George, and his professional diary shows just how successful he was. Throughout January 1908 he earned £20 a week at the Tivoli, the Strand, noting for February, 'engaged three weeks longer', by popular request. A year later, this time for ten weeks, he played the Tivoli again, '3 halls a night, £45', with Marie Lloyd and Little Tich topping the bill. *The Times* reviewer commented approvingly of George that he 'becomes more of an artist the longer he sings'. Lloyd, for her part, paid him the compliment of preferring him over all other performers, according to Morris Abrahams of the Queen's Theatre, Poplar. By the spring of 1913 George was able to record his first three-figure sum, while his last weekly salary, in early 1921, was £300 (£9,860).

Some of the hundreds of posters advertising George senior

The Formby children were privately educated, another sign that their father was by now a wealthy man. George junior was unhappy at Notre Dame, one family story being that his mother left him at the main door of the school one morning only to find him back at home when she returned. He had left by a back door and run home as fast as he could! A report of George's twice running away from school appeared in the local press in 1910. His family felt that George may have been frightened. Certainly he was afraid of Sister Veronica, the nun who taught music, a fierce woman who rapped him painfully across the knuckles for his repeated presence at her piano with dirty hands. He never did learn to read music.

By contrast with school, the home life of the Formby family was a very happy one. George senior was of course often away from home performing on the halls, and as Eliza went with him to look after him, the children were left with their widowed grandmother, Mrs Hoy, of whom George junior was very fond. So vital was she to the functioning of the family that on census night in April 1911, at home with her three grandchildren and an adult niece, she described her occupation as 'Housekeeper'. Eliza and James, along with their brother-in-law Eugene Fawcett, were a long way from home, staying in a boarding house near Portsmouth. In later life George made sure that his grandmother received a weekly allowance from him, periodically increased to take account of inflation. When asked if his father had been a disciplinarian, Ted, his youngest son, replied that he was not because there was no need for him to be. Home was a relaxed place and the children were readily obedient.

George junior remembered 'sitting on horseback at agricultural shows almost before he could talk'. At the age of five he had begun visiting a farm near Martland Mill Bridge in Wigan and it was at this time, taught by his mother's brother, Uncle John, that he began to ride horses properly. He won a prize at Bolton, and his mother always kept an oil painting, copied from a photograph, to remind her of his triumph. There had been jockeys and horsemen on Eliza's side of the family for years. John had been head postilion to King Humbert of Italy and one of George junior's cousins had won the Cesarewitch at Newmarket, aged only sixteen. By 1910 George senior was describing himself on his headed notepaper as 'Fair Gowmless Gradley Lankisheer'. He couldn't have played the northern card much more strongly. The family had moved again, further into the countryside, to Walthew House Farm, Wigan, tel.: Wigan 313, the three-figure phone number testament both to the very few telephones at that time and to the prestige of the family. Louisa described it as 'a very lonely place'.

Top: *George junior aged about six*
Bottom: *Photograph signed by George junior's cousin, Jimmy Sharples*

It was from this large house that George junior rode his white pony to school at Notre Dame. Eliza remembered an incident from this time.

> Holy Communion: What a day! He was dressed in a new suit of clothes. He had a red sash, and he came home that dinner time and he said, 'I'm doing all right, Mother,' and he had a pint pot tied onto the end of his sash… He was not quite seven… came home and said, 'I've got to be a very good boy today. I've not got to swear and I've not got to do anything I shouldn't do, 'cause I've had my first Holy Communion this morning.' And the pint pot was for a little do we were going to have afterwards.

His father had begun buying racehorses and by May 1911 he was ready to send his eldest son to train as a jockey with Etienne de Mestre, a well-known figure in the world of horse racing, at Bishops Cannings, Wiltshire. For years he had had the ambition of turning George into a successful jockey, an idea motivated by kindness towards the reluctant schoolboy; the chance, his father believed, for him to grow up strong and healthy in clean air and to enjoy an outdoor life, even, perhaps, to achieve fame and fortune in a world far removed from the music hall. Some accounts suggest that it was a form of banishment, but that was not the case. 'Georgie', the first precious survivor after three sisters had died, was more likely to be spoilt than punished. The timing throws up a mystery: was this first training course a false start? The admissions register for St Benedict's RC School, Hindley, survives. George entered the school on 20 May 1912 and left on 12 August of the same year, according to the record, to go to a 'mixed school'. So exactly when he left the family home to start his career is not clear. Whenever it was, he may have felt it to be an exile, exchanging as he did a happy home life for the tough regime and loneliness of the stables. While George himself, quoted in the *Empire News* of Sunday, 8 May 1938, accepted that his father wanted to get 'plenty of fresh air into t' lad's lungs' the parting must have seemed harsh. In the same article he spoke of leaving 'our comfortable home' for the racing stable.

Every year George senior bought more songs, but in 1910 he invested especially heavily, acquiring another thirty-nine. In that year he recorded 'Standing at the Corner of the Street', which became his most famous song. He was so popular that others copied his act. This infuriated him, and both his tenacity and hard-nosed business sense are clearly shown in a series of telegrams and letters, some written by Eugene Fawcett acting as his secretary. In March 1911 Eugene wrote on George's behalf to a friend and agent, Jack Hands, about Doris Drew plagiarising the 'Spanish Onion' song, 'Funicula',

Was this the work of producer Tom Arnold?

the previous November. George grew more and more annoyed about her and another imitator, Vernon Watson, who had turned professional in 1911 with his impressions of comedians. In the following October he wrote again to Jack Hands, to ask him if he would track down and stop them. A month later he was describing Watson's behaviour as 'damned cheek' and putting the matter into the hands of the Variety Artistes' Federation solicitors. The 'Spanish song and dance' were always very well received, and George was not prepared to give away this part of his act. 'Laughter never ceased, and ended in a shriek when he stopped and said, "I can't dance. It's all swank."' Plagiarism was always going to be a very difficult problem to beat, but he arranged to meet Hands in a Warrington pub in December 1911 to discuss the matter, writing, 'if I am there before opening time I can get a drink, me being a traveller'. He was portrayed after his death in 1921 as a teetotaller, although he was well known at the 'Cemetery' Hotel, Warrington. Shaun Glenville had an act with his wife Dorothy Ward between the 1910s and the 1950s. He took the comedy role of dame while she was the glamorous principal boy. Appearing on many bills together, the couple became friends of George and Eliza. Shaun certainly thought he was an abstainer.

> He was really a staunch teetotaller, but once in a party in the West End his friends prevailed upon him to have drink with the rest. When the whisky and soda appeared, George declared, 'I'll give way today,' and ordered a small sherry! Later he had another, but no more. When I saw George at the show that night he was nursing his head. 'How do you feel?' I asked, and George replied, 'I don't feel at all well; this "playing the game in the west" doesn't suit me!'

Some performers politely asked permission to use George's material. Ray Wallace sent a telegram asking if he could sing 'one verse and the chorus of "Playing the Game up [sic] the West" as an imitation of you', at the Hammersmith Palace. Wee Georgie Wood, a music hall actor and comedian who, as a 'proportionate dwarf', was cast in the role of a child, like Jimmy Clitheroe later, recalled Formby 'insisting I must add him to my list of imitations and personally teaching me to sing "John Willie – Come On!"' In 1914 the young Gracie Fields wrote to him to ask if she might perform one of his songs. He gave his permission. She was so much in awe of him that she didn't dare to go to ask for his autograph, persuading someone else to do it for her. At one time the two performers were working at the same theatre. As both lots of luggage were stamped with the same initials, GF, it happened that her bags arrived at his dressing room, causing much laughter. On the same bill were two American entertainers, Hedges Mothers and Jacobs Sons. George said, 'I'm told they have their teeth filled with gold. It's funny but it takes me all my time to fill them with meat!'

CHAPTER FOUR

In Need of a Strengthening Bottle!

George's family was growing. They moved on again in late 1912, this time to Hindley House on Atherton Road. A daughter, Ella Magdaline, had been born in July 1910, named after Ella Shields, an American music hall star and male impersonator whose most famous song was 'Burlington Bertie from Bow'. Shields had worked with George at the Manchester Hippodrome, and clearly they had become friends as George asked her to be the godmother of his second surviving daughter. A third, Mary, was born in 1912 and another son, Frank, arrived in 1913, named after both his grandfather and a brother who had died aged eight months from the complications of whooping cough.

George was keen to buy the property because it had fields on which he could train his racehorses in his spare time. Stables were also needed as all the children rode from the age of about three and had their own ponies. Eliza's brother John Hoy helped him, the plan being that eventually young George would manage the stables. This substantial four-bedroomed detached white house with large mature gardens (including a rose garden much loved by their father) and an orchard offered more room for the children to live and play. Moss Empires gave George a £1,000 bonus so that he could buy it. One of the photographs in a family album devoted to views of it shows the slightly blurred figures of two little girls playing amongst the shrubs and flowerbeds. It was in the rose garden that their father would sit, relaxing and drinking in the rich scents and luscious red of his favourite flowers, but also considering his act and writing his songs. It was here that he was at his most creative. The house itself represented the acme of conventional taste in 1913, the elaborate décor and furnishings of the interiors and heavy furniture, silver and china producing

Ella Shields, music hall star

Top: Hindley House
Middle: Hindley House: the sitting room
Right: Hindley House: a bedroom

an opulent, but to a modern eye, crowded, overdressed effect. The fireplace built to represent a proscenium arch was an obvious personal touch. George, a self-educated man and keen reader, even had a library. At a time when art and architecture were moving rapidly towards a modern style the Formby home was entirely, even self-consciously, old-fashioned, harking back, with its oak-panelled walls and massive doors, to a previous century. The album looks rather like the Edwardian equivalent of a *Hello!* magazine photo shoot, though of course the family had no intention of using the pictures for commercial gain. It has been said that for the very poor in Lancashire at the beginning of the twentieth century 'any new possession seemed to stifle fear'. For the boy who told the world that he had sometimes slept in the outside privy during his childhood, these photographs were concrete proof of his achievement and success. His satisfaction, and relief, must have been sweet indeed.

In April 1913 George negotiated a new contract with British Zonophone and was making £300 (£21,000) a year from his records alone. It may have been at about this time that he was given an HMV Model 12 gramophone by the company. While the top case was almost standard, the legs and stretchers were unique and bespoke to the machine. His growing fame made front page news in the *Birmingham Evening Despatch* of 8 May 1913. George Formby, who was playing that week to 'crowded audiences in the Grand Theatre', had been commanded to appear before King George V and Queen Mary when they were staying as guests of Lord Derby at his family seat, Knowsley Hall, near Liverpool, that summer. Music hall had 'arrived' in higher social circles only the previous year when Harry Lauder, the Scottish entertainer and favourite of the late Edward VII, had been requested to perform. George expressed his feelings in a letter written to a Wigan friend. 'I'm pleased to inform you that I've been commanded to appear before the King and Queen on 7 July at Lord Derby's estate Knowsley Hall... I think this is a big honour for me and also for Wigan.' He also wrote for direction to Frank Allen, the MD of Moss Empires. Allen replied, 'Mr Wighton thinks that if you sing your "Spanish" song for your first number and for an encore "Standing at the Corner of the Street" these will be most suitable. Therefore kindly arrange to sing these particular songs.'

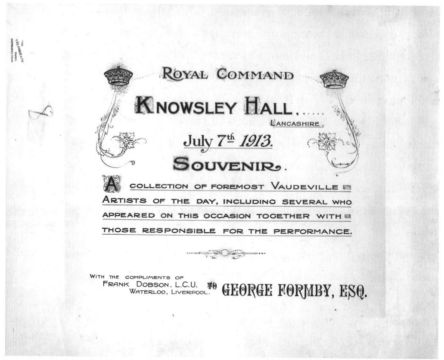

Top: *Knowsley Hall souvenir*
Bottom: *A royal greeting: Knowsley Hall*

The command performance was given at the end of a busy day for the royal couple. A knighting, the opening of the Warrington Bridge across the Mersey and a visit to a soap and chemical works were the main items on their agenda. A huge crowd, including 10,000 local children who sang the national anthem and waved flags and handkerchiefs, greeted the king and queen. One exchange during the royal tour of the works gives an insight into a past age. The king was introduced to the oldest employee, George Gleave, and he asked him how old he was. 'Seventy-two in October,' was the reply. He was asked how long he had worked there. 'Sixty-three years,' was Gleave's proud response.

At Knowsley Hall that evening the king and queen were welcomed by Lord Derby's tenants and their families 'to the number of several hundred' and after dining were entertained at 9.30 p.m. by the artists. The *Daily Mirror* reporter recounted with enthusiasm every detail of the luxurious arrangements. The venue, a converted conservatory, was 'a perfect jewel of a playhouse', the walls lined with creamy-white silk, the chairs gilded, the balcony hung with flowers. *The Times* journalist described the excavations which had been made to accommodate the orchestra 'in front of the proscenium opening but out of the line of vision of the King and Queen and other guests'. The colour scheme was cream and sapphire blue, the French grey carpet spread with Persian rugs. He raved about the 'flow of cool air from an alcove of ferns and flowers in which was set a fountain of ice with electric fans about it in constant motion'.

George was on second. According to the *Daily Mirror*: 'All the artists… excelled themselves before the royal audience, but Mr George Formby was undoubtedly the success of the evening, for Mr Formby was cracking Lancashire jokes to Lancashire people in Lancashire, and his character sketches were superb.' However, an embarrassing unscripted moment arose out of a misunderstanding. George often made a point of having 'confidential chats' with conductors – his 'coughing better tonight' remarks were often made to them – and on this occasion the conductor was George Saker. Just behind the conductor were the royal couple and because the orchestra was hidden from sight in a pit it looked to some members of the audience as if Formby in his chat was referring to the king, disrespectfully and with great overfamiliarity, as 'George'! They got 'very fidgety and inclined to be indignant… Eventually a word of explanation was passed round, and in the ensuing serenity George proceeded to convulse the crowd as usual'. Actually, he picked up the audience's disquiet about the 'gaffe' too and was uneasy all through his turn as he couldn't think of a way of putting matters right. After the show the artists threw a party back at their hotel, but George was missing from it. Eliza absolutely insisted that he went to bed to recover, exhausted as he was from the strain of the occasion. In his obituary in *The Times* it was noted that: 'His broad humour succeeded with unexpected ease and their Majesties praised him very highly after the performance.' As a memento of the great occasion the king presented George with a tie pin. It was this pin, fastened under the lapel of his son's jacket, which made George junior feel 'twice privileged' at his own first command performance in November 1937. He wore it at all his performances with royal guests present, for luck.

In August George senior received a letter from the London Coliseum, the grandest and most opulent of all music hall theatres, referring to the forthcoming charity performance there scheduled for 11 October, during Madame Sarah Bernhardt's season. This was music hall refined enough to attract the middle and upper classes. He was told that the king and queen and a 'large royal party' would attend and that all proceeds were to go to the French Hospital in London and the Charing Cross Hospital, the appeal set up by Lord Lonsdale (he of the Lonsdale belts for boxing). 'The Divine Sarah' was by now nearly seventy and a legendary actress of stage and silent screen. On this occasion she was to give Act II of Racine's *Phèdre*. Seventeenth-century French tragedy might be thought to sit uneasily alongside the item George was to take part in – a 'short skit entitled "Ten Little Nigger Boys All in a Row"'… in which you and your colleagues might first of all appear in black masks, which could be discarded almost immediately when your turn came to sing or dance' – but such was the nature of variety. On 3 October Oswald Stoll, the owner of the Coliseum, wrote of the good progress that was being made with the skit, but pointed out that if it was to be fitted into twenty minutes, each artiste would be confined to a very short slot and might be 'somewhat handicapped'.

Be that as it may, the performance went ahead. The 'Entire Auditorium' was 'transformed, with masses of gold, pink carnations, and fleur-de-lys', and 'brilliantly illuminated'. It was said that three million roses gave their scent. A new royal box was constructed. The tasselled and leather-bound programme for the evening, lined with silk taffeta, reveals that not only Princess Louise but four earls and five countesses were present, with an assortment of marquesses, lords and ladies. Sir Edward Elgar, OM conducted 'Pomp and Circumstance', Sir Henry Wood conducted the orchestra in 'The Marseillaise', and Ellen Terry and W. C. Fields also appeared. George Robey, Fred Emney and Cicely Courtneidge were fellow 'Niggers'. Photographic portraits of all the performers were included, Lord Lonsdale subsequently sending his own copy to George so that he could add his autograph. The day after the show Stoll wrote thanking George for his participation. 'You will be pleased to know that on leaving the King and Queen expressed to me their great delight at the success of the performance; and I think that you yourself would have noticed how greatly Their Majesties and the rest of the Royal Party enjoyed themselves.' Two royal command performances within six months gave 1913 a special importance in George's career.

That year he tried something new, appearing in a serious film, *No Fool Like an Old Fool*, in the character of an old Lancashire man, but the coming of war in August 1914 diverted his course again. George tried to enlist at the age of thirty-seven. He was, of course, turned down on medical grounds. On 10 August, only days after war broke out, he was appearing at the Argyle and on the bill, much lower down, were the Brothers Lawler, dancers. Could the name be simply a coincidence? The following August they were all on the same bill again... It was about this time that George began to run his own shows 'on percentage'. His name was the attraction, and the salaries of the other entertainers were allotted as a percentage of the takings. He had no shortage of offers as his colleagues knew their earnings would be much increased on the back of his popularity.

George in No Fool Like an Old Fool, *1913*

Then began the charity shows for the wounded. George also spoke on behalf of Lord Derby, the director general of recruiting between 1915 and 1916. Derby was very much against conscription and introduced instead the so-called Derby Scheme, whereby men could sign up voluntarily but would only be called up if needed. The pay-off from the government was that married men would be called up last of all. The idea (though ultimately a failure in producing the number of men needed to replace the tens of thousands killed and injured) was launched in a blaze of publicity of which George was a part, recruiting men for Kitchener's army from the stage. He also raised large sums for charity during the war. The role of humour in the face of mass slaughter was thought by one commentator in 1930 to be 'ennobling', helping people to retain their sanity. 'Robey's "Shurrup" to the Alhambra gallery during an air raid had more than a touch of nobility in its magnificent impulsiveness.' In this way both Formbys, father and son, raised morale at times of bitter loss and difficulty for the nation.

George junior had gone to Middleham Moor after about ten weeks at Bishops Cannings, to be trained by George Drake. He was kind to the boy and had him live with the family. Eliza recalled that George 'had a private tutor two hours in the morning and two hours in the afternoon. Sometime he went and sometimes he didn't. So long as he got paid the tutor didn't mind'. He stayed about a year, and it was while he was there that he became the 'music' in a 'barrel-organ'. In the saddle room at Warwick House he would give his fellow apprentices renditions of his father's songs and sometimes played the mouth organ. At Whitsuntide there was a fancy-dress procession in which 'gipsies' paraded with a box on a wheelbarrow, complete with a handle from a wringing machine. George was inside. A tap from his friends told him when the handle was being turned so that he would start playing his mouth organ. A famous photograph survives of the scene, with flat-capped George looking nonchalant and clutching the mouth organ. A less famous one shows him emerging from the box itself.

From Middleham he was apprenticed to Tom Schofield at Epsom, and after three months with him got his first race at Lingfield Park on 6 April 1915. A *Daily Mirror* feature focused on this diminutive child who had become a professional jockey at the astonishingly early age of ten – a record unlikely ever to be dislodged. The comment was mainly about his tiny frame – he weighed only 3 st 13 lb – and his ability, like his father, to make people laugh. His trainer had only one complaint about him. Like many children George had a fondness for sweets and pastry – the jockey's greatest enemies. At this time he was riding his father's filly, Eliza, a three-year-old, and weighed in for his first race at 5 st 2 lb. He was unplaced in the Apprentices' Plate. The official race record noted that 'Eliza dwelt badly at the start'. According to George many years later, she was frightened of the colours on the other jockeys. Two horses began to fight at the post which unnerved her further. Worse, she had never seen a starting gate before and was so curious she stayed there long after the others were on their way. 'We nearly finished in the next race. And to make it worse I'd got mumps – and it was hailing like hail!'

Three weeks later he rode in the Apprentice Handicap over the Dewhurst Plate Course and, after 'plenty of bother at the post', was again unplaced.

Top: *The famous picture*
Bottom: *The less famous one which completes the true story*

Despite this unpromising start, later that year he made his first (silent) film *By the Shortest of Heads*, chosen because the producer, Will Barker, was a friend of his father. It was his first appearance in show business. Film stardom, with his father in control of the enterprise, was to be encouraged.

The five-reel film, directed by Bert Haldane and shot at Epsom, told the story of a child jockey winning a race under the noses of more senior riders, by a very narrow margin. The outcome of the story depended on the success or failure of two horses, one owned by the hero and the other by the villain, in a race. At the last moment, to defeat the machinations of the baddie, the child was given the ride, and a review of August 1915 in *The Cinema* spoke enthusiastically of the intensity of excitement produced by filming the two riders in broadside close-up. 'Both the animals are genuinely racing and not once do they get out of the camera's range... The masterly riding and judgement of the jockeys symbolise the title most accurately.' George was described as 'a typical little hero of a well-ridden race' and the film 'a thoroughly enjoyable melodrama'. His salary was five shillings a week. All copies of the film are now lost, the last apparently sold for scrap in Rochdale by a cinema manager in about 1940. George said later, 'He disposed of it for a few bob. I'd have given a hundred pounds to see it.'

Ethel, George senior's youngest daughter, was born in 1915 at about the time young George was sent to Ireland to the Curragh, County Kildare, the home of his mother's forebears. Racing in England had been greatly restricted by the beginning of war. His father bought five horses in one go and sent them with him to Johnny Burns, the father of the well-known jockey Tommy Burns. In Ireland George was often very unhappy. Life at the stables was hard, and discipline revolved around beatings, of which he seems to have received a good many. The day began at four o'clock in the morning and ended when the horses were tired. To add to his burdens, he was enrolled at the village school at Athgarvan, about a mile away. Before school he had to clean the stables and feed and groom the horses, and he was a reluctant scholar at the best of times. In 1952 when he went back to Ireland he was sent an invitation from his old school addressed 'To the boy who was always late'! He nonetheless made a great impression on his singing teacher, who afterwards claimed he had the best voice in the school.

George formed a bond with a temperamental mare, called What's On, and only with him was she reasonably gentle. He always rode her at exercise, but one morning, unnerved by some fluttering newspaper on the sands, she jumped and kicked, throwing George flying onto a rock. He was picked up unconscious, with damage to his back and a broken collar bone, but soon recovered. He never made a fuss about falls and injuries. There were lighter moments in his life, of course. Thomas Clarke, a props man in George senior's pantomime tour in January 1916, recalled that young George had been able to visit his parents during a Saturday matinee in Glasgow, 'all the chorus girls hugging and kissing him, as he was a chubby boy then'. At the stables he was known as 'Cloggy', the tease being that everyone in Lancashire wore traditional mill workers' clogs. Cloggy often entertained his fellow jockeys by playing the bones and the mouth organ. He was also a mean tap dancer. 'I was a sufficiently quaint little fellow for the owners when they came to the stables to get me to sing my father's songs, which I did in the real spirit of an entertainer, knowing that if I made them laugh the tip would be so much greater.' A fellow jockey remembered that he was 'a mischievous little devil'. On one occasion he had gone into the hayloft which was infested with mice. George was quick enough to catch some and put them in a sack. When one of the boys walked under it he hit it with a stick and the mice fell out on the unsuspecting lad. 'He would laugh his head off.'

For most of the time, though, George was miserable and lonely, and became determined to leave the stables. Aged by now about twelve, he and another lad set off at midnight for Dublin, twenty-five miles away. They had decided to follow the mare, Eliza, who had been sold and was now running in flapping meetings (not subject to Jockey Club or National Hunt regulations) around Dundalk. Obviously if George got involved in such racing he would have been banned from all courses – not what his father had in mind! After covering seventeen miles it began to rain, but, soaked, they got a lift on a donkey cart for the rest of the journey. They spent the night at the digs George's father used when he was in Dublin where the kindly landlady organized hot baths and a good meal. At the station, waiting for a train the following afternoon, they were confronted by two policemen and spent the night in the cells, more comfortable, according to George, than their usual accommodation. Next day they were escorted back to the stables and got another good hiding.

On Monday, 19 June 1916 George senior opened in the revue *Razzle Dazzle* at the Theatre Royal, Drury Lane. *The Times* advertisement boasted of a 'Beauty Chorus of 250' (the programme said 300) and 'The Great Ice Scene' – referred to in the programme as 'Ice Skating at St Moritz' – as its main attractions. The show had been scheduled to open the previous Friday but was delayed by George's 'indisposition', which had lasted six weeks. Some members of his family were staying with him, Eliza, Louisa and one of the babies, with a governess. Unfortunately a rostrum stage used for scene 13, bearing the Beauty Chorus in a 'gathering of the clans' surrounding a lone piper, collapsed. George, on in scene 14, was on the stage underneath. He was badly hurt and taken to Guy's Hospital with lung damage. He suffered his first pulmonary haemorrhage, the doctors there unable to stop the bleeding. However, Eliza, acting on the advice of her mother, who as a midwife must have found it helpful in complicated maternity cases, recommended the use of ice. It was quickly brought from a nearby hotel. George sucked the ice and the bleeding stopped. Louisa remembered that after he was discharged back to his hotel to recuperate the family all crowded round his sickbed as a Zeppelin went over the West End. If they were to go they would all go together. She never forgot the huge silent silver ship drifting over London and over their heads. Her father was to have a further twelve similar attacks from that time onwards, Eliza feeding him crushed ice offstage to try to stop the haemoptysis. Succeeding years' diary entries show the increasing amount of time 'out' he had as his illness became worse. His engagement diary was subject to dozens of alterations as he deleted the shows he did not play and substituted dates in lieu. 'Ill', 'off', 'cold', 'out' are the frequent margin notes during these years.

'Damages against George Formby' read the headline in *The Observer* of 4 April 1917. The Palladium, Southport, was suing him for breach of contract. His barrister argued that he was not well enough to appear there, but he was said to have taken up a more lucrative offer in London. George himself told the court that he had seven children and that it was vital to him to be in London for specialist medical treatment. He was probably trying to make as much money as he could for his family. He lost the case and had to pay £175, despite his counsel trying to defend him with the ominous words, 'My client has one foot in the grave.'

At least his horses were doing better in Ireland. At Leopardstown, in June with Tommy Burns up, his horse Philander won, and at Phoenix Park a month later Burns took another of his horses to an easy victory. The stewards, clearly surprised by this 100/12 horse's performance, required an explanation, but whatever it was, it was deemed satisfactory. At Athlone at the end of July, F. Hunter rode the 2/1 favourite Eliza to an easy victory 'in a canter'. George junior seemed to be doing better too, placed second in six races, but the winning place continued to elude him. By now he was riding Skookum Joe, another of his father's horses. At Limerick in April the horse was the favourite, but George managed only third place, missing second by a neck. Clearly any confidence in the horse and its rider drained away, for three weeks later Skookum Joe was given odds of 20/1 at the Curragh. George was, once again, unplaced. The spring and summer of 1918 saw him still waiting to ride a winner. On Philander he was second at Phoenix Park in April, in a thrilling finish. Jimmy Burns, the younger brother of Tommy and a good friend of George's, won by a short head on Half Caste – an outsider like George's mount – but both of them were in front of the hot favourite, ridden by the notable jockey Steve Donoghue. Disappointingly, though, at Leopardstown in June, riding his father's Iron Orb, he was again out of the prize money.

George junior must have been depressed not to fulfil his father's longing for a winning place, but he had at least the satisfaction of taming one of the horses, Wildwood, by the power of music. Wildwood was always muzzled, but would throw or roll off almost anyone who attempted to ride him. George felt sorry for him, so at odds was he with everyone and everything in his life. 'Just for a bit of company I played my mouth organ to him. I saw him prick up his ears and for the first time he looked as if he would not eat me alive.' He played as he entered Wildwood's box and while he groomed him. Eventually he could just put the mouth organ to his mouth without actually playing it. Wildwood would even let George exercise him as long as he kept playing. His knack with difficult horses was remarkable, but of course there was no racing future for this one – the stewards certainly wouldn't have tolerated George playing the mouth organ while riding him. In a case of art imitating life, he featured in a similar story, taming the vicious Man Eater in one of his films, *Come On George*, in 1940.

In October, terribly homesick, he made a second attempt to get home. During a race meeting he left and went to Dublin, intending to catch the mail boat, the *Leinster*, to Holyhead. He sent a telegram home 'Leaving on *Leinster*' to warn his family of his arrival. On Thursday, 10 October at 9.45 a.m. the boat was torpedoed by a German U-boat fifteen miles out from Dun Laoghaire and sank with the loss of over 500 lives. His father was distraught on hearing the news, and the family endured an agonising wait before they heard by telegram from George that he was safe at the stables. His disappearance had been noticed and two stable lads sent to Dublin to bring him back. They had caught up with him at the dock gates and the *Leinster* had left without him.

Malvern House, Wigan Lane, was the family's next home. This villa, with double bay windows, barge-boarded along the roof line in late Victorian style, proclaimed to the neighbours George's prosperity. Handily, it was next to the infirmary. The war was making it increasingly difficult to get the necessary manpower to train George senior's racehorses, and the Hindley House fields were becoming an expensive encumbrance. But in 1917 the Formbys moved again, this time to Hill Crest, Stockton Heath, London Road, Warrington, a substantial detached red-brick house in a leafy street. Even this new house had a coach house and hayloft. Ella recalled that they had a grand piano and a gramophone in the drawing room and a polar bear rug on the floor. Once again there was a library, a favourite place for her father, who increasingly needed quiet and seclusion from the noise and hubbub of family life. Joe Downing, who knew

George, remembered that he replaced the gas lights at Hill Crest with electricity, a luxury still only available to the rich at the time. 'During the job he said that he wanted an electric bell push on the front door so that the postman and any other callers would know that they had electricity.'

CHAPTER FIVE

Come on, Lads, Give Me a Chord Off!

The last child of the family, Edward, was born in October 1918. According to Mary Formby, each of the children had in their turn been taken on stage as the 'new addition' but Teddy's birth was announced *on record* by his father in a characteristic jokey way – the only one of the children whose arrival was celebrated for posterity. One of the few surviving photographs with them together shows a tired-looking George sitting perched on his son's pushchair, apparently learning his lines, with Teddy, a disgruntled toddler, standing behind him. In June 1918 George had

George senior with young Teddy, c. 1920

caught flu – the devastating strain which was to become a pandemic, killing millions worldwide and over 220,000 in Britain. His engagement diary is marked with a cross next to the words 'Hippodrome Manchester', and annotated 'caught flu here'. It is extraordinary that he didn't die alongside so many others, but as it was he didn't work for over a month. He had to leave his pantomime commitments in both 1918 and 1919 because of illness, and the photo shows him looking thin and worn out. Many years later his daughter Ella wrote: 'I remember he was always ill, and "Don't disturb your father" were Mum's words. My mother worshipped him.'

Six months after his lucky escape from the *Leinster* tragedy George finally succeeded in leaving Ireland. He was having a suit made in Dublin and told them at the stables that he would go to have a try-on, then go to the theatre and get the 'Rattler', the midnight train out of Dublin. He went instead to a friend of his father's, Mr Hamilton, the manager of the Theatre Royal, and asked to borrow some money to get home. He was given £3. This time there was no mishap, and he arrived in Warrington about three o'clock the next morning. George apparently asked his mother anxiously, 'Me dad's not here, is he?' As predicted, his father was far from pleased but at least agreed that George did not have to go back.

Instead he was sent again to George Drake at Middleham and from him went to Newmarket, to the Hon. George Lambton, one of Lord Durham's brothers, who trained for Lord Derby, Lord Stanley and others. The stable had between sixty and seventy valuable horses and there was a nightwatch-man, an ex-policeman, in charge after ten o'clock, responsible for looking after their welfare. There was, as well as the possibility of theft, an ever-present danger of fire. Early one morning there was in fact a fire in the lads' quarters. George had got in at midnight and the blaze was blamed on him. Lambton went into the lads' room when they were having breakfast at 8 a.m. and dragged Formby out by the scruff of his neck. In his other hand he had a hunting crop. He marched him out into the middle of one of the lawns and started cracking his whip. All the other boys thought that George was getting a terrific hiding, as he was yelling his head off – a wonderful lesson to them. Later on in the day George was asked by a chum, 'You had a good hiding today, George?' He said that the Guv'nor hadn't touched him. Every time he cracked the whip Lambton said, 'Yell, damn you, yell!'

As George grew taller and broader, he kept gaining weight, of course. Although as late as 1919 he could get to scale at 6 st 5 lb, he recounted that by the last months of his career he was about 7 st 11 lb. At that time the leading rider of the stable Steve Donoghue rode at 7 st 2 lb. During that time, 'My father did his best to keep me supplied with mounts. The lengths he went to help me to fulfil his ambition to make me a jockey are pathetic as I look back at them,' he said in 1938. Charlie Austin, a music hall artist and great friend of George senior, promised to give young George a diamond pin when he won his first race in England. Despite one or two near misses he was destined never to get it. Towards the end of his flat-racing career he had his colours, those of Lord Derby – dark purple, cerise sleeves and buttons and black cap – and his racing name, Mr George Formby, confirmed for life.

His weight reaching eight stone, 'a disastrous load for an apprentice', he had his last race at Catterick Bridge, Yorkshire, riding Old Chris, a 'dog horse – one of the go-when-you-please sort'. As the winter of 1920 approached he went from Newmarket to Malton, Yorkshire, and started to ride more regularly over hurdles, although (as he later pointed out), he had ridden in his first hurdle race when he was only twelve and a half. 'I was doing a lot of schooling with young chasers-to-be – a sure indication of my too heavy apprentice flesh. One way with another I took a number of bad tosses, but I do not need to tell those who know me that these were the least thing[s] to frighten me, as I never mind falling about.' Despite George's indisputable physical courage and toughness he didn't like hurdling, and his confidence must have been undermined. Not only was *he* anxious about his future, he was worried about his father's reaction if his hopes were unfulfilled. Much has been said about the younger George's domination by women, but it was his father he revered. Even when the lad's potential future career was clearly doomed, even when he could not ride a winner, his father was undeterred and the matter not up for discussion.

George senior continued to do well from his records. In March 1916 he had been given a retainer of £100 and a guaranteed income of £3,150

(£158,000). In December 1917 the Command Performers' Record had been released, George getting as a royalty a farthing per record sold. Others, of course, also profited in his wake. A letter from Will Hyde in 1919 told him excitedly that his song 'Lifted the Latch and Walked In' had earned him £19 13s. 8d. in royalties. More important is that 13,993 copies of the record had sold. In January 1920 George signed a new contract with British Zonophone to run from March, and in November he went to Hayes to make twenty-four new records for them. Coincidentally the Italian–American soprano Luisa Tetrazzini, one of the Gramophone Company's biggest names, arrived on the same day. Judging by a surviving photograph, their respect was mutual. A large part of the charm of George's recordings was his ad-libbing. As *The Voice* of March 1921 commented: 'The improvisations contained in some of his records add greatly to their popularity.' They were wonderfully winning.

In the character of 'The Boxer' he spoke to the orchestra. 'Start off now and let's have some music, because I can't fight without music... Steady

One of George senior's recording sessions. Luisa Tetrazzini is listening
With kind permission of EMI

boys, get your ears well back because I'm going to start as soon as I begin...'
He went on, '...but I stopped every blow. And when he closed me right
eye up I did laugh, I couldn't see, it was funny, of course I were frightened
to open me mouth in case he closed that. I would have looked a bonny
nice thing. Every place closed up and no exits. Have we finished now?
There's a fellow behind me and I'm waiting of him, talking to him all
t' time, he doesn't know I'm talking about him...' Sometimes his humour
had an edge, as in his ad lib from 'Follow Me'. A day out went wrong and
George ended up being escorted to the local court. 'I'm here now. Do you
know I've had the time o' me life today. I've had two ice cream sandwiches...
[A policeman] took me by me hand all t' way and took me in front of a nice
fella with a big wig on. I said, "Good morning," and he said, "Mind your
own business," so I said, "Get your hair cut."'

George 'made a fortune with death standing ever at his elbow',
commented a journalist in *The Voice* in March 1921. He was advised that
emigrating to the milder air of South Africa would prolong his life, but
refused to leave Eliza with their seven children. Understanding better than
anyone else the 'frail hold he had on life', George had always undertaken a
punishing programme of work to provide money for his young family after
he had gone. In his panto season at The Empire, Newcastle upon Tyne, in
the winter of 1920–1 he had the leading comic part in John Tiller's *Jack
and Jill*. Playing two houses daily, at 2 and 7 p.m., he rested after the first
performance in order to be fit enough to do the second. His meticulously
kept engagement diary shows dates booked ahead for as far in advance as
1928. But there are also many dates scored through and the single word
'ill' written alongside. On stage he routinely met and outfaced his demons
with winning humour. 'Coughing better tonight' consciously turned his
ill health to his advantage, but the irony must sometimes have been hard
to bear for Eliza, standing by anxiously in the wings. She was armed with
glasses of water and tubes of ice to refresh him and, later, to stop the haemor-
rhaging caused by his tuberculosis. Towards the end of his life there was an
oxygen tent there too. A friend of her husband's described her at the time as
'his helpmeet, prompter, and above all, his doctor'.

Young George had not lived at home with his family for more than short holidays since he was seven, and by now he was sixteen. He had, however, visited them a month earlier, at Christmas, and had spent a little time with his father between the opening performance of *Jack and Jill* on Christmas Eve and the resumption of shows on 27 December. On Wednesday, 2 February 1921, while George senior was playing 'John Willie', the strain of his exhausting schedule and the seriousness of his illness finally defeated him. A coughing fit tore some blood vessels in his larynx and he haemorrhaged. He was advised by a doctor to go home after his collapse on stage, and he very much wanted to. So many times had he been ill before that he didn't believe this time would be his last. He sent a message to his Newcastle public through a newspaper writer. 'Tell them I think everything will be all right in a few weeks and that I hope to return in my single-handed work this summer. By all means I shall try to do so.' One of the last things he said to Frank Allen, the managing director of Moss Empires was, 'You'll be seeing Sir Harry Lauder; give him my kindest regards.'

After his father's collapse young George had come from Ireland (it is not clear why he had gone back there, having finally escaped), summoned by a telegram, to be at his father's bedside in Newcastle, and Eliza's mother had brought little Edward, to give moral support.

Eliza described what happened next.

> I said to the doctor, he seems to want to go home, so I'll come down with you and help to get him ready at the hotel, and they were very good at the Turk's Head Hotel, they got him to the station, and they hadn't put the private saloon on, which we asked for, I suppose because the War was not long over, and just after Christmas, and the station was full, and on the Friday, four o'clock, we left. We should have got into Warrington at ten o'clock. We had to change at Manchester... instead of putting it [the private carriage] on the front of the train with a communicating door with the rest of the train, they had put it on the end, all locked up. We couldn't even get out for a cup of tea until we got to Manchester. No rugs or blankets, although it

cost £75 and I took my fur coat off, wrapped it round George and travelled with just my frock on in the carriage till we got home. He was on a stretcher, and there was George, Edward and my mother with me. I was frantic; he was being rattled and shook. He was rocked here and there, and I was tucked up at the side of him, wiping his face and doing all that.

Once home, Eliza did all she could to get medical help for her husband, but things didn't go well. George's doctor prescribed strong medicine but didn't visit. A locum advised that the family should employ a 'heart nurse', who proved to be more trouble than she was worth.

On the Monday she didn't arrive; she couldn't do this, couldn't do the other. Sunday we waited all day for her and she came on the Monday afternoon. She had to have two hours off in the morning, two hours off in the afternoon, not to sleep with the other servants, had to sleep on her own, had to eat on her own. I hadn't time to be bothered with her. I said, 'If you'd like to go home, back to your hospital, that's quite all right with me, send a bill in, I don't mind.' I got an oxygen tent for him, £17. I stood on my tiptoes myself and fed him oxygen for an hour and a half at a time, and never moved, and it was an exertion for me to do it.

Eliza recalled two touching conversations.

George said, 'How do you think I am, Liza?'
I said, 'I don't think you're as bad this time as you've been other times, do you?'
He said, 'Don't you think so?'
'No, I don't myself, George; how do you feel?'
Because he seemed quiet... he said, 'Well, I've left you comfortable enough, Liza. Mind you, you'd whip the hair off your head to have me back after I go.'

'I don't want you to go, George,' I said. That was on the Monday before he died, talking to me in the bed. I said, 'Well, if you think that why not pension me off? Leave me without anything if that's what our marriage is.'

'I leave it up to you, if ever I go, what you do. It's up to you, Liza, you might be glad to remarry.'

Later he reminded her, 'Liza, tomorrow's pancake Tuesday, will you make me one?'

I said, 'I will that.'

He said, 'Make it yourself, don't let any of the servants make it.'

I have never eaten a pancake on pancake Tuesday since then because that was the last thing he asked me would I make him. He was very fond of them.

Frank came from Douai Abbey School where he boarded. Much to Louisa's disgust the nuns did not allow her to leave her Somerset convent school until the day which proved to be the day of her father's death, so she was not with him at the end. George died on Tuesday morning at 8.30 in his own bed at home, at Hill Crest, Warrington. His mother-in-law, Louisa Hoy, present at the scene, registered the death. The local newspaper gave the cause of his death as heart failure following bronchitis, his death certificate as pulmonary tuberculosis.

George said years afterwards that he was glad his father had died content in the belief that his son would continue as a jockey, but that was becoming ever less likely. George knew he was facing 'the life of a stable-hand at £2 5s. a week' and was grateful that his father was 'spared the horror to his sensitive spirit of seeing me finally running away from the life'. He didn't want a steeplechasing career, and while a competent and reasonably successful jockey, riding, it is said, twenty-two second-placed horses, he had never had a winner. His father's final plan seems to have been that he would buy a racing stable and, when George was eighteen, would give him day-to-day charge of it, but of course events overtook him. He had always been determined to keep his son away from show business, presumably because the life was hard and unglamorous, involving a great deal of travel and little time at home. What he actually said, famously, was 'One fool in the family's enough', and George had never seen his father perform professionally or even rehearse backstage – he had tried, but if he got close he was booted out. According to his sister Louisa, the children were sometimes invited on stage to take a bow, but George would rarely be at home and was never among them. So all he knew of his father's act came from listening to his records at home. Paradoxically, the elder Formby's efforts seem to have had the reverse effect: not only his eldest son but his second son Frank and his daughters Louie, Ella and Ethel had stage careers. Mary had a circus act and Ted worked in the world of theatre management.

'For a long time he was an idol of the town and he never looked back. His humour was often crude and always simple but it was always true humour, and, what is more, it was invariably clean.' So said *The Times* obituarist in 1921. Ted Granville, his first London agent, spoke to the reporter from the *Daily Dispatch*: 'He has had many imitators but there is only one George Formby. In the aggregate he has broken more records than any other artist in the various Halls.' In a nostalgic tribute evening in 1955, *Music Hall at the Met.*, *The Times* reviewer wrote of the actor impersonating him: '"Mr George Formby" though he was physically more robust than that frail and, alas, only too mortal droll, did the old "fag ends" business with conviction and had us all "Standing at the corner of the street" and "Playing the game in the West" once again in memory; and it was strange and rather moving to hear the long-drawn expectant "Ah!" with which the audience greeted his name – the name of a ghost or spirit – when the chairman called it. No great comedian could wish for better tribute thirty years after his death.' It was going to be a hard act to follow.

★★★

There is an extraordinary postscript to the life of this talented, original and charismatic self-made man, who had risen quite literally from rags to respectability. He was a bigamist. It is likely that Eliza knew at an early

One of George's last characters

stage that their 'marriage' was invalid. His will of August 1906 referred to his 'reputed wife Eliza Ann Booth, otherwise Eliza Ann Hoy' as he made her his sole executrix. She may not, of course, have seen the will at that time, in which case his death may have been shocking in more ways than one. Her children probably never knew that they were illegitimate, though Ella referred in her old age to an acquaintance of her mother's who wanted 'to create a sensational scandal, and if it's not true it's not fair'. In May 1921 'Mrs Booth' was described as 'Eliza Ann Hoy, spinster' in the High Court document granting her probate. So who was really his widow? She stepped into the light in December 1921 alongside Eliza as they attempted to secure £70 (£2,300) from the Variety Artistes' Federation, George's union. The Federation was determined that they should not have it and took the matter to the King's Bench in the High Court.

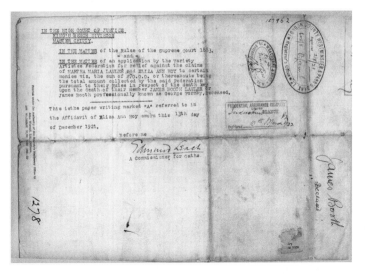

This document shows the names of both Martha Lawler and Eliza Hoy

George's legal wife was a music hall artist named Martha Maria Lawler, née Salter, whom he had married in a register office in Halifax on 3 August 1897. Both stated their age as twenty-one, though in fact she was only twenty. Both gave their address as 39 Portland Road, Halifax. George seems to have been prone to striking up romantic relationships with his landlords' daughters. The couple chose to describe their profession as 'vocalist'. George gave his name as James Booth Lawler, and his father's as Francis Lawler, iron fitter. Her father was not named, which suggests that she was illegitimate. Martha was born in June 1877 in Dudley, Staffordshire. Her mother Hannah Salter married William Morgan, a coal miner, in Dudley in 1881 and the 1891 census shows the three of them living in Wednesfield, Staffordshire. By this time Martha had taken the Morgan surname and was also working in the coal industry, aged fourteen. Small wonder that she was attracted to the music hall stage.

The first, and only valid, marriage of George senior

Why did James and Martha part? There is no evidence to say. Perhaps she refused to travel with him, as she was living with her parents in Halifax in 1901. Whatever the case, just two years later almost to the day, her husband, James Lawler, walked into the Wigan Register Office with Eliza, declaring himself to be James Booth, bachelor. These were the days of Victorian England, and women's rights were being won but slowly. Divorce was out of the question except for the moneyed few who could afford to procure the necessary Act of Parliament. Where a couple parted company and stayed apart informal 'divorce' was widely accepted. But both Martha and James had ruled themselves out of any other legal marriage. Life after James seems to have been dreary for Martha. The 1911 census shows her living alone in Halifax, in one room. With, as she stated, 'no occupation', she was entirely supported by 'one pound from my husband weekley [sic].' Perhaps this was 'hush money' or, on a more generous interpretation, his attempt to do right by her. It must have been sufficient for her to get by: a thirty-five-year-old could presumably have worked if she had felt the need to.

Eliza's pregnancy in 1899 probably forced James's hand. Illegitimate children at the turn of the twentieth century could have a hard time of it. The northern comedian Frank Randle, born illegitimate in 1901 and himself a Wiganer, was taunted and jeered at as 'a bastard' by other children throughout his childhood. James wanted his developing career to head towards respectability, and would know all too well the social price to be paid for 'living in sin'. He and Eliza had to be 'married'. On the other hand, the penalties for bigamy could be severe. At one end of the scale Old Bailey judgments of the time show two days' imprisonment, but at the other, months of hard labour or even years of penal servitude. Clearly James felt that to *conceal* this first 'mistake', and conceal it well, was essential. A prison sentence of any length would probably have killed him. For this reason he had to distance himself from the Lawler name, and from his father Frank. There was no falling out or repudiation of him, but casting doubt on his paternity gave him a plausible reason for taking his mother's maiden name. Frank was as certainly James's father as it was possible to know in those pre-DNA testing days. James even called two of his sons Francis. Had he wished, he could have done as Martha did and left the column concerning his father's details blank. No, he knew Frank was his father but he needed to lose his surname and lose it completely. That was why he gave his father's name as Frank Booth the day he 'married' Eliza. Did James and Martha ever meet again? That may never be known, but Martha seems to have followed his career with interest, or perhaps self-interest, as when her weekly payments ended with his death she was ready, understandably, to claim a substantial sum of money as his widow.

CHAPTER SIX

Chip off the Old Block

George senior, described as 'a thrifty man' by his daughter Ella, left a fortune of over £25,000 (£822,000), including a number of properties. While this was a considerable sum, Eliza needed all the funds she could get. She was only forty-one and all her children except George were under the age of fifteen. Her youngest child was only three years old. Five children were in private education, and George junior was the only one old enough to earn a living. The family income had all but collapsed,

From left to right, Mary, Louisa, Frank, Teddy, Ella, Ethel.
George junior was absent, at the stables

and something had to be done to try to restore it. She could hope to draw a small income from interest and rents, but otherwise she would have to live off capital. Her answer seems to have been to consider her eldest son for a career on the halls, using her money and contacts, and in effect keeping her husband's act going. This sounds like something of a long shot. While he seems to have enjoyed giving little performances for tips as a child, he could scarcely be expected to pull off his father's brilliant stage act, honed and developed over years, as a callow adolescent. Plenty of people in the music hall world eked out a poor living in hard circumstances. But in one way the prospect must have been very tempting, as at the time of his father's death young George was in a dilemma about his future. The family's two horses, too expensive and a nuisance to keep, had been sold two years previously. His flat-racing career was over and he hated hurdling: despite his physical bravery he had been unnerved by several falls he had taken 'over the sticks'. His father's death gave him his release from any filial obligation to succeed in the horse-racing world. In his own words, 'I gave up the idea of becoming a jockey when Dad left us.'

He said in 1937 that as he had a 'passion for speed' he seriously considered becoming a dirt track rider, but in the spring of 1921 Eliza was a woman in a hurry. Why? Her husband had worked himself to death to get as much money as he could for her and she was granted probate of his will in May. She had sufficient funds, it would seem, to consider the family's position, and young George's future, calmly. Instead, within weeks, she was rehearsing the reluctant teenager in his father's material, altering stage outfits and calling in favours. Michael Daly, the writer and musician, has suggested that perhaps she wasn't sure that she would receive her 'husband's' money, or indeed knew that she would not. Joe Hill, who became manager of the Grand and Royal Theatres, Bolton, was quite clear in an interview in 1965 about the family 'secret'. He knew that the Booth children were illegitimate, as the marriage of George and Eliza was invalid. He was convinced that George's actual wife got *all* the money. Is it fanciful to think that Martha held the threat of exposure over Eliza's head to ensure she scooped the pool?

There are some problems with this interpretation of what happened. Firstly, it isn't clear how much actual cash there was. A bank book shows a last entry for February 1921 and a total sum of over £9,000 (£296,000), but there may have been other accounts. Eliza herself spoke of 'thousands of pounds' she had spent on launching George's career and on luxury gifts to him such as a sports car. It is true that she moved out of Stockton Heath and went to a smaller property in Menlove Avenue, Liverpool, shortly after George got married, but that was three years after her husband's death. Did Martha gain a share of her husband's wealth? Why were the two women working together to get money from the Variety Artistes' Federation by the end of the year? Was there a deal already struck that *all* the money was to be shared?

The legend of George's introduction to show business usually goes something like this. He and his mother were returning from Southampton, where they had been seeing off a friend, and spent a night in London. They visited the Victoria Palace where a comedian, George Bass, whom Eliza knew well, was not only using Formby senior's material but using it badly. He was not the first to do it, but now there could be no challenge from the owner himself. Angry and upset, Eliza and George left. He walked for several hours before deciding that *he* would do his father's act if anyone would.

In an interview to a sympathetic reporter at the Palace Theatre, Oldham, he gave his version of events. He explained that Sir Harry Lauder 'told [his mother] to place me where my inclination led, and it has led me to follow Dad'. He decided to appear as George Hoy, using his mother's maiden name which was also his own second given name. Apparently he was influenced by Lauder's further advice not to follow a famous name, but to try 'by hard work to make a name for myself', but the thin cloak of a slightly different name wasn't compatible with using his father's unmistakeable and extremely well-known material while also dressing to look very like him. Furthermore, all the early playbills referred explicitly to the fact that he was the late Formby's son. After all, the managers wanted to sell tickets, and this was likely to be a big draw.

Was he using his father's reputation or not? Did he want to use the connection or not? Psychologically the smokescreen seems to have served him well. As far as he was concerned, if he failed, his father's famous and loved name would not be brought into disrepute. Only when he was top of the bill, he said, would he call himself George Formby. He gave this account many years later in a radio interview in Canada in 1950. He described his father with pride as 'probably the greatest comedian of his generation' and explained that he did not want the name of Formby off the top of the bill. As, he said, he took about eighteen months to get to the top, this meant that their name had been in total for sixty years at the top of the vaudeville bill. It was an exaggeration – fifty would have been nearer the mark – but the point was well made.

This is highly unlikely to have been the way things happened. It was Eliza who had spoken to Lauder about a career for her eldest son in the weeks following his father's premature death and her youngest son, Ted, was in no doubt that she was in control. George, it seems, was reluctant, but she was determined. She took on the task of training him; she had the money and, most importantly, she had the contacts. And she was seeing London bookers and agents before she saw the plagiarized performance which upset her son so much. The reason Eliza and George were in Southampton was that Eliza was bidding farewell to a suitor, Bert, who had asked her to marry him about six months after her husband's death. When she turned him down, 'because I'd got the memory of a very good husband, a loving man, a good partner, and good man in every detail, and I couldn't forget him', he decided to go abroad. On the way home Eliza and her son spent a night in London specifically to see agents, particularly a Mr Jones who worked for Sir Oswald Stoll. They were upset by Bass's performance because the loss of their George was still so raw. But the decision that his son should follow in his footsteps had long since been taken.

George was in no position to impersonate his father, as apparently he had never seen him perform on stage. Eliza, of course, had seen countless performances, and no doubt was word perfect in both songs and patter. Although his mother claimed he had imitated his father's act at home to the amusement of the family, and of George senior himself – 'It was the only time my husband ever saw himself as others saw him, and it was good to see how he enjoyed the lad's acting' – it is hard to see how this can have been true. George later explained that he had learned a couple of the songs from records. It was ironical that George, of all of the children, was the only one not to have seen his father's act. The others were all given opportunities in turns to go along to watch him, and Ella remembered singing along with her father, from the wings.

Over and over again in the Oldham interview George referred to his dearly loved father, who was, naturally, in the forefront of his mind. 'I know I am not a patch on dear old Dad, but he would be pleased to see me in my present role... I intend to use a lot of Dad's stuff. Did you see the little hat I wore on the stage? And the quaint little cape? And, did you notice the stick? Well – they – they – were dear old Dad's, and—' George was overcome with emotion, but Mrs Booth was businesslike. Meeting the reporter cordially in the dressing room of her friends Pierce and Roslyn, also on the bill, she explained that 'they are doing all they can to make the tour of George jun. a success'. Shrewd operator and publicist that she was, she also had plans for the future.

> He is at present rendering his father's songs, but as time goes on we shall be able to give the public entirely new and original songs and patter... I have secured the Moss tour for him already, and when such good judges as Sir Harry Lauder, Miss Daisy Wood [sister of Marie Lloyd and principal boy in, for example, *Jack and the Beanstalk*], Shaun Glenville and his splendid wife Dorothy Ward have given their opinion as in favour of this step, well, I am confident of ultimate success... I have secured the services of a good song-writer for my son, and I mean to spare no expense or trouble to give the public all that my husband would have given them – the best.

References to and reminders of her late husband were deftly made. Eliza could not resist adding her opinion that the real talent lay with her young son Frank, then eight years old. 'You should see little Frankie! That lad has never cried a dozen times in his life. He sees a joke in everything, and as a comedian he has great talent... He is being educated at a famous school and the masters there report that he is a born comedian. I have heard numerous tales of his quickness of wit...' For once the redoubtable Mrs Booth was wrong in her vision of the future.

With the help of Ernest Dukinfield, his father's pianist and sometime songwriter, and Tommy Eden, who had sometimes played for her husband in the free and easies, Eliza coached George in his father's routines. So, in the spring of 1921, George Hoy, once got up in his father's stage clothes and make-up, bore an almost uncanny resemblance to 'the Wigan Nightingale'. The 'eyes' were pencilled on his forehead as they had been on his father's. So similar were they that photographs of young George have frequently been labelled with his father's name. Even the voice, with its distinctive Lancashire accent, sounded the same. For the moment, the old act was all there was. George Hoy first appeared on stage after an intense month of rehearsal, on 21 March 1921 at the Hippodrome, Earlestown, a few miles from Warrington, later described by him as 'a little tin hut near Newton-le-Willows'. The owner Fred Harrison agreed, after some prodding by D. J. Clarke, to give him two weeks in a mixed programme of drama at £5 a week. He performed on Monday, Tuesday and Wednesday between the reels of *Bleak House*, and on Thursday and Saturday in the interval of *The Elusive Pimpernel*, billed as:

George Hoy
Patter Comedian.
The son of the Late
GEORGE FORMBY.
Change of Songs and Patter Thursday and Saturday.

Ticket prices were 3*d*., 5*d*., 9*d*. and 1*s*. Tommy Eden took Eliza to the show along with 'half Warrington'. According to Bert Loman, who later taught him the arts of pantomime, George as a young man seemed to lack confidence. Small wonder that on this evening he was extremely nervous. He said afterwards that he went through the whole of his first performance with his eyes closed, and that he was 'a dismal failure'. While he felt he had inherited his father's sense of humour, he lacked his ease on the stage, even forgetting his

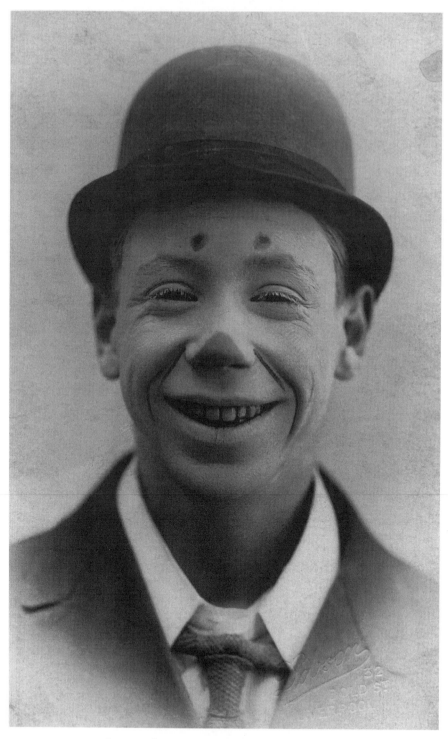

George making a start on the winding road to success

lines in an attack of stage fright. He remembered the audience as 'unforgiving'. It must have been an agonising experience for both George and his mother. But amid the heckling one voice called out, 'Go on, George, you're a chip off the old block.' According to George, 'whoever said that gave me a career'.

While George was still working at Earlestown, his father's old friend Denny Clarke, proprietor of the Argyle Theatre, Birkenhead, gave him three professional engagements – two performances a night at £17 10s. a week, offering him private rehearsal time with the band on Monday for half an hour. He signed him up to a series of shows at Moss Empire halls at the Southport Palladium and St Helens to follow his appearance at the Argyle in the week beginning 18 April. George immediately decided to give ten shillings of his salary to his widowed grandmother – 'my nanny' as he called her. He dearly loved the woman who had been his surrogate mother while Eliza was away from home. The Argyle was one of England's oldest music halls, dating from 1868, and had gained a reputation as a nursery of new talent. Clarke had helped build the careers of Charlie Chaplin, Harry Lauder and Dan Leno as well as George senior. Near the end of his life (on his confessional *Friday Show*), George was very frank about the early days: 'I was first turn, three minutes, died the death of a dog. Oh yes, it's truth night tonight.'

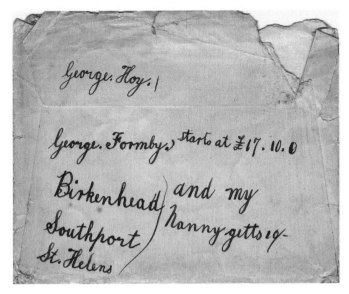

Written in sixteen-year-old George's own hand

Maybe, but the story at the Argyle was different. Clarke's booking record was written at the time, in his own hand. Under the list of turns booked – in this case eight – he wrote in pencil the order of appearance and, often, the time allotted to each performer. On that occasion George went on third. Frustratingly, Clarke didn't, for once, write the timings which would produce a total running time between 100 and 120 minutes – the overall show time he aimed at. But at the Argyle no one ever had less than the five minutes each given to the overture and the bioscope. It is likely that George had twelve minutes, a time clearly pencilled in on his third engagement at the St Helens Hippodrome, with Daisy Wood topping the bill. It has been said that he got a poor reception and that pennies were thrown in derision. But he was given the same sort of time slot as most of the others and he was not the lowest paid. Two of his fellow performers got less than him – one only £12. It was a generous gesture by Denny Clarke in more ways than one.

'He has gained confidence since he literally stepped into his father's shoes and clothes, and he can serve up a Formby number in a very acceptable manner, reminiscent of the lamented famous comedian whose name he bears.' George was happy to quote this critic at the Argyle in his own publicity, but he was being damned by faint praise. The reviewer at the Hippodrome, Ashton under Lyne, seemed to think pretty much the same. 'By hard work he is reproducing something of the great comedian's best talents.' Even his tag, 'A Chip off the Old Block', was a direct borrowing from George senior. There were many references to the likeness of his appearance, and more particularly his voice, to those of his father. Like it or not George was trading on the family name, but even his favourable reviews tended to be only lukewarm. He struggled to advance his career but the going was hard. He said himself he was out of work for three months and nearly starved. His brother Frank later commented that their mother's strenuous coaching efforts were not enough. 'It was as if she was trying to bring our father back to life. George could dress like him; he couldn't be him.' At Blyth, near Newcastle, he was booed and hissed. But Denny Clarke didn't desert his cause. George appeared at another theatre Clarke managed, the Dublin Hippodrome and Theatre Royal, in October 1921.

This time he got £25 for his twelve-minute slot. The following month he was back at the Argyle, and his act was now the longest – twenty-two minutes.

These first months after his father's death were demanding for George, but they also brought benefits while he was at home. Not only was he back with the family, but he was now the male head of the household and the breadwinner, roles which carried considerable weight in post-Victorian northern England. His father's word had been law. If he wanted George to go to the stables, to the stables he went and was never allowed to give up the life. If his father declared that he was never to see or hear him on stage, he never did – no one dared gainsay his wishes. All the other children were sent away to school to receive the education George senior had not had – and Eliza was freed to be with *him*. Ella remembered her mother saying, 'Don't disturb your father,' and he was left undisturbed. This was not an individual's tyranny, but the way things were in hundreds of thousands of homes in the early twentieth century.

Although his mother took control of George junior's early career, in other ways she was something of a pushover. She may have felt some guilt about the comfortless and lonely time he had endured at the stables and his exclusion from so many years of family life and began to spoil him. Far from calling the shots, she gave way on a number of important occasions. Ted commented in a *South Bank Show* interview, 'He could have what he wanted really. Dad was gone and Mother was very vulnerable…' At a race at Aintree he kept pestering his mother to buy him a motorbike. There were only three horses in the race, but because of his regard for George senior the bookie allowed her to place a bet at 10/1. The horse came home and young George got his bike. Eliza taught him to drive, and a car was next on his wish list, an Alvis – elegant, sporty and very expensive. Ted recalled, 'He was a bit of a nagger. He would say, "Go on, Mother, buy me that car, go on, I'd like that car, Mother, I'll work ever so hard…," and he would nag her, probably took him half the day but by that time she was fed up with it. She said, "Oh all right, for God's sake go and get the car."'

On Wednesday, 21 October 1922 the Booth family gathered for the unveiling of the memorial to George senior in Warrington Cemetery. The design of the stone was a replica of the old Manchester Hippodrome's proscenium arch, the 'Hip', said to be George's favourite theatre. The stone itself, in expensive white Carrara marble, stood ten feet high and was topped with a cross. The image of the stage front with swagged drop curtains drawn aside revealed a bas-relief of the comedian's head in three-quarter profile. On either side, above columns, were bas-relief masks of Comedy and Tragedy and in the centre instruments to symbolize music. Formby's name and the single word 'Comedian' were inscribed above the sentence 'After Life's Fitful Fever -He Sleeps Well'. The line comes from *Macbeth*, perhaps chosen for its superficial appropriateness. Denny Clarke officiated at the flower-laden grave, flanked by the widow and children and a large crowd of well-wishers. In the photographs of the occasion young George stands to the right of the memorial, next to his grandmother, his solemn face bearing the inward-looking blankness of grief, his hands protectively on the shoulders of his smallest brother, four-year-old Teddy. Over eighty years later, the day of this memorial service was Ted's earliest memory, etched, as childhood memories often are, by the vividness of an exceptional, dramatic, and often, little-understood event.

Earlier that year George had arrived in Burnley after an exhausting journey to find himself, George Hoy, top of the bill on the theatre poster in the tram station. Then and there he treated himself to a taxi instead of waiting for the tram. The next morning 'George Hoy' was pasted over and replaced by 'George Formby'. So the story goes. Eliza told Rex Blaker in 1967 that Moss Empires *demanded* the name change. Well, naturally. By September of 1923 George appeared on a Morecambe Tower playbill as 'George Formby Junr.', though he was by no means at the top of this one. At Christmas he was using the name in his professional mailings and advertising his recent successes in his father's birthplace, Ashton under Lyne, in Bury and, predictably, at the Argyle, Birkenhead. His publicity still focused on the 'Chip off the Old Block' sentiment. On New Year's Eve he opened for a week at the Hippodrome, Bolton, for a salary of £25 (£1,060).

Beryl Ingham was twenty-two, a pretty, athletic and vivacious blonde, and a capable young woman. She was one half of the dancing duo The Two Violets, her sister May being the other. Their father, John James Ingham, ran the Black Bull Hotel, Market Street, Darwen. For about the previous ten years the girls had been clog dancers of some repute on the northern music hall circuit, and Beryl had won the all-England step dancing championship when she was only eleven. Sometime during 1923, at the Queens, Castleford, she met George Formby. Despite Eliza's best efforts George was not actually on the bill but 'blacked his face' and joined the Swanee Minstrel troupe, which included some friends, performing there in revue. They offered him a lowly £5 for a week's work. Beryl later recalled that his first words to her were: 'Good evening, love, how're you?'

'Mind your own business,' she snapped. She explained thirty years later that she and her sister had been brought up not to speak to strangers. George, deeply attracted to the 'skinny' dancer, himself said that Beryl 'didn't bother with' him for that first week. When he was leaving, in the same train, in the same carriage, he called out, 'Does anybody want an orange?' Beryl put down the paper she was reading, and he said, 'You want the orange?' and tossed it to her. In December she saw him perform at Bolton. Her remark afterwards, that if she'd had a bag of rotten tomatoes with her she would have thrown them during his act, has not been well received by her critics, but at least it had the merit of clarity.

In the spring of 1924 Beryl came to Warrington (perhaps the girls were appearing there) where their courtship began. George pursued her with relentless enthusiasm, dashing off on his motorbike after shows all over the country to see her at home in Darwen. She played it cool. It has been suggested – without any evidence – that she never felt any sexual attraction to him. Could it be that a close association with music hall aristocracy was the defining consideration for her? But the star in the family was dead, and there would have been small reason for her to marry purely for control of his son's somewhat uncertain career. Unless there was something in Eliza's story.

Beryl in glamorous shot, 1920s

> She [Beryl] always knew that Georgie would become a star because Ella Retford [a singer and pantomime principal boy], when she worked the Palace, Blackpool, in 1924 before he was married, and we took Beryl with us, she stayed with me at the Palatine Hotel, and Ella Retford said on the side of the stage while George was working, 'Liza, you've got something there with George' – and Beryl heard it. And from then Beryl knew that if she could get Georgie that he would be a star. He was a star in the making.

But presumably Beryl was not short of other offers. Nor was she ready at her age to turn into George's mother, though her talent for organisation and desire to dominate him were probably reasons why George was drawn to her. Beryl's innermost feelings were, and always will be, private, but there's every reason to believe that her obvious affection for him was complemented by physical attraction.

In August 1924, shortly before they married, George appeared at the Alhambra, Leicester Square, 'the most prestigious variety theatre in the country'. It was to be a momentous booking in several ways. It was there that he first used the catchphrase 'Turned out nice again!' That cheerful expression, commonplace in the north of England, was to be one of the main planks of his success. He was beginning, by short stages, to develop his own act, but on this occasion he was given a leg-up by two of his father's friends. Ernest Dukinfield agreed to play the piano and George Saker, his father's conductor, broke the habit of a lifetime for him. A grand figure, he would not usually demean himself by appearing early in the programme, preferring to give the audience time to settle down. But this time he swept regally down the aisle for the mere warm-up, George.

Eliza was not in favour of George marrying, perhaps because she was, as her son Ted described her, 'a very possessive woman'. But she had put a huge amount of effort – and money – into trying to develop his stage career, and now she would be denied her just return for the family. She also stood to lose a way of life. The transition between accompanying her husband and

A young, happy and loving couple
By kind permission of Canadian Pacific

then her son around the halls had been accomplished almost seamlessly. This was the world in which she had status and influence, but now she'd have to stand aside for a daughter-in-law. It had been a family business too – Louie had acted as her brother's dresser and packer. No wonder there was fierce opposition. George was only twenty and, as he had not attained the age of majority (at that time twenty-one), he needed permission to marry. There was a story, strongly denied by some of George's family, that in order to persuade his mother to consent he claimed that Beryl was pregnant. There's no independent evidence that he ever alleged this, but Ella later said that her grandmother tried to change Eliza's mind by pointing out that she wouldn't like it if one of *her* girls were in a similar position. Given Eliza's devout Catholicism, the prospect of a register office ceremony could only have made matters worse, though *she* had also been married at the same register office (to a man already married!) and was most certainly pregnant at the time. Once again, though, George did what *he* wanted and not what his mother wanted, recruiting her younger sister, Matilda Fawcett (Aunty Tilly), to help him organize the details.

On Friday, 12 September George left the Royal Court Theatre, Warrington, where he had entertained large audiences over the previous week, and went by taxi to Darwen. The story is that in the early hours of the morning he roused the family of his bride-to-be, proposed and was accepted. This *Romeo and Juliet* scene was not quite without preparation, however, nor was it entirely true. According to the *Sunday Chronicle* in an article dated 20 September, notice for a licence had been given on *Wednesday* for a marriage two days later, on the Friday. In fact it was the following morning, Saturday, 13 September 1924, at seven o'clock, when the bride and bridegroom, with May in attendance on her sister, set off in a taxi for the Wigan Register Office. The wedding, at ten o'clock, was witnessed by May and George's uncle, Eugene Fawcett, suggesting that Eliza continued to be hostile. The whole episode suggests orchestration, newspaper article and all, the publicity no doubt arranged by Beryl, who wanted a good story to tell. It has been said that Eliza and Beryl never got along, but shortly after the marriage Eliza bought Beryl 'a diamond watch – it was £50 then! Wholesale!' And Eliza was happy in later years to join the couple on cruises and holidays, though the notoriously difficult mother-in-law/daughter-in-law relationship seems to have kept the temperature between them cool.

The newly-weds couldn't afford a honeymoon. They married with only £70 between them, most of which was Beryl's, and spoken for to pay off George's motorcycling debts. Their wedding night seems to have been spent at George's relatives' home in Wigan and the following day they had to go their separate ways, George to Warrington for his last performance of the week and Beryl back home to Darwen. Money, and the management of it, were to prove important elements in George and Beryl's marriage. As money was so tight they both had to continue their own careers – Beryl's was much more successful than George's at the time – and the week after they were married they were in different counties, Beryl in Northumberland (Newcastle) and George in Lancashire (Morecambe). Beryl wrote that after her performance on Monday the manager came to congratulate her. Typically, she went on to the attack. 'That's champion,' she replied. 'And now what about a part for George?' A wire was sent to George telling him to present himself for rehearsal. The contract that followed was the first that Beryl negotiated for George but there were some difficult months before it actually began. These were the times when (according to their 'man', Harry Scott, many years afterwards) they left their digs in the morning with their lunch – oranges – in a brown paper bag and had to eat outside in all weathers because they weren't allowed to go back to their room till the evening. George's fee was £15 a week, and the first booking, ironically, given that it was the scene of his father's last performance, at the Newcastle Empire.

Thomas Convery, a Newcastle theatre manager and impresario, liked George's act and gave him a revue contract for five years. Convery ran several revues at any one time, but only George's featured his name in the title as the main draw. The first of them was *Formby Seeing Life*, written by Arthur Mertz and advertised as featuring singing, acrobats and comedy. However, there was no mention of the ukulele, even as late as November 1925 when he was playing the Palace, Oldham, in *Formby Seeing Life*. 'Quip and crank and merry jingle' were noted by one reviewer, but no ukulele… at Oldham what they wanted, still, was his father's old material. In February 1924 George and his mother had visited the HMV recording studio and George recorded

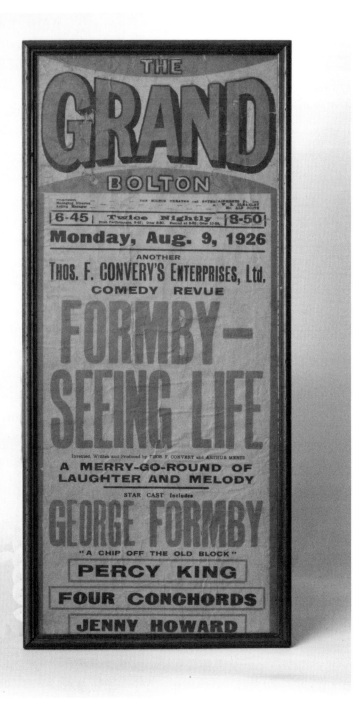

A poster for George's first Convery revue

'Rolling Around Piccadilly' as an audition piece. It was rejected, and only released two years later when he re-recorded it along with a further five songs. Some were in his father's repertoire; all owed much to his style and were released on the Edison-Bell Winner label. None was a success. By contrast, in 1926, five years after his father's death, the HMV catalogue was still listing no fewer than thirty of *his* titles, available to fans for three shillings each. That was what his Oldham fans wanted too.

By January 1926 George was described by a critic as 'the life and soul, the electric force' of the show. By now his stage persona was classless, sophisticated and cheerful, his broad smile contrasting with his father's assumed melancholy. Beryl had persuaded him to abandon the John Willie costume while keeping the character. Beryl and May were still doing their 'sister act' and also got their picture in the publicity. It was quite a family affair, as two of George's sisters, Ella and Louie, had responded to an advert for 'supers' and were signed up as dancers. There were sixteen scenes, with Jenny Howard the leading lady. 'George poses as a simple Lancashire lad – from Wigan.' But there was more – he 'possesses all the artistry of his father (as a comedian)' – *and* at last, there was the ukulele! George played the Argyle in May 1926, Convery and Denny Clarke sharing the takings. It was in this revue, appearing at the Shepherd's Bush Empire that George made his London debut.

CHAPTER SEVEN

John Willie's Jazz Band

'He was always strumming. He loved Dixieland, my Georgie,' his mother, aged one hundred recalled in a newspaper interview. She always insisted she bought George his first stringed instrument, a ukulele, a La Foley, from the department store Gamages, London. She bought one for his sister Louie as well. Influenced by the radio and records, he liked jazz and the hot Latin American dance music of Edmundo Ros and Xavier Cugat. The ukulele was to the Twenties and Thirties what the guitar was to the 1960s. An important influence was Frank Crumit, the American vaudeville singer and ukulele player among whose best-known numbers were 'Abdul Abulbul Amir' and 'The Prune Song' (1928). The latter has a modern feel:

Nowadays we often gaze on women over fifty
Without the slightest trace
Of wrinkles on their face.
Doctors go and take their dough to make them young and nifty.
But doctors I defy
To tell me just why

No matter how young a prune may be, it's always full of wrinkles.
We may get them on our face;
Prunes get them every place.
Nothing ever worries them, their life's an open book.
But no matter how young a prune may be, it has a worried look.

A large number of Crumit's records were found at George's home after his death in 1961 and a La Foley ukulele with a simple tutor inside the case was sold at the Beryldene auction. But according to Ella, writing in 1990 to the George Formby Society, he had actually been *taught* to play the ukulele by an American, Ukulele Ike, when he was on the bill with him. Ike's real name was Cliff Edwards, and he was later the voice for Walt Disney's Jiminy Cricket in the 1940 film *Pinocchio*. In that same film he sang 'When You Wish upon a Star', which won an Oscar for best song. Unfortunately there is no evidence that he and George ever met. George said years after the event that he had acquired his first ukulele from a chap he happened to be sharing a dressing room with, buying it, for a lark, for fifty bob.

His first 'banjulele', (the Keech brothers' 1917 invention and trade name), with ukulele frets and tuning and a banjo body, was probably made by Alvin D. and his brother Kelvin – publicity shots from 1923 show him holding one, and a 'Keech ukulele' was listed amongst George's effects after he died. He had seen it in the window of a junk shop when driving through Manchester earlier that year with his brother Frank and bought it for fifteen shillings. George's mother told the George Formby Society in 1961 that he had had lessons from 'an American gentleman who had a studio in the West End'. This is very likely to have been Alvin D. Keech, as George's syncopated style had much in common with the ukulele tutor produced by him.

It is easiest to refer to the instruments George played throughout his career as ukuleles, as that was the way they were billed at the time. He developed his own unique style. Much ink has been spilt on the discussion of just how good a musician and player George was. His musicianship has been sneered at because of his lack of ability to read music. He was accused of having a number of ukuleles tuned in different keys because he could not even 'tune a string'. Wartime newsreel films give the lie to that second accusation. His playing benefited from hands and wrists made strong and supple during his career as a jockey. Eddie Latta, one of George's songwriters, told the Decca record producer Kevin Daly in 1966: 'George had a natural, quick ear; very quick ear but no music... Rhythmically he was bloody good.' Joe Cooper, writing in *New Society* in 1974 also thought he was pretty good. 'Nobody has ever reproduced the casual devastating right hand syncopation, which so delicately synchronised with deft left hand chord fingering. His strumming rhythm was essentially an eight beat bar reduced by syncopation to seven and embellished by various roll strokes and characteristic flourishes.'

There are also a number of versions of the story about George first incorporating the ukulele into his stage act. His brother Ted recalled that it was a suggestion of a theatre manager, Charlie Lawson, at home in Warrington. Another, widely recounted, was that as George was unwilling, Lawson instructed Frank, then aged about twelve, to take it onto the stage in the middle of George's act and say: 'The management have told me you've got to play this.' Yet another account was that he first took it onstage for a shilling bet with a couple of singers who had been friends of his father. They had said they liked almost every musical instrument except the ukulele. So, in whatever circumstances, George walked onto the stage at the Barnsley Alhambra in 1925 and played it. Beryl's reaction was, apparently, 'You'll never go on stage without a ukulele again!' From then on he practised hard, but at first performed only one number, one he knew really well.

From the beginning Beryl had never made any secret of her low opinion of George's act. She felt that it was old-fashioned and needed a new, more exciting angle. She could see ways forward for him and the ukulele was to be the first major element in his act that owed nothing to his father. The second, Beryl's insistence that George remove literally and metaphorically the 'cloth cap', led to the development of a new glamorous persona which would not only deeply impress the northern audiences to whom George was to play but be acceptable to southern audiences too. Beryl quickly picked up the need for colour and spectacle which was proving so popular in America in burlesque. A letter from Beryl in the late 1920s shows how important the ukulele had become to George as it appears stylishly on the letterhead. Incidentally, Beryl also showed an early tendency to 'text-speak', signing off, 'Yours as B4…'

Joan Stoker, a young and impressionable member of a Blackpool Opera House audience in the early 1930s, was to remember vividly seventy years later the immaculate costumes, sophisticated evening dress, sparklingly bright beribboned shoes and the glamorous make-up and hairstyles which so captivated her in her front-row seat as a little girl at a Formby show. She

Beryl in costume

also remembered the excruciating embarrassment of her family's slightly late arrival and the friendly banter from George – 'you'll have been to Yates's Wine Lodge' – as she and her parents shuffled conspicuously to their seats. That survival from George senior's act, the wonderfully easy, natural and warm rapport with his audience, was what most appealed to Joan's father. The glamour of the occasion, George's elegant appearance and immense charm were the most enduring memories for Joan. These elements melded together were to prove wildly successful. Eddie Latta maintained that George used to say of his risqué jokes: 'If I went on in a check coat and baggy pants they'd be blue. People wouldn't take them. But in evening dress they're all right.'

George after his 'makeover' by Beryl

By the summer of 1928 the new revue was *Formby's Night Out*. Denny Clarke signed up the show for four separate weeks between August and the following January for £400 or 50 per cent of the takings. The Stoll publicity machine described this as a 'new laughter show' when he appeared that same January at the Manchester Hippodrome. It comprised eleven scenes. Stoll Attractions threw everything at the publicity, to cover all the angles. George was billed (still!) as 'A Chip off the Old Block' – in bold, then 'son of a famous father, The Lad Fra' Lancasheer', and, most importantly, 'a born comedian with a distinctive personality and inimitable methods all his own'. In case the paying customers hadn't got that last message it appeared again in a reference to his 'unique style and original "touches"'. The final promise was that 'his star is definitely well in the ascendant'. That at least was indisputably true.

It has been wrongly assumed that George was struggling to make good in show business in the late 1920s. His roles in the long-running Convery revues suggest that his work by that time was regular and lucrative. A 1927 photograph album shows that he was able to afford a luxury special-bodied Morris Oxford built at Morris Garages in Oxford (hence 'MG'), only one of numerous cars George was to own which had bespoke coachwork. This was definitely not 'off the peg' motoring. The photos also show an elaborate portable radio, very much an expensive new gadget at the time. Not bad for a young man of twenty-three! It was around this time that George and Beryl took Eliza and Louisa on one of their first cruises. In 1928 they also became homeowners, buying a semi-detached house at 836 Lancaster Road, Barton, near Preston. *Formby's Good Deed* was the third of the Convery revues, featuring not only Beryl but Mickey Dripping, the latter described as George's 'very clever canine companion'. He was a mongrel who did an act with George in all the glare of the footlights. He tended to wander off before the show but would always reappear on time for his performance.

The Twenties brought, on both sides of the Atlantic, deep poverty for many working people. It was a time made the more bitter by the disillusionment that followed the 'war to end all wars'. Lloyd George's promise of 'a land fit for heroes' quickly rang false, and the Twenties saw unemployment on a

A rare shot of a pensive George

large scale. The Wall Street Crash in 1929 ushered in a particularly severe economic depression in the north of England. In that year in Wigan one in three was on the dole. By 1931 the hated Means Test had been introduced, officials arriving to check people's homes to assess their eligibility for unemployment benefit. Without a national health service and with a visit from the doctor charged at five shillings, many could not afford health care. Escapism was desperately needed. At the other end of the social scale the 'Bright Young People' danced, drank and drugged the pain away. Drink was often an anaesthetic for the working class too, but so, more innocently, was a visit to the cinema or the dance hall.

George's 1929 recordings were the first to feature the wooden ukulele, on two tracks – 'In the Congo' and 'All Going Back', but neither was very successful. It must have been a bitter pill that at the same time his mother was receiving from Associated Copyrights Ltd a 'Mechanical Royalty Statement' detailing the sales of fifteen of his *father's* records. But the economic downturn had profound effects on the emerging record companies. Commercial songs – sentimental big band numbers and catchy tunes – were in demand, and on 1 July 1932 George made his first successful record. The song was written by Jack Cottrell and backed by the Jack Hylton Band who were working with George at the Palace Theatre, Manchester. Hylton had a huge reputation in 1932. As long ago as 1924 he had been leading his band in the Piccadilly Hotel. His records sold in large numbers and 'Happy Days Are Here Again' (1929) became closely associated with him. George was singing 'Chinese Blues' (as it was called then) and the boys in the band took a fancy to it. Hylton suggested that George record the song and Decca agreed, but the band leader was cautious, keeping his name off the label in case it was a flop. Another 'safeguard' was to make 'Chinese Blues' the B-side and the harmless 'Do De O Do' the A-side, but it was 'Chinese Blues' that sold the record. It was an immediate and long-term success. George was still singing about Mr Wu in his last panto at the Hippodrome, Bristol, in 1961. According to Dorothy Cottrell, her husband Jack was paid £10 for the song while George, out of the royalties, bought a new SS Jaguar. Not only *she* was sore: Jaguar cars smarted from the fact that George jumped a waiting list to have a new car and then sold it within six months of his ownership.

Such was George's growing success that in early 1932 he had hired a valet who also worked as a butler and handyman, dresser and stage assistant. Harry Scott (born Harry Scothron) had appeared in local circuses and the smaller halls as a young man. In 1966 Scott wrote that when he began his work with the Formbys his salary was £5 a week and thirty years later it was still £5 a week. In that way he contributed, apparently 'from the horse's mouth', to the idea that George was mean. But a letter from the Formbys' accountant refers to Scott's salary as £8 in 1955 and Beryl's cheque stubs from 1959 show clearly that he was by then receiving £10 a week. Some of his remarks come with a health warning! Still, he said, he was not complaining. He had stayed in wonderful hotels and knew that if he'd wanted caviar and champagne he could have had them. After the deaths of George and Beryl he said openly what is in any case clear in his memoir, that he was much closer to Beryl than to George. He described himself and Beryl as like brother and sister, and, as such, subject to the occasional 'family' rows which, after great stormings-out and much fuming on both sides, were always made up. By the end he seemed half in love with Beryl. George was more distant, less confiding, except perhaps in the immediate aftermath of Beryl's death. In his articles in *The Vellum* (the George Formby Society's magazine) Harry made much of his status as friend and confidant but Ted Formby insisted that he was really always only an employee.

In the winter of 1932 George appeared in his first pantomime, *Babes in the Wood*, at Bolton, and it was to be the beginning of a lifelong love affair with the genre. George later confessed that he looked forward to it all the year round because 'it permits you to go crackers... pantomime is ageless and it makes you feel ageless to appear in it'. He also loved all the things that could go wrong. In 1938 he described an incident in Birmingham the year before. 'The Captain had to propose to my wife and she had to be very coy about it. In the middle of his proposal the scenery suddenly began to fall down. I made frantic efforts to keep it up and shouted as I did so, "Go on – fall for him – the scenery is!"' Panto season over, in March 1933 the first *George Formby Road Show* began to tour the north of England. George and Beryl themselves hired the hall, the company and the band. This was a rehash of the old percentage system which George's father had run during the First World War. The first show netted only a £14 profit but they were to continue for the next four years. Harry Scott recounted the difficult moments of a performance in 1934, although he recalled it as the first ever evening. The compère was disgruntled about having to run up and down stairs to his dressing room and walked out just before the curtains opened. George wasn't dressed and there was no one to announce the acts – except Beryl, already in her stage outfit. Whereas the 1933 posters proclaimed that Beryl 'Talks and Taps', by the November of the following year her new role was billed, on the advertisements for the Hippodrome, Darlington, gender appropriately, 'Commère'. George later claimed she was the first ever woman in 'British Theatreland' to do the job.

The year 1933 saw a major departure for George as he went into the film business. Technically this wasn't a first as he had appeared as a child jockey in 1915, but he had no real experience of film and simply said that he would 'give it a bash'. The Mancunian Film Company had been founded in Rusholme by John Blakeley, a local businessman, in 1920, the first film he made being a silent comedy starring Wee Georgie Wood. He realised the potential of recruiting music hall stars for films and George Formby was only one of a number he employed with great success. Despite wishing to work in Manchester, which would have been much cheaper than in London, until 1947 he used a small studio above a garage repair business in Albany Street, near Regent's Park. A bell was rigged up to ring in the garage when filming was due to start so that the banging of metal on metal downstairs didn't upset the sound system.

It was while George was playing the Royal Court Theatre, Warrington, that Blakeley approached him and signed him up to star in *Boots! Boots!* According to an article in *The People* (1952), George and Arthur Mertz had spent three weeks in Blackpool two years before, writing the script. Mertz was not credited, but Jack Cottrell and George himself were. The film was made in fourteen days and cost a little less than £3,000, as that was all Blakeley could afford. Beryl negotiated a salary for George of £100 a week and 10 per cent of the profits. His mother Eliza claimed that, 'When he made *Boots! Boots!* he sent for me to come to London. He sent to me for everything – they don't think I was as much in contact with him as I was.'

The film has been described as 'no-budget' rather than 'low-budget' and, lacking any substantial plot, is now something of a historical curiosity. *Film Star Weekly* summarised it as a 'comedy of the rise to fame in cabaret of an hotel "boots" and a scullery maid', but for the most part it simply strung together the sort of short acts characteristic of music hall and revue, showing a new technology harnessing the appeal of a well-established entertainment genre. Because Blakeley wanted to recreate the music hall experience, most of the film was taken by a static long-shot camera. Professor Jeffrey Richards has commented that the real value of George's first two films is that 'they preserve for us the raw unrefined pre-cinematic Formby. They're a marvellous photographic record of a music hall persona and a music hall tradition'. George said of *Boots! Boots!*: 'Continuity went west. Nobody cared though because the picture was just a series of gags. If anyone thought of a new one it went in the story whether it fitted or not.' He recreated his father's comic character, the gormless simpleton John Willie, the 'Boots' of the title, playing a wooden ukulele and singing four numbers, 'Baby' (the first song he sang on film), 'Why Don't Women Like Me?', 'Sitting on the Ice in the Ice Rink' and 'I Could Make a Good Living at That'. He performed 'We'll Go Gathering Nuts in May', a song of his father's (entitled then 'We'll Go Gathering Nuts and May') still in the HMV catalogue in 1926, as part of a comedy routine. All through his film career George kept the direct rapport with the audience which he cultivated on stage, by singing straight to camera. In that way he recreated the sense that everyone was special, and the smiles and winks were for them alone!

Beryl (co-starring to save money) was the scullery maid and object of John Willie's affections, tap dancing expertly to the tune of 'Chinese Laundry Blues'. This sequence is probably the only surviving record of the dancing act that had made her famous. A well-known story told against Beryl was that she was unkind to a young actress, Betty Driver, later queen of the hotpot in *Coronation Street*'s Rovers Return pub. The usual version has Beryl, shortly after the thirteen-year-old Betty had finished recording her song and dance number, shouting out, 'Either that kid goes or I do'; apparently out of jealousy that Betty might steal the limelight or even attract

George's sexual attention. Apparently Betty was dismissed, her scene cut and, mortified, she cried all the way back to Manchester. The ogre, Beryl, meanwhile took over Betty's part.

It's a good story but not a wholly true one. Betty was credited in the cast list published in July 1934, and by 2001 a longer version of the film had come to light which actually includes the whole of Betty's 'deleted' routine. Eleanor Dugan, in *The Vellum*, has pointed out that the plot would not in any case have allowed Beryl to take Betty's role as the youngster was quite obviously still a child. But thus are myths created. Betty herself said in 1992, when interviewed for the *South Bank Show* devoted to George, that she met George and Beryl again on the lot next to her at Ealing when she was about eighteen. On one occasion Beryl had asked Betty and her sister to keep an eye on George at lunchtime and make sure he had only an egg. As Beryl departed through the gate George asked the girls what she'd said. 'He replied, "Oh to hell with that. I'm going to have a hotpot or something," and he'd have a great big meal.' Betty used to talk to George 'quite a lot, because he was a very inoffensive man', and they met up again a couple of years later. She had to share a dressing room with Beryl and she remembered Beryl saying 'Wasn't I a cow to you when you were a little girl? And I said yes, but never mind Beryl, let's leave that now, let's be normal, and from then on she was fine'. Betty thought her: 'A very disliked lady, I'm afraid. But saying that, had she not been a very firm person George wouldn't have been a star... she drove him, she was fantastic, no one should make eyes at him... but George was very sweet... he used to give everything away and that's why Beryl was so very strict.'

Despite the humblest of origins – its world premier was at the Palladium Cinema, Burslem, Stoke-on-Trent, in July 1934 – *Boots! Boots!* earned ten times its outlay, audiences in the Midlands filling the picture houses to see it. These venues often lacked sophistication. Never were 'fleapits' better named, as the staff tried to ensure a hygienic and deodorised auditorium by ostentatiously operating the Flit spray with its perfumed disinfectant *after* the audience was seated! They had a pretty clear idea of where the problem lay. Nevertheless, cinema audiences would spend their few coppers on a seat at the pictures where they could forget their troubles for a while in the warmth, smoky darkness and superficial glamour of the coloured lights playing on the swagged curtains.

Basil Dean, the Liverpool-born founder and head of production at Associated Talking Pictures, had already signed up Gracie Fields and was quick to see George's potential; in his own words 'here is another personality that seems to bounce off the screen'. He signed him up to his recently formed company, which filmed at Ealing, on a seven-year contract. George was to star in eleven films for Associated Talking Pictures, but before that he had another picture to make with Blakeley. Between times he didn't desert the live stage. Revues and his 'all-star road shows' were his bread and butter, and on his birthday, 26 May 1934, *Formby's Good Deed* opened at the Shepherd's Bush Empire. Introduced as 'a New Star from the North', George was able to capitalise on the imminent release of his film and sang three numbers from it.

George and Gracie Fields with bandleader Henry Hall
With kind permission of EMI

CHAPTER EIGHT

I Could Make a Good Living at That

In the 1930s comedy was king, and British films often starred music hall stars. The censorship of films was very strict and themes of social and political realism were not allowed by the British Board of Censors, who listed forty-three banned items. So escapist comedy had a clear run. George's second and last film for Blakeley was *Off the Dole,* described as 'A Musical Merry Burlesque' and released in July 1935. This time, as George later said, Blakeley 'lashed out' and spent £7,000 on making it. Arthur Mertz directed, George singing a song written by him, 'I Promise To Be Home by Nine O'clock', which his father had noted in his professional engagement diary in 1917!

The publicity blurb tried to widen the film's appeal. 'It is an established fact that periodically the whole English speaking world turns to the North of England for an exclusive brand of humour. At given intervals we become "Lancashire Conscious", for there is in Lancashire humour that blend of simplicity, of wistfulness, of "mugdom" (to coin a word) scoring a triumph over sophistication, that is irresistible.' Maybe. The film was wonderfully received in the north of England, with queues stretching all the way round the cinemas, but made little impact in the south. In the top hundred films in Bolton, Lancashire, in 1935 *Off the Dole* was number 27 – nationally it was number 566. It grossed £30,000 in seven weeks. The title, of course, would appeal to many in the audience who undoubtedly were *on* the dole at the time. Once again George played John Willie, struck off the dole for moonlighting and for his lack of interest in getting a proper job. Accused of hawking firewood on a handcart, John Willie replies, 'That's our furniture!' Soon afterwards he becomes employed by his uncle's detective agency to catch the 'villains' in a convoluted and flimsy plot interspersed with snatches of revue and touches of rather broad social comment. His character had more edge and cynicism than later roles would allow him though naivety was the overriding trait.

George and Beryl (Miss Seymour, in her last film role) sang two of the numbers together. The film included six songs – among them 'If You Don't Want the Goods Don't Maul 'Em' and 'Isn't Love a Very Funny Thing?' as they were deemed to be such an important ingredient – but the most famous (or notorious) became 'With My Little Ukulele in My Hand'. In 1933 Decca sent out test pressings of the song to reviewers. It was considered obscene, and Decca quickly withdrew it, re-recording it four months later under a new title 'My Ukulele'. Twice little words caused problems: 'playing *with* my uke' was replaced by 'playing *on* my uke' and the baby boy, who originally had '*a* ukulele in his hand', finally had '*my* ukulele', softening the innuendo.

The offensive lines in the first version revolved around an encounter with a Welsh girl, Jane, sitting in the sand hills:

> She said your love just turns me dizzy
> Come along big boy get busy…

These were replaced in the second version with some awful cod Welsh:

> I felt so shy and bashful sitting there
> For the things she said I didn't understand
> She says 'Your love just turns me cuckoo
> Aye indeed to goodness look you'
> But I kept my ukulele in my hand, oh baby…

Later, when the song was filmed in *Off the Dole*, all mention of Jane was omitted. Spencer Leigh notes that when in 1963 (the 'Swinging Sixties'!) Joe Brown tried to broadcast the original song he was prevented from doing so not only on *The Billy Cotton Band Show* (because the BBC thought the lyric was too suggestive for a Sunday) but also on *Thank Your Lucky Stars* and *Five O'Clock Club* on ITV, presumably because of their early evening scheduling. It would not be the last time that George and the broadcasters were to clash.

A scene from No Limit. *Jack Hobbs, the villain, driving a 1935 M.G. 'P'-type and trying to stop George racing*

Later in 1935 George made his first film for Basil Dean and Associated Talking Pictures, earning, at the outset, £30,000 per film. (£1,540,000) 'Super slapstick was what counted in those days. So, before asking whether I could act Basil asked if I could swim, ride horses and motorcycles, and, if necessary, jump off a cliff. I said I could do all that with the possible exception of the cliff and he signed me up for my first movie, *No Limit*.' George was presented as very much a Lancashire character and the script was co-written by Walter Greenwood, famous for his 1933 novel, *Love on the Dole*, which had been a great critical and commercial success. Himself born in Salford, of radical working-class parents, Greenwood was an ideal choice to write for northern audiences.

No Limit is highly rated by George's critics. He himself considered it 'the best bit of slapstick ever made' and his personal favourite. Filmed in the Isle of Man, it was the perfect script for him, with his lifelong love of speed and motorbikes. One of the extras, Harold Rowell, described the 'resourceful' director, Monty Banks. Monty, an Italian with a pencil moustache and dark curly hair, was a distinctive figure at only five foot five inches tall. He 'had obtained permission to take shots of the crowded grandstand. He ran up and down the road dressed in a canary coloured sweater, white plus fours, and black and white checked stockings... The crowd's gaze followed him. They turned their heads like a Wimbledon crowd and in ten minutes he had obtained some wonderful scenes – all for a small donation to the hospital box'. Rowell was sitting with a couple of friends after a chaotic morning in which all the arrangements had gone wrong. Next to them was 'a little bloke wearing an old-fashioned brown leather suit. We told him just what we thought about the lack of organisation and asked him who was the actor fool enough to take the star part in this lot. He quietly replied, "I am"'. Rowell thought George 'a thorough gentleman. He was always considerate and like all really great entertainers he never spared himself. He gave of his best ALWAYS. If he had any failing I feel without the restraining hand of his wife Beryl he might have been far too generous and become the soft touch'.

George did most of his own riding on his bike, 'an old AJS which I had built myself and called the Shuttleworth Special'. Rowell realised that George was a capable and enthusiastic motorcyclist and also that he was prevented from doing most of the stunts.

Although every precaution was taken to preserve George in one piece, I remember one particularly difficult piece of riding he did himself. Personally I consider it to have been the most dangerous of all the motorcycling scenes. It was planned to get pictures of him riding up the Cronk-y-Voddy straight, passing us, his rivals. In order to keep the camera focused on his face they fitted a solid tow bar to the back of the camera truck, and from this a short flexible section of about eighteen inches was attached to the steering head. You can imagine what would have happened if it had been pulled up taut... George rode under these conditions without turning a hair: in fact he seemed to enjoy himself.

George described another similar stunt. At a speed of over 70 mph (he claimed) he had to keep close behind the camera van, but to avoid bumping into it on corners. At the same time he had to keep his gaze on a white patch trailed from a rope from the van which marked the distance he had to maintain to stay in focus.

At the climax of the film, George, desperately trying to win the race, runs out of petrol and has to push the bike the last 500 yards. The scene was shot and reshot fifteen times. The last time, overcome by the heat and encased in heavy motorcycle leathers, George genuinely collapsed. Dean called it 'perfect' and it was the version used in the film, but a doctor had to be called for George. The filming was something of a nightmare for Beryl in two other respects as she 'was scared stiff of bikes – she called them the tools of the devil – and never liked George riding them'. Nor did she like Florence Desmond, George's co-star. The feeling was mutual. There had been a row because Desmond, mindful of her co-star billing, was angry that the Ealing Studios' billboards on the side of their vans only mentioned George. She was apparently assured by Basil Dean that the matter would be rectified but nothing was done. She said later, 'George Formby's attitude did not help me to swallow my pride and let the matter rest, and so one day I got mad and told Monty Banks… that unless the boards were changed I would not go on with the picture… the offending objects were removed. George Formby was furious.' Desmond was the last of George's leading ladies to sing on film, in this case a solo number, 'Riding Around on a Rainbow'. Beryl probably insisted after this that George should be the only singer in his films. In November George went to the Regal-Zonophone studios to record four songs, including, from the film, 'Riding in the TT Races'. *No Limit* was an immediate box office hit on the national circuit. A permanent memorial to this most enduring of films – shown every year at the TT races – is the statue of George leaning on a lamp post at the corner of a street in Douglas, Isle of Man.

Harry Gifford and Fred E. Cliffe were the most prolific of George's songwriters, responsible for about 90 of the 200 or so songs he recorded – 'Fanlight Fanny', 'Our Sergeant Major' and 'Mr Wu's a Window Cleaner Now' among them. Fred Cliffe had, in the early years of the twentieth century, appeared on the music hall stage with Charlie Chaplin in *Mumming Birds*. Harry Gifford also had music hall roots, having collaborated with George's father towards the end of his career on 'Bertie the Bad Bolshevik' in 1920. Their association began in 1932. George rarely met up with them in person and their relationship was dominated by his demands by letter for changes to the songs, but their partnership was a happy one, some letters including racing tips and one a request for their prayers before George played the dreaded Glasgow Empire! In July 1936 George found himself protesting to them that they would have to alter another lyric which would become a favourite.

> Dear Lads,
>
> Very many thanks for your song but I am very sorry to have to send it back to you as it is really too blue, you are getting too much on the sex stuff, try and clean it up a bit and send it along again, alas you will have to clean up 'with me little stick of Blackpool rock' for I cant [sic] work it in the state it is in, the Records have refused to do it as it is, so you had better get busy making them cleaner.
>
> > You couple of muckey buggers
> > > All the best wishes
> > > > Yours Faithfully,
> > > > > G F!

Earlier that year George began filming *Keep Your Seats Please*, which featured 'When I'm Cleaning Windows', though some lines of the original song, 'The Window Cleaner', were omitted.

> Pyjamas lying side by side,
> Ladies' nighties I have spied,
> I've often seen what goes inside
> When I'm cleaning windows.

And the lines below from 'Window Cleaner No. 2', recorded only days after the film's release, were also *not* included in the film version:

At eight o'clock a girl she wakes
At five past eight her bath she takes
At ten past eight my ladder breaks
When I'm cleaning windows.

Despite her determination never to work with the Formbys again, Florence Desmond was persuaded by Basil Dean to co-star. Her first reaction when he asked her, at lunch, was, 'Cancel the cutlets, Basil. I won't do it.' The prospect of a generous salary, proper co-star billing and Dean's vow to keep Beryl off the set must have sweetened the bitter pill, though nothing and no one could have carried out the last promise. Beryl was there, as large as life. Desmond was full of complaints. 'I seemed to spend all my time running across the screen saying "But George". When the cameras were not shooting over my shoulders I had to carry a child of three in my arms, and as the picture progressed she grew steadily heavier.' Well, children do...

The summer and early autumn of 1936 were spent in Blackpool, George's spiritual home, for a season in *King Fun*. Stan Evans for the *South Bank Show* remarked, 'I think that George is like Blackpool... bright, breezy, free and easy, simple, full of life, full of enjoyment, and fish and chips – that sums George up – fish and chips, and his songs and his ukulele seem to go well with it.' His energy is summed up in the bet he took to climb the 518-foot-high Blackpool Tower. Jack Taylor bet him £5 he couldn't do it. George took him on and at the appointed time a crowd of 10,000 turned up to watch him. He was very enthusiastic to get started and only dissuaded when his film manager at Associated Talking Pictures, Ben Henry, threatened to sack him 'if I dared set one foot on any part of Blackpool Tower except the lift'.

In October George gave a charity performance and a donation of £25 on behalf of Barnsley miners whose pit had been involved in a disaster two months before in which fifty-eight miners were killed. He was to attend a civic reception after going down into the pit itself and, later, distributed grocery vouchers to the bereaved families. George assured the reporter, 'If ever there's a man on this earth who deserves everything we can give him it's

On the Blackpool sands

the miner. I've lived among them and I know.' It was this sort of comment that reinforced his working-class northern image. If he had lived 'among them' it was only in a general sense and not for long: the family had left terraced housing behind by the time George was six.

Ben Henry became involved in a lengthy correspondence with Fred Bailey. Fred, the son of a Wigan greengrocer who had once proposed to the widowed Eliza, was George's close childhood friend from the Stockton Heath days and a keeper of the flame for him, recording everything he could of George's career. He had gone with George to his first professional engagement at Earlestown, to encourage and support him. Fred's father had made a considerable fortune and he and his wife Jessie had the resources to travel and to spend time away from the day-to-day running of the business. They went on holiday with the Formbys and helped them in innumerable ways – meeting them at the quayside after a cruise, for instance, and giving them a lift home. Fred attended the trade shows, arranged for members of the film industry and journalists before a film went on general release, and afterwards conducted informal research on the size of the audiences, the length of the queues and the sort of reception the films were getting. George liked to refer to his friends on stage and in songs. As part of his opening patter in the 1950s he asked 'How are you doing, Fred?' and in the song 'The Old Cane-Bottom Chair' one line speaks of 'Jessie and the twins'.

On holiday in Jamaica. The central four figures are Fred and Jessie Bailey, George and Beryl

George and Beryl also sought the opinions of Fred and Jessie about songs. In a letter to them from the Queen's Hotel, Birmingham, dated 9 March 1937 George wrote: 'You are quite right it is entirely different to either of the other two I have done. I am glad to hear you like "Leaning by [sic] a Lamp post". Yes I think it is a very nice song indeed. I have not recorded it and I don't think I will as Regal Zonophone don't care very much for it. They say it is not funny enough for me to record.' Lacking his characteristic double entendres, it is one of the most charming and winning of all George's songs, with a hint of melancholy that recalls his father's style, and it's extraordinary to think that it might not have been recorded. Beryl had as usual wanted to get George's name associated with the composition, but the writer, Noel Gay, who had written the song originally for *Me and My Girl*, would have none of it. Apparently thwarted, Beryl was not done yet – she ensured that during his lifetime *only* George was legally entitled to perform it.

As the goose laying Associated Talking Pictures' golden eggs, George had gained quite an influential position, which Beryl determined to use to her young brother-in-law's advantage. Teddy, by now a teenager, was given a chance to work for Ben Henry. Beryl's letter was full of bracing advice.

Dear Teddy

We sent off to you yesterday a dinner suit and some shoes, and now its all up to you to do your best, and very best, I had to do some talking to get you the job, so I don't want you to let me down, I told Mr. Henry what a fine boy you were, and that you would do what you were told so now get busy – use your own brains – don't listen to the twaddle of other people – keep a still tongue – don't run other people down – always do the right thing and always say the people who you work for are the best thing that ever happened – for don't forget they are the ones who are giving you your bread and butter.

Best of love from George and self and above all the very best of luck and health.

Yours Faithfully,

Beryl Formby

Keep Your Seats Please was released in March 1937, and by April Ben Henry was writing, 'The picture is doing amazingly well wherever it is playing and it looks like establishing George in the front rank of screen comedians.' Binkie Stuart (real name Alison Fraser), who was only three when she appeared with George in the film, recalled many years later that she had 'great fun' with the man she called Uncle George, when Beryl wasn't around – but she usually was, standing right behind him. Binkie believed that Beryl was annoyed whenever the little girl stole a moment of the spotlight from George. She also remembered the volatile relationship between Florence

Ted Formby as a young man

Desmond and Monty Banks, George's director again and (from 1940) the husband of Gracie Fields. Desmond wanted to have her breakfast on set, but when Banks refused she slapped his face. Binkie was hustled off quickly by her mother. She recalled, George 'used to fluff his lines a lot and Monty would get quite exasperated with him. So did Florence Desmond. She could be quite catty and sometimes had no patience with him'.

By this time George was making about three films a year so it was not long before the next one appeared. *Feather Your Nest* co-starred the beautiful Polly Ward, a niece of the music hall star Marie Lloyd who had admired George senior's work so much. It was released in July 1937. In September Ben Henry was able to tell Fred Bailey that the film was selling very well and playing for two-week slots at theatres in Manchester. 'Leaning on a Lamp Post', recorded at last in September, became one of George's best-known songs.

Shortly before the film was released George and Beryl had established the George Formby Club, annual subscription one shilling, whose object was declared to be 'to aid deserving charities'. The first was the British Wireless for the Blind Fund. George's poor eyesight, and his awareness that he had been born blind, gave him a special affinity with such charities. It was said that, 'In his younger days there was a possibility of his losing his sight altogether,' and the fear of this never left him. There was to be a monthly magazine with a letter from George and competitions with prizes. All this was arranged under the auspices of Associated Talking Pictures. *Keep Fit*, George's next film, made in the spring and early summer of 1937, cashed in on the current rage, as signalled by its unimaginative title. This was the heyday of The Women's League of Health and Beauty, whose members were distinctive in their short black satin pants and white shirts. George's leading lady was Kay Walsh, who, it has been said, enjoyed a brief fling with George 'during one of Beryl's rare absences from the set'.

It's true that during the making of the film, in June, Beryl was admitted to a private clinic where she had her appendix removed following a fall from a horse. She had been appearing with George at a gymkhana, on a horse sixteen hands high. In legging her up, the hand pushed her too hard and she fell clean over the horse. For a fortnight she was in pain, particularly when sitting, until it was decided she must have inpatient treatment. There was much speculation at the time in the hothouse of the film world, where gossip was always rife, that this was a cover for the real reason for her admittance – a hysterectomy. The story has often been repeated since by Beryl's detractors. The argument ran that, fearing George would be tempted to dalliance with his beautiful co-star, to whom he was clearly attracted, Beryl had a hysterectomy to offer George 'sex with no consequences' so that he would not stray. This seems nonsensical. Why should Beryl, aware of his attraction to Kay Walsh, leave the film set where she had been keeping her customary guard on George's virtue, if not for an emergency? If gossip is to be believed it led to the very fling she feared. In any case, after major surgery Beryl would presumably be unable to offer sex on any terms to anyone for some weeks, so such a stratagem would seem 'not fit for purpose'. How extraordinary that anyone would think that she would have her own body mutilated and her sexual self compromised to stop her husband from 'straying', particularly if her absence catapulted her would-be adulterous husband straight into Walsh's arms. Kay Walsh herself recalled that Beryl was taken off in an ambulance and that George 'spent a busy night with ravishing film extras'. Not, one hopes, ravishing the film extras. But the most straightforward and obvious evidence about what was really going on comes from a letter to Fred and Jessie Bailey. Beryl wrote, with a nice touch of self-awareness, 'I am feeling nearly my old self again, anyway it won't be long before I start telling them how to run the Nursing Home... By the way will you ask Fred if he would like me to bring my appendix up for him to stick in his book, he must at least keep a record of it.'

Perhaps Beryl might be allowed the most sensible interpretation of her actions: that she was doing exactly as she said she was, though from her point of view the timing couldn't have been worse. And the fling? It seems unlikely. Walsh had fallen in love with director David Lean the previous year and began living with him. One of Lean's wives said of her that she was 'terribly in love with him'. In her autobiography Kay wrote of the early days of their affair: 'We worked all day and danced all night and slept through the

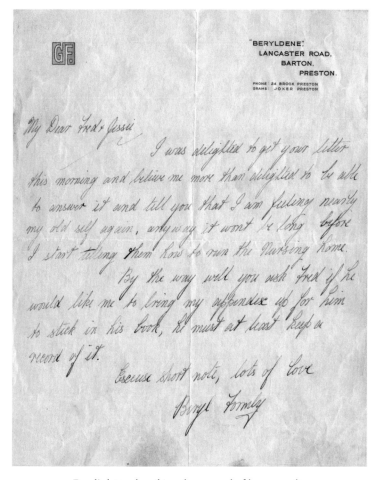

Beryl's letter describing the removal of her appendix

weekend, waking late on Sunday to make love, to read the Sunday papers and to breakfast on eggs and bacon... We were asked everywhere – we were an attractive couple, we enjoyed life enormously.'

CHAPTER NINE

Trailing Around in a Trailer

After *Keep Fit* was completed George opened at the Opera House, Blackpool, in the revue *King Cheer*, without Beryl, who was still convalescing. The show, with a cast of a hundred, was described as 'easily the largest spectacular' in the town, and ran for sixteen weeks. That summer of 1937 he bought Garthallen, Little Singleton, five miles from Blackpool, a five-bedroomed house with a tennis court, set in four acres of carefully landscaped garden. It immediately became Beryldene. Beryl told the George Formby Club that it was bought to cheer her up (or to appease her?), and they moved in on her birthday, 9 September. She also mentioned that the Preston house, though quite large enough for them, 'wasn't quite suitable'. It was semi-detached and apparently the neighbours hadn't been too enamoured of George's habit of turning the radio on at all hours of the night to listen to jazz. Meanwhile, George's mother had not given up show business or promoting her children. In May she made a personal appearance at the Hippodrome, Aldershot, with 'The Famous Formby Family: Frank – Louie – Ronnie'. Ethel was also performing separately, with a pianist. Eliza recalled:

> I worked for twelve months as an act with my children, with Frank, with my eldest girl and her husband, and me. We did a four-handed act and Sir Oswald Stoll put the show on for us. A very well-dressed act and very nice. But it upset George – he didn't like it... He felt very hurt because I had not told him they were going to put the show on, but I did it to help my other children. When you're left with seven, you don't know who to help or what to help, do you?

116

"BERYLDENE" NEAR SINGLETON VILLAGE.

An artist's portrait of Beryldene, Little Singleton

By this time almost the entire family was benefiting from the Formby name. Eliza said:

> We worked for two years on and off – we worked in revues,
> Moss Tour, Stoll Tour, and then Georgie came round and said,
> 'What did you do it for, Mother?'
> 'Well,' I said, 'to get a bit more money.'
> 'Well,' he said, 'don't bother, I'll allow you something.' Then
> he put me on an allowance. It was stopped the hour he died!

The year was crowned by George's first royal command invitation. In November 1937 he performed before the king and queen at the London Palladium, alongside, amongst others, Gracie Fields, his friends Max Miller and Norman Evans, his former leading lady Florence Desmond and The

117

Crazy Gang. The show was broadcast on the National Programme and described by the *Radio Pictorial* as 'the radio high spot of the year'. George told the reporter he was nervous – 'I'm not a bit ashamed to admit it' – and that his appearance in the show would be 'the greatest thing that has ever happened in my life'. The account continued, 'If only his father were alive to see his son's triumph. I'm too young to remember George Senior, but they still talk with reverence about his genius, of his battle with ill health… George Junior has a proud tradition to uphold and upholds it grandly.'

Playing in *Dick Whittington* in pantomime that winter, on the stage at the Newcastle Empire where his father had given his last ever performance, George was told that the show had broken the theatre's box office record. He and Beryl marked the success by presenting to each of the twenty-five little girls of the chorus who appeared with them an inscribed silver bracelet as a memento. Gestures like this, gifts of flowers and chocolates, always of course organized by Beryl, were part of her management strategy.

> Inside the studios he was hard working and cheerful except when rowing with his wife. There was no getting past Beryl when she had made up her mind. She was quick to make a fuss whenever she thought George was being put upon, such as when he was asked to play a scene he didn't like or didn't understand. Everyone was a bit scared of her.

So wrote Basil Dean in his autobiography, *Mind's Eye*. Dean was one of many who thought George was tight-fisted. 'One day George was seen to produce a ten shilling note at the refreshment counter to pay for a drink for one of the staff, a procedure so unusual that all movement ceased and all eyes were focused on the phenomenon.' He did not think him a would-be womaniser though: 'To do him justice I don't think girls bothered him very much. But as a precaution Beryl was on the set at every take, keeping ceaseless watch.'

By this time there was a special Formby unit set up at Ealing Studios under the directorship of Anthony Kimmins, and films were to appear at frequent intervals. Work began on *I See Ice* in mid-October 1937, with Kay Walsh, to

Beryl's chagrin, once again providing the love interest. The theme reflected the craze for ice hockey at the time. The songs were 'In My Little Snapshot Album', 'Noughts and Crosses' and 'Oh Mother What'll I Do Now?' In February 1938 George was thrilled to receive the matrix, or master disc, of 'The Window Cleaner', framed, as a gift from Regal-Zonophone to mark a hundred thousand pressings of the record. Beryl wrote a reply for him to Sir Louis Sterling. 'It is something I shall value more than words can express... there is nobody more delighted than I am that the particular song has been such a success...' At the end of the month, about a week after the trade

George with the matrix of 'The Window Cleaner'
With kind permission of EMI

show for *I See Ice*, Ben Henry commented to Fred Bailey, 'I am inclined to agree with you that it is the best yet!' *Film Weekly* summed it up well. 'This is just the kind of hearty fooling that it is almost impossible to resist. It has plenty of rough edges, but it doesn't give you time to think about them... George preserves his dogged optimism and gets across his essential human touch.' The film went on general release in July. Back home again in Blackpool and replying to her friend, Hilda, who had, as ever, remembered her birthday, Beryl was more modest about it – 'I think it is just as good as the others don't you?'

In May George had topped the bill at the London Palladium for a week. This personal milestone passed, he bought his long-promised first Rolls, *the* symbol of his success. Thereafter he bought a new Rolls or Bentley every year until his death – twenty-six in total – always personalised GF 1 or GF 2. The Rolls-Royces were Beryl's cars, and she was occasionally asked why the number plates were not her initials. George felt that those who asked hadn't thought about it enough. BF?...

George even serviced his own Rolls-Royce

Two stylish and successful young people enjoying the fruits of success.
Note that the car had two spare wheels!

That year he had to miss his usual summer season at Blackpool as the film makers of *It's in the Air* had to make the most of the fine weather for flying. Instead for one week he played Newcastle and was touched when a chara-banc load of Blackpool fans came over the Pennines to see the show. While the Formbys were there they heard of 500 unemployed men from the North East who had saved up eight shillings each for a week's camp in nearby Redcar. George and Beryl sent each man a large packet of cigarettes and in return received a model ashtray in the form of a horseshoe made by one of the men out of all the silver paper inserts from the cigarette packets, with a letter of thanks signed by all of them. George described it as 'a gift which has always remained with us'. He revealed around this time that for him an ideal week's holiday was to go up to Middleham or Beverley and live again the life of a stable lad. His love of horses and the open-air life, he said, gave him 'complete relief of the mind' from all the pressures of filming and the stage. He also recalled that it was the boxing matches at the stables which awakened his love of seeing fights, which he would go to Blackfriars to see if he found himself in London on a Sunday.

George found the outdoor life with horses relaxing and renewing

By 22 August *It's in the Air*, described by *Boy's Cinema*, a tuppenny weekly, as 'a splendid British comedy thriller', was finished. To coincide with its release early the following year the whole story was told in the magazine in excruciatingly small print, over ten pages, each of three columns. The film was hugely attractive for thousands of young men who would have loved to join the glamorous 'boys in blue'. *The Times* reviewer, writing of it in January 1939 thought, 'He may not be a smart guy… but he somehow gets along; he may not know his left from right, but he does know right from wrong… In its [the film's] own unpretentious way it suits Mr. Formby's unpretentious personality.' His belief that George appealed to the maternal instinct of the female audience was spot on. From the first scene when George gave his gas mask to his engaging little dog Scruffy and was turned down for an Air Raid Warden's uniform, his childlike disappointment set up the contrast between men of action and a character appealing to women. Many cinemagoers at the time considered this film his best, and the title song *It's in the Air* became the number one RAF song of the Second World War. The sequence with George in a runaway aeroplane shouting 'Mo-other!' was one of the most popular moments in all his films. A sad footnote was that in June 1940 J. M. Wells, the airman who had actually done the wonderful crazy flying in *It's in the Air*, was killed in action.

George's popularity at this time can scarcely be overestimated. By 1938 there were nearly 5,000 cinemas in Britain and more were being built. In September he was booked to open the new £100,000 Avion Cinema in Aldridge, near Walsall. Huge queues formed hours before the 2.30 p.m. ceremony.

> From the conversations in the auditorium it was quite clear what everyone had really come to see: what was far more important than the business of opening a cinema was the personal appearance of George Formby. His name was being spoken everywhere. People could be heard saying 'Our George' and 'Good old George', and the excitement was at the level which we now imagine was only achieved with the advent of the post-war pop star.

A short film programme was played before:

> The much-awaited face peeped round the curtain and George Formby made his entrance. The crowd was ecstatic. His first task was to hand a cheque for twenty-five guineas from the Avion Directors... for the Walsall General Hospital Fund. He added a further cheque for £10 from himself and his wife. Loud cheering turned to a roar as someone produced a ukulele! George obliged with a song about his snapshot album and saucy pictures he had taken with a concealed camera. He managed to relieve himself of the ukulele and prepared to make his speech but a second instrument was produced as if from nowhere and he sang, 'When I'm Cleaning Windows'... He then tried to leave the stage in order to depart via the auditorium. Everybody tried

to press into the aisle to touch him, and to try and shake his hand. A crippled ex-serviceman who had hobbled nine miles to the cinema on his crutches managed to shake his hero's hand. Afterwards he found that George had passed him a pound note! George Formby specialised in these tricks when meeting the public at events like this, and this added to the excitement felt by the crowd. After Mr and Mrs Formby had driven away the audience sat down to watch *I See Ice*...

All sorts of 'opportunities' came George's way in the late Thirties. He was pictured in *An Album of Film Stars*, produced by Player's cigarettes, alongside Errol Flynn and Valerie Hobson and priced at a penny. *Film Fun* published a cartoon series, *The Great George Formby*, which ran into the early Fifties. Looking urbane and elegant, he advertised the stylish De Reszke cigarettes in the magazine *Radio Pictorial*. His radio career began in 1936 with an excerpt from *King Fun*, but was established in two series, *A Lancashire Lad* and *A Formby Do*. In October 1938 Beryl commented in writing to a fan that they 'enjoyed making the Feen-a-mint programmes very much'. The makers of Feen-a-mint, a laxative, sponsored a series of radio shows which were broadcast on Radio Luxembourg. At about this time, George, weighing in at 10 st 3 lb, had been granted a licence to ride under Pony Turf Club Rules and took part in a hurdling race at Northolt Park. Unfortunately his horse, the odds-on favourite in a field of four, and ironically named Lucky Bert, refused at the last fence and he was disqualified. Perhaps a win was something of a long shot as George had only seen the horse for the first time that same day. Beryl said that it was 'a great shame George didn't win at Northolt as he had set his mind on winning with it being his first race after so long'. Not to mention the fact that it would have been his first win ever.

George's career seemed to be going swimmingly when the risqué lyrics of one of his songs gave offence at the BBC and they effectively banned 'When I'm Cleaning Windows'. At that time the Corporation saw itself as an active guardian of the nation's morals and a range of songs and music were banned for a variety of reasons; they could be deemed too sentimental

An image of elegance and sophistication

or unacceptable because they included references to drugs or prostitution. With George, whose songs offended the Dance Music Policy Committee more than once, it was a matter of 'tastelessness', 'vulgarity' or 'smut'. On this occasion Dick Bentley, the compère of the feature *You Asked for It ...*, a radio request show, wouldn't play the record because 'the windows aren't yet clean enough'. George was furious.

> It is a damaging thing to say about any artist and I am quite definitely taking legal advice on the matter. The song is always in great request and I have broadcast it dozens of times. Why, I sang it before the King and Queen at the Royal Variety Performance and I have sung it almost every Sunday at charity performances sponsored by hospitals, churches and other organisations. Recently I went to a hospital to sing to sick children from about five to fifteen years of age... Afterwards I was told that the nurses played it on the piano and all the kiddies sang it in chorus. Even the matron approved.

A formidable ally indeed, but it was the reference to the Royal Family that was the clincher. With them lined up alongside the rest of the nation, the BBC was completely out in the cold.

On the following Saturday George appeared in *Sing Song*. Before the programme began the announcer said: 'As an extra attraction we present George Formby, to whom we owe an apology. An unfortunate reference was made to one of Mr Formby's songs in a programme last Monday. We are sorry this occurred but we are still the best of friends, which is borne out by the fact that George is with us tonight.' The apology was given at peak time, just before the nine o'clock news. But George and the BBC managers were simply not going to see eye to eye. The manager of the North Region wrote in 1942, 'The man is essentially vulgar and he seems to be incapable of producing anything that is not objectionable.' Not only was he apparently keen to censor the biggest star in northern England, but he somewhat overstated his case. No one (except him), then or now, has found 'Leaning on a Lamp Post' to be 'objectionable'.

The pantomime season found George at the Palace Theatre, Manchester, in *Dick Whittington*, but he fell ill halfway through. A letter dated 23 January 1939 to Beryl at the Midland Hotel, Manchester, reads, 'I am very sorry indeed to hear this afternoon that George is ill and has had to come out of the show. Mr Carne is away from the office so that I am writing to you to say how sorry we are to hear of George's illness, and very much hope that it is nothing serious.' It was serious enough to result in a five-week cruise to the West Indies, George's first major break since 1934.

In early 1939 the *Sunday Express* began 'George's Laughter Page' to 'make your sides shake even if Hitler makes your head ache'. Full of corny gags and 'Songs I Should Never Have Written' not to mention tips such as 'How to knit a Gas-mask for your canary', the humour was of the mildest, but the feature was an explicit attempt to make people 'forget their worries and troubles' on the eve of war. George's role was cut out for him.

George's next film was *Trouble Brewing*. In the five weeks it took to make, his co-star, nineteen-year-old Googie Withers, recounted that he never said one word to her. One day something went wrong in the middle of a scene and they were told to keep their places until it was fixed. 'There he was, alone with me for the first time and not being watched by Beryl, and he said out of the corner of his mouth, "I'm sorry, love, but you know, I'm not allowed to speak to you." It was very sweet.' She thought Beryl a 'funny woman. I don't know why she was like that. I don't think any one of us young girls wanted to get off with George'. But famously he took his chance for a passionate kiss in the vat of 'beer' at the end of the film. 'He quite inadvertently put his hand on my knee and suddenly felt a girl's thigh… and then he kept it there and he started to visibly sort of shake… and then we had the kiss, and my goodness it was quite a kiss that he gave me! But then Beryl was in on it like a flash. She said "Cut!" after it had lasted about three seconds. I remember Kay Walsh said to me that she had to run along a street and then they both fell down on the ground, I think, and then they had their kiss, and she [Beryl] did the same thing: she ran along with them, fell on the ground with them – out of shot of course – and said, "Cut!"'

It has been said that one reason Beryl did not like George playing romantic scenes was that they were unpopular with children in the audience, who found them soppy. A young fan confirmed that: 'Any suggestion of romance was greeted with inattentive chatter and the ultimate sin of a screen kiss earned itself a chorus of raspberries.' Both George and Beryl were keenly aware of the importance of the youngsters who were fans. *Cinegram* even suggested that George had censored some of the charlady's lines in the film as being unsuitable for children.

Ben Henry was honest enough to write, 'A tremendous number of people think this picture is better than *It's in the Air*, but this is not my opinion.' It wasn't the opinion of *The Times* reviewer either. 'The early sequences are laboured and rather humourless but the film gradually warms to a most amusing climax.' Nevertheless he gave an insight into George's appeal: 'It is a tradition among clowns that they must always seem more stupid than ourselves; just a little more muddle-headed, a little more clumsy and a little more destructive than we could ever be and thus we delight in their antics with a warming feeling of superiority. Yet the clown must be well-intentioned; he must have a good heart and he must triumph in the end. Mr George Formby is such a clown.'

George habitually looked at the rushes of his films from near the front because he was short-sighted. He and Beryl always sat with an empty seat between them. Everyone else sat at the back, which made it look not only as if he and Beryl had no friends, but that they were not on speaking terms. But they always sat that way since the early Ealing days – George, then his distinctive light grey trilby hat, familiar from so many of his films, next to him in its own seat – then Beryl. The hat was developing a life of its own. It even had its own chair in the corner of the studio restaurant. By this time it was much the worse for wear. Bought in Manchester for ten shillings, it had been worn first in *No Limit* and in seven films subsequently. Though carefully cleaned after each film and stored in a special steel hat box, its career of absorbing custard pies and studio snow had nevertheless taken its toll. The hat band had come away, the crown was wearing thin and there was a hole in the brim where it had been nailed to a wall. But George swore to wear it until it fell to pieces on his head.

Come On George posed the problem of moving a racing stable to Ealing Studios. Six horses were brought in from Mr Younghusband's stables, and the star of the show was the obedient Diana, ridden by George in many of the scenes. Despite George's background as a jockey the studio insisted on insuring him for £60,000. Pat Kirkwood, aged eighteen at the time, was his female lead, and her relationship with George was famously difficult. As a singer of some reputation she expected the opportunity for a solo. In fact she was not allowed to sing at all. Beryl insisted that her long hair be cut and her clothes be of the plainest. Kirkwood couldn't understand why George ignored her. 'There was no communication from [him] – not even a cup of tea or a "good morning".' The director Anthony Kimmins eventually told her that George had probably been warned off by Beryl 'who was apparently very jealous of George and still madly in love with him. I felt rather sorry for her in spite of her making me look like a scarecrow, because she must have suffered a lot of pain'. To achieve the final close-up kiss Beryl was lured from the set by a 'telephone call'. Kirkwood recalled, 'All was ready to go, and I was instructed by Tony to: "Grab him and let him have it and don't break till I say *cut*." As I was so utterly fed up with all these capers, together with losing my locks, looks, and entire persona, I decided to do just that.'

CHAPTER TEN

Guarding the Home of the Home Guards

After finishing *Come On George* in June 1939 George and Beryl were off to the Palladium for a week. *The Times* carried a review of the show. 'Mr Formby sings his little ditties with a bashful and engaging smile. He is a cheerful friendly fellow who seems quite as pleased to be in our company as we are to be in his, and when the verse takes a downward dip towards the liberties which the music hall allows, he treads the thin ice with all the schoolboy's glee in his own bravado.' 'In these days the gift of laughter is a gift of the gods', another journalist wrote. Just as the Depression of the Thirties demanded light escapist entertainment so the coming of the war spotlighted the need for that essential ingredient of the British character – humour. The late Thirties and early Forties saw George at the height of his career. According to the *Motion Picture Herald*, he was the top British male star at the cinema box office between 1937 and 1943, and from 1938 to 1942 the highest-paid entertainer in Britain.

As George later put it, 'I knocked Gracie off her perch in 1938 and James Mason knocked me off mine in 1944.' *The Times* commented in 1939, 'the unchallenged favourite of recent years should be Shirley Temple. Gracie Fields, Will Rogers, Marie Dressler, and George Formby are others who have headed the popularity lists. These have not been welcomed for their glamorous qualities but rather for those warm-hearted virtues which are most easily understood by the bulk of their audiences... To nearly every man his entertainment is a means of escape; in the hero he sees himself and he therefore will most delight in the escapades of one who succeeds in doing all that he himself most wishes to do but cannot'.

Shortly after war broke out George signed up with ENSA, the Entertainments National Service Association – 'Every Night Something Awful' – to play to the troops. At first all the shows were free but later this policy was reconsidered, bearing in mind that human nature values more what it pays for, and on the basis that the fees could be ploughed back into providing more events and programmes. A scale of modest charges was introduced, from a shilling down to twopence. George's Blackpool show was suspended for a short time at the beginning of the war but resumed to European record-breaking takings for twice-nightly performances.

Seven weeks into the war *Come On George* had its trade show. George played a stable boy who alone could calm Man Eater, a jittery horse. The moment George jumped onto the horse's back his skill as a rider was clear. This film had a different distribution from the usual 'London first then the "suburbs and provinces"'. It was shown to the troops in France as a morale booster *before* it was released to the general public. In December *The Times* reviewer contrasted it with the latest offering from the Marx Brothers. Their film was touched with cruelty, George's with pathos. In a patronising paragraph northerners and the 'industrial proletariat' were both sneered at but even the writer conceded that 'this makes a sufficiently amusing farce'. Elspeth Grant, writing in the *Daily Sketch*, thought the 'French would get as many horse-laughs out of the film as you – for it is pictorially so funny that the language doesn't much matter. From some of the lines that got by the Censor I gather he must share this view'. George trod the line between family fun and music hall 'coarseness' but the delicate balance didn't suit everyone, even a critic well disposed towards him. In a very warm review praising George's genuineness and friendly nature, written by Hubert Cole in the *Picturegoer and Film Weekly* in December 1939, there was a sting in the tail. He found 'two or three jokes in the worst possible taste' in the latest film, 'so blue that they staggered' him. His advice was that George should 'give them up at once before they do him serious harm'. In truth, apart from the occasional (and not very original) innuendo 'I must first take down your particulars' and some suggestive lines in 'I'm Making Headway Now' there was little to cause offence. In any case George had the last laugh: by the end of the Thirties he was earning £100,000 (£4.6m) a year.

An ENSA publicity shot

In January 1940 the BBC began to broadcast to the Forces. *Break for Music* became the 'most effective of all the Radio ENSA programmes'. It was recorded in factories to which the entire company of artistes, musicians and even a Bechstein grand piano decamped, and broadcast once a week. The entourage even ventured as far north as Manchester and Bradford. Conditions could be harsh. George had to abandon one show in an aeroplane hangar because his hands were too numb with cold to play the ukulele. Pantomime that year was *Dick Whittington* at the Empire Theatre, Leeds, and George made sure to be topical. 'The first entrance of Mr. Formby is the signal for jubilation… he is especially funny in his rendering of "Run, Rabbit Run".' Robina Hinton, who as Bobbie Wood was the Cat that year, remembered George's generosity. 'To work with George was wonderful. He was awfully nice and a very kind man while being a true professional.' The producer Tom Arnold demanded that the Cat be in character throughout the performance, even in the finale which involved her descending a flight of steps on all fours while wearing a mask. 'I was always conscious that the audience wanted my entrance over so that George would come down… he was very thoughtful, knowing that his entrance would cut off any applause for me. He would wait until the very last moment so that I got full benefit.' Combining stage and charity work, George started a branch of the OK Club for Kids, in this case to raise money for cigarettes for Yorkshire soldiers serving in France. The children bought a badge for a penny, or whatever more they could afford, and photos of George were also on sale. If they saw George on the street or on the stage they were encouraged to greet him with the club's war cry – OK George!

In the first autumn of the war George gave a concert at Southport for the Fleetwood trawlermen, a cause that became special to him, recorded by Pathé News. By December fourteen trawlers had been sunk and in January *The Times* announced that he hoped 'to raise 100,000 florins [a florin was two shillings] for the dependents of trawler men [sic] who have lost their lives at sea. A part of this money he will raise by giving a series of concerts… the rest, he hopes, will be made up by florin subscriptions from the public'. In 2001 the son of one of the theatre managers who

Dick Whittington, Leeds 1939–40. Robina Hinton as the Cat
By kind permission of Robina Hinton

organized Sunday concerts in Sheffield wrote to the *Daily Mail*. 'Only one star gave his services completely free – George Formby.' The first of this series of Sunday charity concerts happened on 22 January, at the Blackpool Opera House, and was 'practically sold out'. Ben Henry, going to the concert on 8 February, 'Like everyone else, got held up with the weather'. Considering that late January and early February that year were extremely cold, with temperatures one night of minus 19°C in places as far apart as Kent and Cumberland, it was surprising that so many people were prepared to turn out.

George's generosity with his time and the extent of his commitment sit strangely with his legendary meanness. Opinions about it vary widely. His sister Ella didn't see him as mean at all – on the contrary, she thought him too open-handed, careless with money, a trait deriving from a luxurious childhood where cost wasn't counted. Even in the racing stable he had worn handmade clothes and boots. According to her, he needed Beryl to manage his money; otherwise he would have frittered it away. Certainly she believed that he was fully in agreement with the claim that Beryl allowed him only 'five bob a day' as a ploy to turn away scroungers. But even she had to admit that, like his father, he wasn't a naturally generous man, and after his death seemed to forget her earlier comments. His co-star Garry Marsh agreed that Beryl protected George 'from the shysters and lend-me-a-fiver types who were always hanging around. If he'd had his own cheque book he'd have been a soft touch for anyone with a get-rich-quick scheme'. The whole matter was complicated, but seems to have hinged on his estimate of the worthiness of the recipient. He wouldn't buy drinks for those who could well afford them. And he was no socialist. He expected everyone with ability to work as hard for their money as he had done. When they did he was generous. In his last summer season at Blackpool in 1960 he gave the stagehands a ten shilling note every week – this for youngsters on about £4 a week. And he was compassionate to those who were vulnerable – the sick or disabled – and fully understood the need for soldiers to lay aside the demands of war, to relax and laugh. There was no limit to the time and energy he would give for those who needed him. He was also thoughtful towards his mother. A letter survives that was written between 1937 and 1945 while he was living in Little Singleton, near Blackpool.

Dear Mother

I have had a talk with Beryl and we have decided to send you £10 to remove you and help you over Xmas and Beryl says she is going to bring your money up from £2 a week to £2 10s so that will help you a bit more. Its nothing to do with me mother but I think Frank should help you a bit now. He seems to be doing very well now he has a film contract and he spent most of your money. Ask him see what he says...

Happy Xmas from both, Georgie

The sums of money sound small, and in comparison with his annual income they were, but of course in 1940 they were worth much more in real terms. Under the surface the family resentments were simmering – in this case Frank's spending of his mother's money. Clearly Eliza still had not given up hope of a sparkling career for her second son and had been backing him financially. He had sometimes appeared in Morecambe on the same bill as George, alongside a young Ronnie Ronalde in the *Silver Songsters* – until one day in 1940 the police arrived to question him about some black market silk stockings...

In his memoir *The Theatre at War* Basil Dean noted that 'as the war progressed, the demand for living personalities to relieve the tedium of military training and the strain of watch and ward grew'. The ENSA parties filled this need for colour, humour and escapism. On 12 February *The Times* announced that George would be taking a company to France under the auspices of NAAFI to entertain the troops, pointing out that 'he has declined many professional engagements so that he may remain free to give as many entertainments as possible to the Forces'. George told a reporter that he didn't regard this as a sacrifice – 'What's the good of making a lot of money these days? After all, Beryl and I can't buy more butter with it than the man next door.' Once again he was identifying himself with his public. A number of the newspapers noted that Beryl was going to accompany George, most repeating her heavy-handed attempt at humour: 'Somebody's got to do George's washing if he's going to hang it on the Siegfried Line.'

Gracie Fields had gone to France ahead of them and at Christmas 1939 was already entertaining the RAF in Rheims. George was scheduled to follow on 2 March with other artistes and even whole dance bands, such as Jack Hylton's. In the event he went a few days later, such was the disappointment at Castleford when it was announced that he would have to miss the planned show there. Castleford had special associations for the Formbys, as that was where they had met. George took to France with him 'three bags full' of scarves, socks and balaclava helmets, each with a personal message from the sender pinned inside, knitted by the chorus and juveniles of that year's pantomime, *Dick Whittington*. Beryl had organized a weekly knitting prize of perfume and chocolates, as well as providing the wool and needles. She departed with a dartboard under her arm, contributed by twenty-four Leeds telephonists.

Basil Dean, never generous in his appraisal of George's talents, commented in his memoir that the concert parties 'were popular because their well-balanced entertainments, if not of high artistic merit, were always good value for money'. George did not want to take the pay – £10 a week – for 'making the boys laugh', but it was pointed out to him that while he was overseas he would not be able to get money from England. So he accepted the fee, but frequently paid back some of it into the Cigarette Fund for the Forces. Before he left he took the sensible precaution of acquiring specially made boots – made to measure, of Moroccan leather, with a light ankle fitting, fully leather lined and with waterproof treated leather soles. They cost him £9 (£364) at a time when good quality shoes could be bought for £1 15s. His outfit was later described by Beryl: 'I have never seen anything so laughable in my life as George's dress. It was an army tunic, riding breeches and a tin hat. He wore it everywhere he went and the troops seemed to like it.'

On 16 March Ben Henry wrote to Jessie Bailey that 'they both arrived quite safely in France... everybody seems to feel that theirs is the best party of any kind that has ever been out there'. Ten days before George had recorded a troop concert in France in which he performed a sketch with Beryl from *Dick Whittington* and sang four songs, 'When I'm Cleaning Windows' and 'Chinese Laundry Blues' among them. Near Douai he performed in the local cinema. One soldier walked five miles in very severe weather conditions with his group of friends to see him perform, as petrol for army transport was strictly rationed. Another, arriving on the *Duke of York*, remembered forty years later being welcomed by George and Beryl on the quayside.

A letter to Daniel Wiles, the producer of George's *South Bank Show*, said the writer was entertained by George in a farmyard, then shortly afterwards was taken prisoner and was a POW for five years. On that occasion George sang a new song, 'Imagine Me in the Maginot Line', which he maintained had been composed by Beryl at the time when he was trying to join up. 'She says she kept thinking "Imagine George in the Maginot Line" and for some reason or other it struck her as funny.' Newspaper reports of the time claimed that George had written it. Assignment letters, however, tell another story. In fact he had paid Gifford and Cliffe £16 in November 1939 to write it. He gave a number of performances in the Maginot Line, one of which was filmed. The song illustrates exactly why he was so popular with the men – he was always totally on their side.

> Imagine me in the Maginot Line
> Sitting on a mine in the Maginot Line
> Now it's turned out nice again
> The army life is fine.
> The enemy we had to chase
> But my gun it got out of place
> I went and shot the Colonel in the base
> Down on the Maginot Line.

By early April George was performing in a little French theatre in Cherbourg. He sang his famous songs, told some jokes and then a trampoline was brought on to the stage. He and Beryl 'showed us how it should be done, then invited we service men to have a go, with hilarious results. The next day he sailed for home at the end of his tour, giving an impromptu performance as the vessel cast off'. The Formbys' tour was forced to a conclusion as the advancing German armies pushed forward to Dunkirk. George's party, in France for five weeks, made their escape out of Brest, in Brittany, the Formbys being among the last civilians to leave. The party returned to England, thanks to the intervention of an admiral, on an otherwise empty troopship. George, not a good sailor, commented cheerfully that he could be ill in every room.

He described his time in France as the 'happiest I ever had in my life' and 'the greatest experience of my life'. Newsreel film shows his huge enjoyment of the company of the soldiers. One newspaper writer spoke of George as 'a glutton for work. It's no rest cure driving for miles on end in five-ton lorries, shaving in cold water, being up at seven in the morning and playing in damp theatres. But far from grumbling, George seems to thrive on it...'. His first engagement on his homecoming was at the Hippodrome, Coventry, on 29 April, and he was just as popular in England as he had been in France. Newspaper reports described the show as 'the stuff to give the troops or any other audience for that matter. George was called for encores after every song'. He was also anxious to publicise his defence of the ENSA arrangements which some of his fellow professionals had criticized. 'They did all they could for us and even if we did have to spend half the night on two occasions sitting on petrol cans in a lorry it was through no fault of the organization in London... After all you expect to rough it a bit...'. He condemned his colleagues' own conduct. 'I have been told of occasions when hotel rooms have been practically wrecked by some artists who treated the whole trip as a sort of gala holiday, and found the wine pretty cheap to buy.' For a man seen by many as henpecked and 'gormless', these were outspoken remarks.

In May 1940, at a time of real risk of invasion, a message was broadcast asking for men to join the Local Defence Volunteers. The government hoped for a total of 150,000, but 250,000 signed up in the first twenty-four hours. Their motto, with strong overtones of the previous world war, was pretty straightforward: Kill the Boche! In August Churchill changed the name to the Home Guard, by then already standing at over one million men. George was one of them – a dispatch rider with the Fleetwood platoon. Combining his three nights on duty with standing in for Arthur Askey for a week at the Blackpool Opera House towards the end of the summer kept him busy. His topical song, 'Guarding the Home of the Home Guards', was a huge popular success. The aftermath of Dunkirk at the end of May led to a huge administrative headache in the southern counties of England as men of Britain, France and Belgium poured out of the 'little boats'. Where were they to be billeted, fed and watered? How were they to be kept entertained? Cinemas and theatres were kept open all night as sleeping accommodation. The exhausted rows of men slumped in their cramped seats must surely have been George's quietest audience ever!

This was the desperate summer of the Battle of Britain, the threat of imminent invasion replaced only by the horrors of the Blitz, which began in London in early September. Against the backdrop of death, injury and the shattering of homes and lives, George brought humour. *Let George Do It*, a comic propaganda film produced by Michael Balcon (Anthony Kimmins being in the Navy), was released in Leicester Square on 12 July and generally from 11 November 1940. Jeffrey Heskins for the *South Bank Show* commented 'what he enabled people in the nation to do was to laugh at their enemy, and that's a very powerful thing to do... make something that you're afraid of seem very ordinary and commonplace and this was the effect that he had when he entertained troops during the war and certainly in his films'.

Ben Henry wrote to Jessie Bailey: 'I'm glad you liked George's new picture, which I personally feel is about the best one he has ever made.' Almost all the critics, then and since, have shared his view. In terms of the impact on the Allies' morale it was certainly the most important. Starring Phyllis Calvert and Garry Marsh alongside George, *Let George Do It* became one of the most popular films of the war. Its attempted topicality misfired, though, as by the time it was released Norway had suffered invasion in April 1940 and so was no longer neutral. *The Times* film critic went straight to the point. 'Rather shamefacedly, this film has to explain that it was made before the invasion of Norway, for it shows the British Secret Service employing the artless and imbecile Mr. George Formby, as the result of a frightful blunder, against German agents in Bergen. It is a typical daydream of wartime... for there is an incidental sequence, which describes an actual dream in which Mr. Formby... captures Hitler himself and removes him from his rostrum in the midst of a speech. But whom ought this daydream and the arrival of Mr. Formby in Norway to comfort, the British or the Germans...?'

But all this was too clever by half. It was not the topicality of the jokes that made them funny, according to a Mass-Observation survey. The non-topical jokes in the same sequences received much more audience laughter. The theme of espionage, George's character and the insult to Hitler in the dream sequence all played to the public zeitgeist, though, perhaps surprisingly, in the Mass-Observation analysis the press actually liked the film better than the public said they did. 'Mass-Observation recorded that the fantasy sequence in *Let George Do It* in which Formby landed at Nuremberg and knocked out Hitler was one of the biggest cultural morale-boosters of the early war years, the visual encapsulation of the people's war with the English everyman flooring the Nazi Superman.' In some city areas, though, the most popular joke was the Storm Troopers' cheering *after* George knocked out Hitler.

The dream sequence provoked strong reactions of dislike as well as approval. While 58 per cent of the public answered 'Like it' to the question 'What did you think of the scene with Hitler?', 42 per cent answered 'Dislike it'. Acted jokes rather than spoken jokes were highly regarded, and this played to George's strength. George wrapping a petticoat round his head and later landing in Mary's arms after being shot from the torpedo were loved by the audiences. The last lines of the film were:

MARY (Phyllis Calvert) George, say something!
GEORGE Turned out nice again!

These were not the original lines, according to George's copy of the script – there was constant reassessment and revision during shooting. At first he was to pull out two fish from his jacket pockets and say 'Anybody fancy some fish and chips?' But in the end George's upbeat catchphrase won greater favour. The film was a strange mixture. The story line was far-fetched and the inclusion of four very good songs, 'Grandad's Flannelette Nightshirt', 'Mr Wu's a Window Cleaner Now', 'Count Your Blessings and Smile' and 'Oh, Don't the Wind Blow Cold', which between them took up nearly a quarter of the running time, twenty minutes in all, sat oddly with the 'realism' of genuine newsreel footage. The producers had been lucky to be able to include it, as a ban was imposed during the making of the film.

On 14 July the critic of the *Sunday Chronicle* commented: 'I can sit through the film again and again just watching his artistry.' His co-star

Phyllis Calvert also commented on an aspect of his brilliant technique. 'I watched him with admiration and fascination. He didn't act. He played himself. He was a personality chap. There's a scene where he goes to five doors in a nightclub, finding his way blocked by the villains, and he's singing and playing his uke all the time. The song ends when he gets to the last door. He had to do this several times during shooting, and on each occasion he finished the song at the exact moment he reached the final door.'

Phyllis recounted how the studio 'grapevine' maintained that George would make passes at the girls if he could. She was a little disconcerted that he never made any approach to her. But, 'on the very last day of filming, just before Christmas, Beryl had to do some Christmas shopping. I was in my dressing room at the lunch hour and a knock came at my door. George was standing there, rather like a little boy, and he said "Ee I'm crazy about you!" That was all. I think Beryl appeared the next minute. It was rather extraordinary how he couldn't resist trying to make it with his leading ladies'. Despite this tendency, Calvert thought that George and Beryl were happy together.

In the first month after release *Let George Do It* took more money at the box office than the Hollywood epic *The Grapes of Wrath*. The film was shown by a Royal Navy film unit to British sailors in Murmansk and Archangel on the convoys. It seems that a few Russians were present at the original showing and the next evening the British forces could not book a seat – they had all been taken by Russians! Copied by Studio Mosfilm in 1942 and released in 1943, it ran for a year in Moscow with dubbed dialogue and a new title, *Dinky Do*. *Russia Today* claimed that next to Stalin and some leading military men George was the most popular figure in the land, and during the war it was said to be the favourite film of the Russian soldiers and sailors. The songs were often performed by orchestras and jazz bands with Russian words and variations. It played in America, too, under the title of *To Hell with Hitler* – nothing if not direct.

Seventy years later this film, so important in its own time in raising morale, has been largely forgotten by those who compile programmes

George and Phyllis Calvert in the final scene from Let George Do It

recalling the early years of the war on the British Home Front. In such ways history is subtly distorted: the root of this omission lying in the snobbishness of the establishment then and now towards a northerner who was a working-class, not a middle-class, hero.

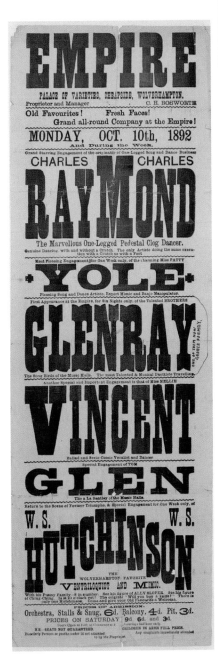

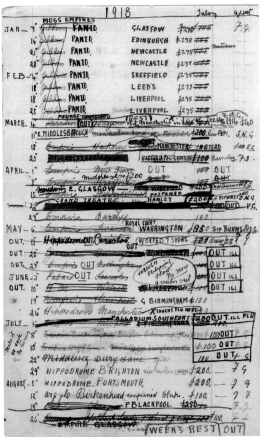

Left: *One of George Formby senior's first professional engagements*
Top Right: *Formby senior's Engagement Diary showing that he caught Spanish Flu*
Bottom Right: *A cartoon signed by George senior*

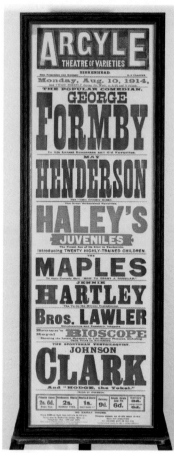
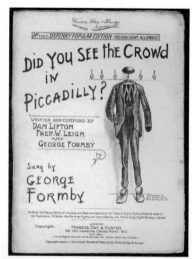

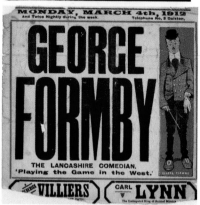

Top Left: Who were the Brothers Lawler?
Top Right: Sheet music for one of George Formby senior's 'London' songs
Middle Right: Record with George Formby's name and Wigan inscribed
Bottom Left: Cylinders and Edison Red Gem phonograph
Bottom Right: One of the many posters advertising George senior's bill-topping shows

Top Left: *George junior aged six, taken from a similar photograph and kept by his mother*

Top Right: *George Junior rode under the colours of Lord Derby*

Middle Left: *George Formby senior's gramophone, presented to him by his record company*

Left: *Eliza's Lady Ratling brooch*

Above: *The last entry in George senior's bank book, February 1921*

147

Top Left: *George junior's sisters in costume*
Top Right: *George junior's first contract, the Argyle Birkenhead*
Middle Left: *Oil painting George aged 17. His mother had this in her bedroom until she died*
Bottom Left: *Ukulele Ike. Cover of record produced by Kevin Daly (With kind permission of Michael Daly)*
Above: *George's personal hand-tinted front-of-house picture, given to him by Associated Talking Pictures*

Top Left: *George's personal hand-tinted front-of-house picture, given to him by Associated Talking Pictures*

Top Right: *Programme for George's first Royal Command Performance 1937*

Bottom Left: *The lamp was given to George by Noel Gay, the composer of 'Leaning On A Lamp Post'*

Bottom Right: *Regal Zonophone artists (With kind permission of EMI)*

Top: *The remarkable popularity of father and son is illustrated by the fact that both were honoured on cigarette cards*

Middle Left: *Italian poster for* It's In The Air — Vorrei Volare

Middle Right: *Collage from* Let George Do It. *Amongst the items is George Formby's personal script*

Bottom Left: *This little toy went everywhere with Beryl throughout the war*

Bottom Right: *George signed autographs on all sorts of things*

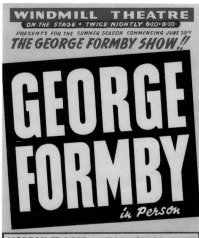

Top Right: The poster for George's Australian tour, 1947
Left: Windmill poster advertising George's sell-out show 1959
Above: Celebrating a new boat on Beryl's birthday, 9 September 1958, Horning, Norfolk
(With kind permission of Jarrold and Sons Ltd)
Bottom: George in 1959 in the programme for his show at the Windmill Theatre, Great Yarmouth

Top Left: *The programme for Aladdin 1960/1. George's last pantomime*
Top Right: *George and Larry Adler (with kind permission of Phil Argent)*
Middle Left: *Pastel picture by Audrey Pawson of the exhumation of George's Jaguar, crashed at East Winch in 1959 (With kind permission of Audrey Pawson)*
Bottom Left: *The Formby family grave, Warrington Cemetery*
Bottom Middle: *Ted and his son Alan 'A Tradition Nobly Upheld' – an obsession with lifebelts!*
Bottom Right: *Ted and Win Formby Booth*

CHAPTER ELEVEN

Swinging Along Singing a Song

In September 1940 George and Beryl, again working with ENSA, visited a huge ordnance factory in Chorley, Lancashire, for a week as part of an effort to raise factory workers' morale. They toured the canteens, giving shows at midday and midnight. Each audience was made up of a different group of workers, which indicates the size of the place. Dean believed that 'the regular break with routine, the chorus singing and general air of jollification, the looking forward and the looking back, brought succour to the tired human spirit'. George's patriotism was simply expressed. 'I know you will carry on doing your jobs, and the people who make the bombs will carry on doing theirs, and the people with the planes will keep on dropping them, and I will keep on coming round the works to cheer you up, and one day when the lights go up again it will still be "Rule Britannia".'

'Phyllis', a reporter for the *Blackpool Gazette*, wrote of such a concert, which saw 2,500 workers crammed into a canteen designed for 1,000. 'Girls perch precariously on the top rungs of ladders, reaching nearly to the high ceiling, to get a better view. Round-faced women, wiping perspiration from their foreheads after hurrying so as to be in time, hold each other up on mineral water boxes. Some still have their sleeves rolled above strong elbows. Pretty blondes add colour to this gathering of toilers in the country's cause. Vivid scarves are twisted round their hair and scarlet fingernails are much in evidence as they hold their mugs of steaming coffee.' It was said that both work output and appetites for lunch increased noticeably after such ENSA shows.

Beryl referred to their factory shows, and to George turning down an invitation to go to the US and Canada to raise money for evacuees and Spitfires, in a letter from Beryldene:

George says there is no need for anyone to leave this country at all for there is enough work here to do if they would only go out and do it – why don't they do the same thing on this side – enough money could be got for Spitfires here if they would only try.

P.S. George and I are doing munition works again this week during the workers lunch hour, and we may do some midnight ones as well while we are at it – it keeps the workers happy.

The Blitz began in London on 7 September 1940, and for the next fifty-seven days London was attacked by day or night. Drury Lane was bombed in October. George owned a factory producing Pilot radios which was destroyed. He was the first big-name entertainer to perform in the air raid shelters during the Blitz, on 27 November. Basil Dean recalled, 'I had gone across to the Aldwych Tube Station to attend the first ENSA concert to be broadcast from an underground shelter. From a little stage mounted in the middle of the track, just large enough to take a piano and himself, George Formby was making the shelterers forget their anxieties, as they sat on the tiered beds along the platform, or on the track itself, laughing and joining in the choruses.' Arc lights were set on long poles held by men stationed around the platform while Vice-Admiral Sir Edward Evans, 'London's shelter chief', in his uniform, acted as compère. George sang four songs, including, appropriately, 'Guarding the Home of the Home Guards', the biggest hit of the evening. He told his audience that the studio had been bombed twice earlier in the year during the making of *Let George Do It* and his ukuleles 'left floating about in the water'. In his rallying goodbye speech he commented that 'we've a got a king and queen, and I think they're marvellous people for us lot to look up to. I think the way they're carrying on, well, if Hitler was... They've got as much good in their little finger as Hitler and Goering and all the damn lot put together'. On his way home, while the bombs were dropping and the guns going, he saw in the deserted street a man with a barrel organ. He was playing 'There'll Always Be an England'.

Beryl wrote from the set of *Spare a Copper* at Ealing Studios: 'Well we had it jolly hot again here last night after having it quiet for two. I think they came back again and just gave us all they had – but we can still say HA HA never touched me' (a catchphrase from several of George's films). Later, the theme in a letter to Fred and Jessie was much the same.

> Yes we are still having a rough time of it down here – last night was a B… I must say they never left us alone until we were going to work this morning – they have been at us again this noon – it is a bit of a devil when they won't even let us have Saturday afternoon off isn't it, they are with us at the moment but I can't be bothered to go out and have a look…

Charlie Chester boasted in his autobiography that he was one of the few who found a friend in Beryl. He and George discussed film scripts and Chester visited him in his flat in Baker Street during the Blitz. There George showed him his collection of 'dozens and dozens of the world's most expensive pens and watches'. He said that the only thing he couldn't get was a bottle of whisky. 'I managed to get him one. It cost me £3 – more than a week's pay to me – and he never paid me for it!' Eventually, because of the continued disruption of life – and sleep – by the raids, Beryl and George went to stay in the countryside about twenty miles from the studios, but there they had four land mines dropped in three days. Beryl, writing to Fred and Jessie, commented with her customary sense of irony:

> My my did they shake the place… my typewriter flew from off the table… anyway we are still here to tell the tale and appear very brave while we are telling it… then we had bombs on the studio which set fire and through it we nearly lost all the instruments and all our stuff.

From mid-November blitz tactics were being used in other major towns and cities; the first being Coventry where the destruction of most of the Gothic cathedral became a poignant symbol of loss. Southampton, Portsmouth, Sheffield, Glasgow were all attacked and the evacuation programme to remove children from these areas of danger got into full swing. By 1941 George's hectic schedule was noticed by the diarist of the *Yorkshire Evening*

Press, who described him as 'one of the busiest people in England'. He had fitted in his visit to France between film commitments and variety engagements. He entertained the troops wherever he could, in camps, hangars or garrison theatres. He performed for workers in munitions factories, between recording and broadcasting. All the time he was fundraising. When he had a spare moment on Sundays he put on his Home Guard uniform and was off to do his duty in Blackpool. There is no doubt that the war was *his* finest hour, but the pace he set was shattering.

The New Year found George apparently on top form and on top billing in pantomime as ever – *Dick Whittington* – at the Blackpool Opera House, cheering people up just as he did in his ENSA role. But this time he was doing himself a bit of good too. His salary was to be not less than £500 (£18,400) a week and a clause in the contract covered possible cancellation because of the 'war situation'. Beryl, by contrast, was employed for the same eight weeks at £45 (£1,650) a week 'including all matinees'. George's performance of 'Bless 'Em All' was deemed by *The Stage* to be 'The Greatest Panto Song of the Year'. But this famous number was by no means new. Written by Fred Godfrey in 1917, its earliest performances were by Godfrey himself, playing the piano and singing to his RNAS colleagues, who often, as many have done since, took liberties with the first word of the title. George, by now aged thirty-six, went to the Blackpool Employment Exchange to register for military service. When he received the results of his medical in March, to his surprise and chagrin he was listed Grade IV – 'not even a place!'– because of sinusitis and stiff toes. He hadn't expected this echo of his father's rejection, saying that he'd thought he would be at least Grade II.

Spare a Copper, filmed the previous summer, was released in April 1941. John Paddy Carstairs, the director, thought George 'a genuine honest person with no pretensions'. He also considered him naïve because he 'didn't like cheques and wanted cash' and carried around with him a suitcase for the banknotes. The suitcase would become notorious, George and Beryl studiously stashing as much as they could away from the clutches of the Revenue. *The Times* reviewer remained unimpressed with this latest film. 'Mr. Formby… is left to fall back on his own inspired "goofiness", his bashful charm, the beguiling vacancy of his expression and his talent for playing the ukulele. All these are excellent in their way, but they are not enough, even with the support of Miss Dorothy Hyson, to carry a film as heavy in the hand as *Spare a Copper*.' It has been widely reported that George took advantage of Beryl's rare absence from the set to get her hair done to ask his (married) leading lady if she'd like to pop into his dressing room for 'a bit of fun'. She replied, 'I'm sorry, George, but I just don't do that sort of thing, I really don't.' To his credit he didn't try to persuade her. 'Oh well, I'll go and have a cup of tea instead,' was his recorded reply. In August *Turned Out Nice Again* was released. The role of George Pearson was a more serious one for George, and the first in which he played a married man. There was also an outstanding song, 'The Emperor of Lancashire', and a risqué number, 'Auntie Maggie's Remedy', which would become one of his comic standards.

Does anyone know where the car is?

Now I know a girl who is putting on weight,

In a spot where it just shouldn't be

So I said to Nelly

"Now you rub your knee-cap

With Auntie Maggie's remedy."

It was his last film for Ealing Studios as his contract had expired. He had formed a new company in March, Hillcrest Productions, through which, in a deal amounting to £500,000, (£18.4m) he would distribute his future films – two a year – in partnership with Columbia Pictures. In this way he hoped to break into the huge US market which had always remained psychologically daunting to him. The deal was also portrayed in the press as Formby making his contribution to the war effort by bringing in US dollars. He was to make seven films over the next six years.

Alongside film-making George continued his charitable work. Eddie Latta gave all rights to George for his song 'Spotting on the Top of Blackpool Tower' and was paid £10, a sum he promptly returned to George for his recently launched Blitz Fund. On 24 May Ben Henry wrote to Fred Bailey: 'George and Beryl are coming to London to organize a series of concerts in aid of the Air Raid Distress Funds in the blitzed towns and the nearest one to you will be Liverpool on June 16.' George threw an informal cocktail party, with, as a newspaper reporter put it, 'the inimitable Ben Henry hovering in the background, smiling paternally', to announce this next venture to help air raid victims. He expected the fund to raise £50,000 – £1,000 for each of the ten shows and £40,000 from a wireless appeal to BBC licence holders. It would involve a 2,000-mile tour in a 'Flying Fortnight', visiting ten major towns and cities which had suffered the worst of the bombing, performing matinees. The idea was firstly that those in safer areas could contribute money to those who had suffered in the Blitz, and secondly that communities could help their own members who had been so dreadfully affected. Starting at Manchester then Coventry, he went on to Southampton, Portsmouth, Plymouth, Bristol, Liverpool, Sheffield, Hull and Glasgow. In the event, Exeter, Walsall and Edinburgh were added to the itinerary. Every mile (over a thousand in the first week and almost as far in the second) he drove himself. All salaries and expenses he paid himself. He insisted to a reporter that this was not a publicity stunt, telling him 'you needn't use my name if you don't want'. Beryl was deeply involved, as ever, in the organisation of the venues and the recruiting, through ENSA, of the artists. Oscar Deutsch, the MD of Odeon Theatres, loaned cinemas in the towns, including two for profitable Saturday afternoons.

After Portsmouth George's campaign was given a much-needed fillip by one of his keenest fans, Queen Mary, the mother of the king, who donated for auction a George III silver cream jug, a Georgian silver tea strainer and an agate and silver *étui*. The latter is usually a small, decorative needle case, but this one was variously described as containing ink, pen and scissors, or, in another version, a lady's knife, fork and pen. George had appeared before the Royal Family at Windsor in early May. He was given a pair of gold cufflinks and Beryl a powder compact decorated with the royal monogram. The king apparently urged him to 'wear them, not put them away'. George regarded them as a most treasured possession. Shortly afterwards he was entertained to tea by Queen Mary at her home, Marlborough House, in the West Country, after performing in the village hall to some soldiers. She handed him the items at the end of it and had her photograph taken with George and Beryl on either

Queen Mary with George and Beryl. She was a great fan
With kind permission of Windsor Castle Archive

side of her. 'Eh,' said George, 'it'll cost anyone a pound to speak to me when I get back to Blackpool.' He was able to say at the Coventry show that he would sing the same ten songs as had been requested by the Royal Family.

It was at Plymouth in June that Lady Astor arranged a surprise. George's young brother Ted, then a Lance Corporal in Kingsbridge, Devon, was summoned to his Colonel, much to his anxious astonishment, and told to put on his smartest uniform and polish his boots. He was then picked up in a chauffeur-driven Lincoln Zephyr and taken to Plymouth Hoe. Mystified and overawed when the grand front door was opened and he found himself in the presence of Lady Astor, he was just worrying about whether he should salute or shake hands with her military companions, when 'she got hold of me as if I was sort of a long lost son' and took him to see George and Beryl. George was a little shy in the company he was keeping, but 'as usual Beryl was in charge of the situation'. He quickly discovered that Beryl had arranged for him to come to see them as they were performing for charity there. Leaning over to Teddy and giving him a big kiss, she said, 'That was a nice surprise, wasn't it? I got you a weekend off!' Ted recalled one of the five shows George gave there. 'They loved him. They wouldn't let him get off!' Part of the show was an auction. The cream jug made £50, and was given back for reauction in one of the other towns. (In Liverpool George's former patron, Lord Derby, attended the three-hour matinee and bought a number of items which he then offered for resale.) Some much less covetable items went under the hammer too. Lord and Lady Astor, who had organized the Plymouth show, paid £10 for some onions. Beer brewed forty years before for Edward VII went for £7. A signed photograph, some sheet music given by Oscar Deutsch and even George's tie, a violet number that day, were auctioned. The tie went for £5. (£184) Ted's evening was completed with dinner at Lady Astor's – lobster – 'and then at the end... when I was being transported home Beryl slipped me the usual ten pound note, which was very welcome, and Lady Astor put about six or seven hundred cigarettes in the car for me to go back with, so I had a wonderful day'.

The second part of George's Flying Fortnight project was a radio broadcast to be made by him on 9 June, asking forty million members of the public to contribute a shilling apiece to swell the coffers. If 800,000 of them each sent a shilling it would realise £40,000. But this aspect of the plan proved a huge disappointment. Charity slots were hard to come by and the BBC had filled them for six months in advance. As no regular Sunday evening times were available George agreed to speak on *Monday Night at Eight*, unaware that he would be given a script which he would be obliged to deliver. The major problem was that there was no address announced for people to send their shillings to. George was also irritated that he had driven to North Wales from Blackpool for the show and then had to drive through the night to Southampton, nearly 300 miles away for his matinee the next day, a nightmare journey as it proved, through the Welsh mountains with fused car headlights, 'crawling along in inky blackness'. A week later the BBC had received only about 200 replies, but after George's article in the *Sunday Dispatch* he got more donations in one day than in the previous week. At the end of the fortnight George expressed his anger that less than half the money he had hoped for had been raised, though the estimated yield from his ten shows was £9,725, nearly reaching the target. He complained of lack of cooperation from the BBC and lord mayors of some towns, specifically of Bristol and Liverpool, who had not promoted his appearances there. His determination to give his all for charitable causes was unabated, though. In July he organized a special matinee at the Coventry Hippodrome for the Emergency Appeal for the Coventry and Warwickshire Hospital, destroyed by enemy action. He was able to hand over a cheque for £1,040 7s. 3d.

In the summer George went on a tour to Orkney and Shetland under the auspices of ENSA, appearing with film actor Jack Buchanan. On his way north he popped into a cinema in Inverness which was showing *Spare a Copper*. He was delighted that the full house showed his popularity had spread to the Highlands and found it interesting to see the audience's reactions to his work. He and Beryl were waiting to set off for the Shetland Islands when they were told that there were ten men on a gun site perched on a cliff who hadn't had much fun recently. George went over to them – against orders – and sang sitting on a box under a cloak held over him to keep off the heavy rain. He began at 10 p.m. and finished at two in the morning. In 11 days he gave 55 performances, one in front of an audience of 10,000. There two big army huts had been arranged in a V-shape with the platform at the apex. George had to sing first in one direction then in the other, thus entertaining two audiences at once. One sailor, aged sixteen at the time, remembered George coming on board the HMS *Punjabi*, a destroyer, to sing to about forty of them. 'The sentimentality, it got to them a bit. Those old tunes and the fact that they were tired and weary… one or two of the lads really felt it and you could see that in their faces… they were the sort of songs that lads would sing at the guns anyway – the modern version of "Tipperary".'

August and September were devoted to the filming of *South American George*. In October 1941 ENSA asked George to do a tour of Canada, but after considerable thought he turned down the invitation. 'I've decided that I ought to remain with the lads in this country, singing to them whenever they want to hear me. Sorry, but there it is,' he wrote to Basil Dean. The same month he went to the Ministry of Supply with a cheque for £2,776 19s. 8d., the proceeds of his appearance at the Tank Matinee No. 1 held at the Odeon, Leicester Square, in July. He was told that the money would buy 6 caterpillar tracks, 4 gun turrets, 6 heavy tank guns or 480,000 rivets. 'Righto then,' he said, 'I'll have the rivets. I believe in getting plenty for me money.'

Between 16 and 18 December 1941 George and Beryl gave a short series of army concerts at Salisbury, playing two or three camps per night. George, looking 'spruce and jolly', topped the bill at the first concert and confided gleefully to the audience, 'At the moment I'm the only person who doesn't know where I'm going!' Beryl told the press, 'George will only go to the small units… He is happiest playing to a few boys miles from nowhere.' The *Daily Film Renter* described George's popularity as 'phenomenal' and it was little wonder. He offered to deliver any parcels or letters for soldiers in the area and found himself inundated with requests. Undaunted, he delivered each and every one in such spare time as he had. On their way home they called at St Dunstan's Home for the Blind to give a £50 cheque to boys, men and women blinded in the war.

Fred and Jessie Bailey spent Christmas with George and Beryl at Little Singleton, but there was not much rest for George. On 27 December he gave a command performance for the king, the queen and the two princesses,

George's distinctive features made him a caricaturist's dream

Elizabeth and Margaret, at which he gave the first ever public performance of 'Frank on His Tank'. On the 28th, a Sunday, he sang and joked at the Albert Hall in aid of King George's Fund for Sailors, at 'that august home of music where few, if any, comedians of his type have ever appeared before'. On the bill were Vera Lynn, John Gielgud, reciting a poem specially written by John Masefield, Geraldo and his orchestra, and the massed bands of the Royal Marines, 110 strong. Afterwards George reported that he had tried to find a quiet place to tune his ukulele. 'But it's such a low-brow instrument that everybody scowled at me. Eventually I had to go into a cloakroom.'

At the show George met Sir Malcolm Campbell, who had broken the world land speed record on nine times between 1924 and 1935. One of the topics of conversation was the 1939 Ford Mercury 'Bluebird' which Sir Malcolm had used as a team car and personnel carrier for his speed record attempts. The station wagon had been modified so that the rear seats folded down to make a sleeping area at the back, and George, thinking ahead to his projected ENSA tour to North Africa, bought the car. REME fitted sand tyres and painted over some of the clear glass. George also had a lean-to tent made to fit onto the offside, to provide accommodation for his pianist and his dresser, and blinds fitted to the windows. He and Beryl slept inside.

On 29 December 1941 *South American George*, his first film with Columbia, was released. The change of company was signalled by a new sort of role for George's leading lady, the dark-haired beauty Linden Travers. She was cast as a career woman, agent and legal adviser to an Italian singer. Reflecting her status, she was even allowed to deliver one punch line. Unusually, Linden got along well with Beryl. 'She and I eventually became good friends, and she helped me a lot with my clothes. She was very good for him, and I think she realised that she had helped to put him where he was and didn't feel that someone younger and prettier than she was should get hold of him. I think she was very sensible.' *The Times* critic noted the change of film style with the change of company – 'it attempts to tell a coherent story...' which 'at least relieves Mr. Formby of the strain of having to hold the screen with nothing but his grin, his affectation of shyness, his "gormlessness" and his banjo to help him. He gains from a script which insists on the co-operation of others, and the pity is that it is not funnier in itself...' On the same day that the film was released George and Beryl paid £500 for a film script entitled *Talkie Mad*. They seem to have been looking forward to a future without Columbia.

In the New Year George undertook a twelve-day tour of Ireland, having turned down a £1,000-a-week pantomime offer. By now he was the highest-paid performer in Britain, but as, he said, he was earning only sixpence in every pound, he thought he might as well work for nothing. He expressed a wish to play to lonely units and was expecting to give three shows a day. Touching down on Saturday from Liverpool Aerodrome, by four o'clock he was in the wards of a military hospital singing to the wounded. In the event the tour was extended for another week. George devised a motto which, he said, he wanted to be observed while he was in Ulster. Noting that a number of civilians had been at some shows, he announced that from thenceforward his watchword would be 'the troops, the whole troops and nothing but the troops'. This was also a signal to the officers and their wives who in his view 'hogged' the best seats. But they refused to take the hint. Eventually he asked Beryl and Harry Scott to go outside to where the soldiers were waiting and tell them to leave only the front row free. A threat by one of the top brass to report George to the War Office left him completely unmoved. As a civilian giving his services free they couldn't touch him. To compensate the general public he gave a charity show in Belfast at the Hippodrome which raised over £500. After three weeks and 72 shows, with audiences ranging from 1000 to just 9 Lancashire lads who had written to him asking just to see his 'dial', he and Beryl departed, George commenting that this was 'the pleasantest tour I have ever undertaken'. Dropping in to the Isle of Man, he entertained troops guarding the internment camps. On his return home, as if he didn't already have enough to do, he joined the Herbert Morrison Brigade with its 'war on waste', driving a lorry and helping to collect and salvage waste paper, clothes and scrap metal, work he fitted in where he could, for much of February and early March.

George continued his charity work, raising £8,000 for a tank fund. He was keen to do another ENSA tour abroad, but nothing was offered. Instead he relied on his films and radio work to lift morale. He was busy with both in early 1942, broadcasting six programmes to the troops. The fee was £30 a show, all of which he gave to the Fleetwood Trawler Distress Fund. From early March he was also making *Much Too Shy*.

In an article entitled 'On Leave', of March 1942, *The Times* leader struck a sad note. The writer made a comparison between the two world wars and two generations. The image used to span the decades was that of George and his father and it was drawn vividly.

For some at least there are the ghosts of the past, of other leaves a quarter of a century ago, which were enjoyed by a young man so like, and so different from, this young man of today. Father and son, seated side by side, with the rest of the family, at some entertainment, may scarcely see the same thing. For one there is, perhaps, a wildly comic film about a young Lancashire lad, while for the other the screen, with its rushing and roaring of aeroplanes or motor-bicycles, will fade and reveal instead a shabbier stage with, alone upon it, a pathetic cough-racked droll – whose name was also George Formby.

CHAPTER TWELVE

Monty and Me

George took up a new role in the spring of 1942, that of associate producer of a film starring Vera Lynn entitled *We'll Meet Again*. But by the late summer he was back in a much more familiar place, in front of the camera, as the making of *Get Cracking* got under way. Designed to spotlight the Home Guard, it was filmed in a little over six weeks. On 12 October 1942 *Much Too Shy went* on general release after an August showing in London. George recounted how his co-star Jimmy Clitheroe, like Wee Georgie Wood, a 'proportionate dwarf', who played his younger brother in the film, was more than once accosted by police concerned that a child was driving a car.

In early 1943 George went on a tour of North Scotland and Scapa Flow. Beryl described the flight, during which she and George 'practically lived on Fleetwood fish which I had cooked. We ate it cold'. It was, she said, 'rough travelling'. At Lyness he entertained the men to an impromptu concert on a 'shaky old wooden pier... There was quite a lot of jostling and singing and many a sailor was jostled off and into the drink and had to be fished out by his pals'. One sailor remembered, 'I was a young lad serving in the Merchant Navy on board oil tankers on the Russian convoys coming back from Murmansk. A ship came alongside our tanker and we were told that it was an ENSA ship for entertainment. My mates and I went on board. After the show we met him and his wife Beryl. We talked to him but I thought he was a bit shy. But his wife Beryl did a lot of talking... He gave us hope to sail back again to Murmansk in the cold and winter seas in gales of Force 12 and waves up to 60 ft high.' Another, Chester, a marine boy bugler, not yet fifteen, met George and Beryl in the Navy canteen at Flotta. They went walkabout around the base ship, the *Iron Duke*, and Beryl, spotting a particular marine, Mortiboys, approached him. 'He had the most beautiful head of fair curly hair, how it had survived the service barber I do not know, how he even got it all under his cap was a mystery, but when Beryl Formby saw it she rushed up to him, hugged him to her bosom and kissed him, saying 'what lovely curls!' This to a "Bootneck" was the height of indignity and Mortiboys never lived it down.'

Get Cracking was on general release by May 1943. Still *The Times* reviewer damned it by faint praise. He concluded that 'although a distinct improvement on other films in which Mr. Formby has appeared [it] is cut too closely to fit the demands of an individual technique to achieve any real life of its own'. One of George's co-stars in the film, Irene Handl, commented many years later that had George been given an ace director 'they'd have got something really special out of him'. It was a generous remark, but beside the point. Beryl instinctively understood the concept of 'branding' and was not remotely interested in trying to 'rebrand' George. George, for his part, did not love film as he did live theatre and wouldn't have wanted to experiment in that way. The *Picture Show and Film Pictorial* revealed that a number of the adventures which happened to him in the film *Bell-Bottom George* were based on anecdotes he heard from troops on his tours of North Scotland and Scapa Flow.

Most of the summer George spent working on *Bell-Bottom George*. He played the Garrick Theatre, Southport, for a week following the August bank holiday, then on the 20th, after a long wait for an overseas tour, he and Beryl flew to Fez in Morocco via Lisbon and Gibraltar. This was the beginning of the most extensive tour undertaken by a British artiste during the war. For it they wore the official khaki-coloured ENSA uniforms, recently introduced to be worn overseas in war zones, and known affectionately as 'Basil dress'. It was felt that the uniform would make it easier for the performers to use service transport as it would be clear that they were members of an accredited organisation. Some disliked the militarization they felt was implied by it, but George and Beryl, ever alert to new possibilities and being good clothes horses, were enthusiastic. Basil Dean remembered, 'Without waiting for confirmation of the forthcoming "dress-up" they hurried round to Moss

Bros. and selected uniforms of a highly decorative character, complete with 'guardee's' buttons and ENSA badges in gold on the coat lapels. Two days later I was escorting a number of M.P.s across the stage when, rounding a corner by some scenery, we came upon George and Beryl in full regalia, posing for a Press photographer!' It's a good story, but if it's true, these photographs were never published. The first press photograph of the couple in their uniforms, held back by the censor till three weeks after their departure for North Africa, appeared in the *Daily Mirror* on 10 September. Their uniforms had neither gold badges nor special buttons. They were army issue and on their return were handed back.

Beryl kept a meticulous diary of the fifty-three-day tour, listing the venues George played at, the number in the audiences and even keeping a note of the jokes he used in his performances. Each day, in sometimes three shows a day, he entertained outdoors, in hospitals and cinemas. At Sousse, on the North African coast, a soldier recalled: 'We rigged up a stage on the back of a lorry with sheeting for a backdrop. There was a howling sandstorm blowing at the time and he went on entertaining until the whole lot blew down.' The First

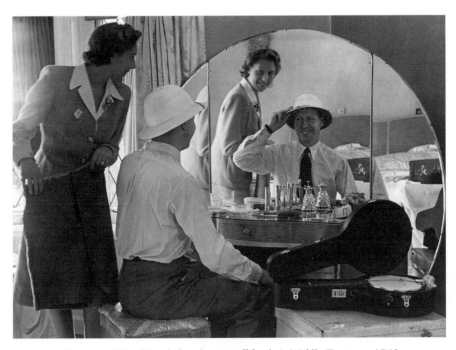

George and Beryl just before they set off for their Middle East tour, 1943

Army was in sand dunes near Tunis. One soldier remembered: 'Rumour had it that we were to be entertained but we were very suspicious as no one had been out to see us at that time. Then out of the desert came an army truck. The tail board was dropped and there playing his ukulele was George with Beryl at the piano. He sang all his old songs and we cheered them to the echo… I remember George was wearing a pair of voluminous trousers with elasticated tops. He pulled these out, stared inside and said "Coo, I can see my toes!" Unfortunately before the show was finished the sirocco arrived, the canvas on the truck started flapping violently and in no time we were blinded by the stinging sand. We lost sight of George and Beryl completely. So ended our first and only entertainment for months.'

By 30 August Beryl had counted a total of 25,300 troops at 20 performances, some at hospitals where George played to wounded soldiers. The conditions were punishing: temperatures of 125 °F in the shade, with flies, which George hated, getting into his eyes and mouth. One soldier wrote home that a locust joined him and Beryl for their cross-talk act, George trying to hit it with his cap. No doubt he was serious but the audience howled with delight. From Tunis they went to Malta in early September,

With the troops in the Middle East

where George performed at a roller skating rink. On a street in Valletta he stopped two soldiers because he recognized their Lancashire Fusiliers badge (he was in the Home Guard of the LFs). They said afterwards that it 'made their day'. At one of his shows in Malta, of about one and a half hours, one in his audience commented: 'I doubt if he would have left then but for Beryl. A wonderful performance, one I shall never forget, the fact that we never had many visits from artists made it all the more appreciated.'

On 3 September the Allied forces under Generals Montgomery and Patton had crossed the Straits of Messina from Sicily to Reggio di Calabria. George and Beryl moved on to Sicily two days later, where they entertained 2,500 members of the Eighth Army at Catania. Afterwards they were offered a tent and after seemingly endless 'goodnights' from the soldiers they finally got to sleep, worn out after three nights of little rest. The next morning

A makeshift arrangement, North Africa

they were brought a cup of tea and when they looked out of the tent they were alone on the plain except for the cookhouse. The army had crept away quietly in the night. The following day George and Beryl dined with Brigadier Grey who wanted an autograph for his son. 'In return,' said Beryl, 'we wanted permission from Monty to go into Italy.' At 1 a.m. there was a knock at their door and a despatch rider was waiting with the necessary permit: 'Please admit bearer to Italy.' They had to leave their entire luggage in Messina: 'Beryl just had the dress she wore' – but they took the piano!

Beryl later told an Australian audience that they crossed the Straits of Messina in barges with the boys and travelled ninety miles up the toe of Italy by jeep. This 'official' version has been challenged. It has been said that they bribed a fisherman to take them across. At one point their convoy approached a bridge which had been blown up. The detour was through the river bed between white safety lines, an area from which mines had been cleared. Ahead of them was a group of Italian prisoners. Several of them walked over the white safety line to give the oncoming vehicles room. One stepped on a mine. Two of the men were blown to pieces and three badly injured. George later recounted how shocked his party had been to experience so suddenly the horrors of war, though he felt the soldiers with them, humane as they were, took it in their stride. It seems that Beryl couldn't resist the temptation to embellish her tale. Her contribution was, 'Harry our dresser can't stand the sight of blood. I said, "Harry, don't faint, it's our job to keep up morale." We got out and helped a man whose arm had been blown right off.'

George and Beryl were the first civilians into Reggio di Calabria 2 days after the invasion, entertaining 3,400 troops there in a 90-minute show on 9 September. One of the welcoming party remembered that George told him he was most keen to be the first entertainer to visit the troops on mainland Europe. The show was given within two hours of landing, in a bandstand in a public garden, while the fighting was still going on three and a half miles away. At the end George told his audience: 'This is the proudest moment of my life. I'm glad and honoured to be the first British artist to play to you fighting lads in Italy. You've gone a long way and I've had a bit of rushing to catch you up!' These performances, while the Eighth Army was advancing in Italy, were the highlight of the tour for the Formbys. Beryl's boast that she was the first woman to go so far forward with the troops was widely reported in British newspapers, as were George's comments. No doubt both were competitive. A hostile critic claimed, without evidence, that being first was much more important to George than entertaining the battle-weary men and that he had left behind a lot of disgruntled 51st Highland Division men whom he was supposed to be entertaining. Another reduced his efforts to a simple competition with Gracie Fields. If that was his motivation then he was the clear victor.

By this time Beryl's diary noted '20 days 41 shows 68,400'. A soldier recalled that in the local theatre-cum-cinema she managed to 'tip our Brigadier, with herself, into the orchestra pit'. He added, ungallantly, 'I, with other liaison officers, had to make a big fuss of her, but our concern really was with our Brigadier.' That night the Formbys slept on the floor of the Town Mayor's office. On Friday (10 September) George was giving a show to over 2,000 troops in the market place at Reggio when a British soldier with a dozen Italian prisoners came along. When he saw what was going on he lined up his prisoners against the wall, indicated they could sit down and made them wait while he watched. The Formbys then set off in a Jeep sent for them by Montgomery. He clearly believed that George was a key morale-booster, and was his strongest ally. The next day, Saturday, George and Beryl had lunch with him – bully beef, tinned sausages and fruit – and he autographed an Order of the Day for Beryl. Her diary reads: 'Monty's show Vi-Bo [modern Vibo, Calabria] 2,300.'

They then returned by ferry to Sicily and on to Tripoli. On the 14th George played at Leptis Magna, on the Mediterranean coast in the Tripolitania region of Libya. Leptis (now a World Heritage site) is one of the best preserved Roman cities. George played in the huge and magnificent Augustan amphitheatre. One member of the audience, of the 4th Armoured Division, the Desert Rats, remembered that they had to wait about three hours for George to arrive. 'When he did he said "I'm sorry I'm late, boys, I've been waiting for the girls!" The lads all shouted out "Bring them on, we've been waiting for *them* for years!"' George played and sang for about two hours until he lost his voice. Myles Hildyard, a decorated soldier and in civilian life a man of letters and an aesthete, wrote in his diary:

George and Beryl with General Montgomery

My last night there I went to see George Formby at Leptis, he is a man very popular with the troops, a rather Edwardian banjo-strumming figure but he makes them roar. Half an hour before it started the theatre was full, over 6,000, and soldiers were being turned away. I sat on a column behind the stage with a 20-foot drop and looked up at the half circle thick with soldiers. There was a girl first who played for the men to sing and it sounded very fine and Hollywood, with the footlights lighting up the ruins behind us and the moon rising over the capitals, and a thousand little cigarette ends glowing in the towering black mass.

George and Beryl moved on to Cyrenaica, then by road to Tobruk and on to Cairo. Of his arrival there Basil Dean wrote, 'Later came George Formby with an assortment of ukuleles, encouraged and restrained alternately by the redoubtable Beryl.' But the first thing Beryl did was to go to bed – sent there on doctor's orders. By now the strain was beginning to tell on George, too. The entry for 'Monday 20 Sept.' reads 'No Show (ill)'and the following two days 'Cairo no show (ill)'. Echoes of his father's engagement diary. But by Thursday he was filling the venues again. Barbara Sand was the pianist for an ENSA show which was criss-crossing Egypt in 1943. George and Beryl joined that same troupe in the Suez Canal area. She recalled:

George and Beryl in Egypt, 1943

Nothing fazed him... He was, however, dominated by his wife to a ridiculous degree, and she protected him from his adoring fans in every circumstance despite the fact that many times the troops had endured so much just to see him. He was idolised not only by the English audiences but the Australian and New Zealand soldiers as well. One night we played to ten thousand [Beryl said 8,300] N. Z. soldiers in an open air theatre near Cairo and they almost went wild with delight when he finished his act... He was a superb artist with a wonderful sense of North Country humour and a dialect that was the same both off and on stage. I shall always carry a very warm place in my heart for him.

A soldier in that audience was sure that they 'would have kept him all night'. The only thing that prevented him staying was that he had to give another show, this time to the South Africans, immediately afterwards. The soldier was especially pleased that George didn't have to worry about the 'niceties', mentioning a song 'about the Middle East – very funny and need I say smutty – and another entitled "No Matter how Long a Stocking is the Top is always nearest the Bottom"'. He commented, 'I don't know when I laughed so much last.'

Another gunner remembered George performing in Egypt and his quip about the 'hazardous journey out. What a crowd of troops, doctors and nurses. Never in the field of human conflict have so few been chased by so many for so long, for so little'. A member of a small unit a few miles up the 'Blue' from Mersa-Matruk appreciated George's arrival. 'He gave us an impromptu concert by the side of the road. We all sat in a circle around him on jerry cans. It was one of the experiences of the desert I will never forget. At least he did come up the Blue to entertain us and not stay down in Cairo or Alex.'

In late September the Formbys travelled to Ismailia in the Canal Zone and on to Port Said where George gave six shows at the Britannia Club. By 3 October they were in Rafah, in the southern Gaza strip. On they went to Damascus, then briefly to Beirut for a rest. One gunner recalled that he met George while they were both swimming in the sea. George asked him where he was from and promised that when they were at the Leeds Empire in November they would give a message from him to his wife. George told him to go and have a word with Beryl, who was sitting on a bench surrounded by 'six or seven officers, like bees round the honey'. The soldier didn't want to approach the officers, even though George assured him that they were there first and foremost to entertain the rank and file. Instead he went round to George's caravan afterwards. The message was duly given to Beryl, two complimentary tickets sent to the gunner's wife and she was in the audience in Leeds to hear it. Afterwards she was invited for a chat in George's dressing room.

On 10 October, only days before their return, the *Sunday Dispatch* reported an interview George had given to the *Union Jack*, a Forces newspaper, while in Algiers:

> Most of the stars are where we left them – in the West End. Some of them give concerts to the troops provided such concerts are not in some dreadfully remote camp where there is a shortage of red carpets and cocktails. Some of them appear in an occasional Sunday concert in London.

Then his remarks began to get more personal, and, presumably, recognisable.

> At least one of them, a healthy young man of military age, has had his calling-up deferred provided he gives a number of shows to the troops. He gives the shows, but sees to it that they are all in or near London and suburbs. One famous music comedy soprano is always twittering how awfully pleased she would be to sing to 'the dear boys' in uniform but is always finding that proposed dates are inconvenient. A comedian whose name you all know adopts an even simpler policy. He does absolutely nothing at all beyond starring in a West End show, the seats for which are far too expensive for the soldier in the street. Two celebrated comedians were not long ago booked to appear at a show in the north of England. They went along, and because the arrangements for their reception were not up to pre-war standard they threw a 'temperamental' and scurried back to London.

This seems to have been part of a crude campaign of self-congratulation, as he went on to remind his readers of the £250,000 income tax he had paid without 'moaning about it'(!) and that he and Beryl were 'supporting 100 widows and orphans of Fleetwood trawler men who have been lost at sea. At Fleetwood they call us "The town's godparents"'.

After 53 days, 106 shows in 13 countries – sometimes as many as 5 a day – travelling over 24,000 miles and entertaining 207,150 troops, by Beryl's reckoning, the couple returned home. They met George's critics in the Waldorf Hotel, London. He had 'put the cat among the pigeons' with his comments. 'No other star... has caused so many tongues to wag, so many tempers to rise, so many conferences to be held with the Press.' He defended himself by saying he had not attacked anyone who had been out there, and explained he was trying to get the boys the best entertainment. 'They are fighting for us. If they weren't we might all be behind bars.' He did, however, also remark that, 'It's a case of when the cap fits.' Apparently mild-mannered, George was outspoken when he didn't like what he saw, but his bragging on this occasion compromised his message. He always refused to identify the fellow artists he had criticized, despite a cable from the Variety Artists' Federation, who had challenged him to put names to his 'black list'. His trump card at the Waldorf was Montgomery, whom he quoted to good effect: 'This is the best job you've ever done... Tell them in England we want more stars.'

That uncomfortable encounter behind them, George and Beryl began, with the help of Tom Arnold the impresario (who wanted George in his pantomime), to organize cinema venues for the friends and families of the servicemen and -women who had asked them to pass on their messages. From early November through telephone or letter and in cinemas in Birmingham, Manchester, Liverpool, Leeds and Newcastle, George and Beryl tried to cheer their audiences by describing the leave camps which were 'always on the shores of the Mediterranean, set out like a Lido with tables and Italian prisoners as waiters. The officers go to the same leave camps but there's no distinction and no saluting'. Then, as promised, they relayed an estimated 400 messages from sons, daughters, sweethearts, brothers and husbands in hearty terms. They were, many of them, brown as berries and fit as fiddles.

The boys were steering clear of the girls and missing their fish and chips, steak and kidney and beer (or mother's cup of tea). They were 'browned off' as well as brown, missing all at home, looking forward to seeing everyone again and, occasionally, touchingly, asking after babies they had never seen. One – 'and he was the only one I found who did' – liked it out there very much. Those in hospital were invariably recovering well and feeling grand. Sid in Sicily was enjoying sport, swimming and more fruit than he could eat – he only wished he could send some home. A husband hoped his wife had forgotten their quarrel and sent his love, a sweetheart asked for an early answer to his question which would make him the happiest man in the world. Arthur in Malta requested more letters – supported by Beryl – 'as they have nothing else to look forward to'. These messages must have given great consolation to the worrying mothers and wives at home, seeming as they did to come directly from their loved ones.

Beryl with her mascot.
This little toy went everywhere with her throughout the war

CHAPTER THIRTEEN

Up in the Air and Down in the Dumps

In January 1944 George was asked to make a broadcast for the BBC about his experiences in the Middle East. Initially he was daunted by the prospect of a live show – at peak listening time, straight after the nine o'clock news – in which he just had to talk. He'd had little experience in that sort of unscripted role and his reading difficulties probably undermined his confidence. But he proved to be a natural, speaking in a simple easy style as if giving a 'fireside chat'. The programme received glowing notices. Shortly afterwards he had a bout of illness during his stint in *Dick Whittington* at Nottingham's Theatre Royal, recalled in 1999 by Josie Roberts, a dancer in the show, then aged seventeen.

> We made our way to the stage but as we passed George's dressing room we noticed that he was sitting doubled up with pain. We thought nothing of it as he quite frequently suffered with tummy ache.

But this time George was too ill to perform. Josie remembered:

> The show limped until the interval and not a laugh had been heard... Then suddenly a familiar voice rang out. 'Hello everybody, I'm back,' boomed George... One second elapsed and then it started – clapping, stamping, cheering and shouts of 'Good old George' filled the air and he just stood there laughing and joking for about five minutes. It was so emotional that we all gazed at one another and many tears were shed.

The previous autumn, between radio, his theatre visits and pantomime, George had turned again to filming and early in the New Year *Bell-Bottom George* was released. The songs were 'Swim Little Fish', 'It Serves You Right (You Shouldn't Have Joined)', 'If I Had a Girl Like You' and the title song 'Bell-Bottom George'. Three of these were to cause George trouble when a Home Office team of propaganda experts investigated them as being 'enemy-friendly'. George never discussed the investigation, even with his closest friends and relatives. He referred to it afterwards only as a 'nightmare'. It is very hard now to see why any of the songs could be seen as suspicious. 'Swim Little Fish' may have been thought to be belittling the efforts to attack the German U-boats which were sinking ships in the Atlantic, but the scene in which George sings to his goldfish, Egbert, is so charming that any deeper interpretation seems perverse. 'Bell-Bottom George' could, at a great stretch of the imagination, be regarded as critical of the Navy with its notion of a girl in every port. But it was a very old and commonplace comment about sailors. 'If I Had a Girl Like You' expressed sweet but harmless sentiments, only one line having any possible connection with the war at sea. 'Single-handed I'd rescue ship and captain and crew...' For George, who had spent a huge amount of time and money in supporting Britain's war effort it was mystifying and mortifying to be in any way associated with treachery. The accusation would threaten his projected return to France and ultimately, if it was upheld, his whole career. He and Beryl were on the set of *He Snoops to Conquer* when the conclusions of the preliminary committee were made known to them. George was called to London to perform the songs and after an agonising seven-day wait he was told that they could be sung, provided they were not altered or added to in any way. No one had reason to scrutinise the songs more carefully than the committee, and they could find nothing wrong with any of them. George had been set up, probably by some of the artistes he had criticized for not contributing much to the war effort.

The Times reported on 29 June that the invasion troops involved in the D-Day landings were to be entertained by the first ENSA contingent in an operation that amounted to a formidable invasion on its own account.

It comprised 'twelve mobile columns, complete with sleeping coaches, portable lighting sets workshops, and radio rediffusion vans'. According to Basil Dean, all the songs and patter had been carefully vetted 'by a qualified committee to avoid the possibility of affronting standards of good taste, and while there had been few instances of rejection, in certain cases alterations in material had been firmly insisted on'. Despite George's previous comments about his colleagues, when there was a prospect of returning to France, 'There was no lack of volunteers among the stars. They were so caught up with the fancy of landing on the beaches that we were compelled to allocate them weeks in advance, so many stars to each sailing... The irrepressible George Formby and his wife were to be in the first sailing...'

George waited for that sailing on the south coast for three weeks, giving concerts there to pass the time. As ever Beryl looked after him and drew any criticism from him. One soldier recollected a show in a field near Corsham. 'After a long applause he gave two encores and was then practically pulled off the stage by his wife Beryl, much to the disappointment of us all. We then dispersed saying "the miserable old rat bag" or some other army phrases.' There was also a huge build-up of troops waiting for the delayed advance and desperate for entertainment, but getting to Normandy was difficult. No branch of the armed services could spare the transport or take the risk of transporting ENSA parties. The officer who finally took the Formbys to France recalled, 'In the two days we waited at the port of embarkation George sang quite literally under a lamp-post at the corner of the street to while away the tedium of our waiting.' Unofficially, any units willing to co-operate could take over individual artists, and eventually an army unit attached to the RAF, and so not subject to the direct command of either, was requested to take an ENSA entertainer to Normandy as a passenger in a jeep aboard a vehicle-landing craft. George posed no problem, but the officer in charge was disconcerted to see Beryl there as well. Not only was space a problem, but there were no facilities for a lady.

George had been determined to travel in the same way as the soldiers, but it was a trying voyage, with the roughest seas he'd ever travelled in. Beryl, in an interview with the *Lancashire Daily Post* said, 'When George was singing the ship was rocking to about 75 degrees and it took me all my time to hold him down and keep the mike to his mouth.' Because of all the extra personnel, some servicemen slept on stretchers on deck until, interrupted by a fierce storm, they scrambled for cover wherever they could find it. By dawn they were high and dry on the beach, trundling ashore with George on the back of one of the tanks.

George and Beryl stayed on the beach at Arromanches as the troops were unloading from their landing craft, George with his ukulele entertaining and raising morale. One soldier remembers asking him for his autograph, 'which he signed on a 100 franc note because we didn't have a piece of paper between us. We had a chat, pulled each other's leg a bit, wished each other good luck and we parted... He was a very nice bloke'. The first concerts were often in the open, with the men sitting around him in shell and bomb craters. Many of the soldiers said afterwards that these events, with George and Beryl chatting after the show, helped them forget the war for a little while. Stages were fashioned as best they could be – even the back of a three-ton Bedford truck (an ENSA lorry) was brought into service –

A difficult crossing to France, July 1944

while audiences varied in size from several thousand to fewer than a hundred. On the Arromanches to Bayeux road George's stage was a farm cart and he played to about 200 exhausted men resting for a few hours on the way to Rouen. Another was in a farm barn, the area being bombed day and night. 'This didn't deter them one bit,' one member of the audience recalled.

An early concert was in an improvised theatre in a brick-built barn, for 600 airmen. The first half-hour was almost drowned out by the roar of aircraft – Typhoons of the 2nd Tactical Air Force loaded with rockets – landing and taking off from a nearby front-line airfield, only one hundred feet above their heads. Beryl resorted to a home-made megaphone while George shouted to her from ration boxes in the front row of the audience. George said afterwards, in a hoarse voice, that he didn't care if he had to repeat himself ten times. 'The sound of those planes meant much more than the show and I'd hate to steal their act.'

George's first official performance was a two-hour concert to sweeper crews in the little cinema on board the former minesweeper *HMS Ambitious*, by then being used as a headquarters ship. He seems to have enjoyed driving the DUKW (Duck), a six-wheel-drive amphibious vehicle, out to the vessel himself. Always mindful of those unlucky in the draw for seats, he later repeated the whole show for them before his party went on into France. According to the *Daily Sketch*, he took up his ukulele to give a rendition of a new song 'which George had written himself' – 'Rolling Into France'. George acknowledged that the words were by Fred Godfrey but claimed he wrote the music. Thoughtfully Beryl had taken all copies of the previous Sunday newspapers she could lay her hands on, which were much welcomed. Another soldier met George 'aboard the *Black Prince* anchored off the beach-heads in Normandy. The day before *Black Prince* had been hit by German bombers and the authorities tried to deter George and the ENSA party from going on board, but he insisted that the men shouldn't be let down, telling us from the makeshift stage that they were the last party out at the evacuation of France and they would be the first back and they were'.

Basil Dean described the storms which had turned the ground in northern France into a quagmire. 'George Formby and the parties in the first section had been stirring things up, playing here, there and everywhere, never less than two shows a day and sometimes three.' The Theatre Municipal, Bayeux, was crowded nightly. The Formbys went into Normandy with Field Marshal Montgomery and were invited to a meal with him. George quipped to his audience later that he didn't know whether it had been an invitation or an order he had received from the great man. Monty spoke to him about the plight of the 6th Airborne Division (Gliders) who had been in France holding a vital bridge for fifty-six days without relief. He felt they would much appreciate a show from George, who readily agreed. Beryl enjoyed recounting the next part of the conversation on more than one occasion. 'Of course Beryl can't go, Monty said, but I said that if I couldn't go George couldn't either, and Monty said, "All right if you like to risk your neck".'

Dean was impressed by the Formbys' determination. They were prepared to set off in a jeep, without a piano, pianist or costumes.

> Early the next morning [17 August] I found George Formby, impatient to carry his uke across the Orne, waiting by my car, and his wife with him. I tried to dissuade Beryl, but she would not be denied, and so became the first woman of the invasion forces to cross that river... The little Normandy towns and villages through which we passed had mostly been blown to pieces, their tiny streets buried under piles of rubble... Everywhere the stink of long-neglected dirt, blown from the rafters of ancient build-ings, and the still fouler sweetness of death.

They discovered the airmen in an orchard next to a farmyard, hiding in foxholes. The Germans were about 120 yards away. Beryl sat under a tree and George stood with his back to a tree or a wall of sandbags, ready to dive into a slip trench, with the men squatting on the ground in front of him. They were a silent and sometimes invisible audience, the men bobbing up and down from time to time showing 'thumbs-up' appreciation. Beforehand the couple had been given advice as to what to do if things went wrong. 'If anything comes over, *duck!*' George was told. 'Don't feel embarrassed, because if you don't you'll be the only one standing! We don't think anything *will* happen because they'll be able to hear you.'

185

Between 12 noon and 3 p.m. on that day George gave six shows to the men of the Airborne Division, none of them more than 300 yards from the German lines and, in one case, a mere 80 yards. As he performed his nine songs and a comedy routine with Beryl he recalled only one stray bullet signalling the presence of the Germans. Dean's memory was a little different: 'He sang song after song, screwing up his face into comical expressions of fright whenever shells exploded in the near distance, and making little cracks when the firing drowned the point lines in his songs.' The audience laughed silently. George maintained that the shooting mostly stopped because the Germans were listening too. He always remembered and often described this 'most weird' performance. 'On the long drive back to our camp, whenever sufficient numbers of men were gathered to warrant a performance, in stables and in courtyards, out would come the uke,' Dean recalled. By the end of that day Beryl and George had given nine shows. When a radio interviewer commented approvingly of their achievement George modestly replied that they 'didn't sacrifice what the boys did – we did nothing wonderful'. Beryl, however, commented feelingly afterwards: 'I don't think I could go through all that again. While one was doing it it always seemed when one awful day was over that the next wouldn't be so bad. And when the next day was just as bad we felt the following one might be better.' Their courage was fully appreciated by their audiences. One soldier had thought the advertising posters were displaying a Conference Code Name and so was particularly surprised and delighted to see George in the orchard.

George's energy and commitment to the forces he'd come to entertain went far beyond merely entertaining. After the battle for Noyers and Thury Harcourt in early August the 7th Battalion South Staffs 59th Infantry Division had suffered heavy casualties and were pulled back to rest. As they arrived at their destination, about a mile from the front line, they were greeted by George and Beryl. George asked if they'd like to see a makeshift show straight away or wait half an hour and see a proper show. They decided to wait and in no time at all George had taken off his jacket and shirt and was erecting a stage. Meanwhile Beryl handed out cigarettes. Half an hour later they were watching 'a first class show'. George and his party also entertained a Guards tank brigade in the Ardennes, just behind the front line. At the end the CO commiserated with the Left Flank Squadron who had missed the show as they were at the front. George requested some transport to take him to where they were.

> That is how I met George. In a cramped shallow dugout, between the track of our Churchill tank with a couple of smoky oil lamps for illumination, a mess tin of sweet compo tea and George plucking away at his ukulele and singing 'When I'm Cleaning Windows' but with much more risqué words than the public had ever heard! A lot more even risqué-er jokes followed. After lots of hand shaking and back slapping George left to slide down into the dugout below the next tank leaving a very happy crew. The next morning we discovered that George spent nearly all night out of one dugout and into the next until he had entertained the whole squadron.

After their four-week tour the Formbys returned home to begin filming on *I Didn't Do It*. But George was keen to continue his work to keep up military morale. At the end of December 1944, from his home in Lancashire, he went to entertain the women at a WAAF camp at Weedon, near Morecambe. They were snowed in and conditions were very bad – so bad that this group of girls were to be the last, as the Commandant had decided to close the camp after two women died of pneumonia. For one of the WAAFs there it should have been a special day. Barbara Pelling was celebrating her twenty-first birthday, but not even a card had reached her and she felt totally miserable. George's concert transformed her mood. One of Barbara's friends told him that it was an important birthday and he got her up on stage, 'really lifted my spirits, dried my tears and sang to me. I shall remember dear George forever'.

In January 1945 *He Snoops to Conquer* was released. George's leading lady this time was Elizabeth Allen, the oldest of all of them at thirty-six and a well-established actress. Her part was, to say the least, undemanding and she recalled 'cycling to work one foggy drizzly morning during the blitz, and I thought to myself "Dear God, it's come to this"'. By now public taste was turning away from humour and towards melodrama. The most popular films of 1945 and 1946 were *The Seventh Veil* and *The Wicked Lady*, both of which starred James Mason. Good looks and a smouldering presence were his stock-in-trade, and glamour back on the escapists' agenda. An edition of the *Picture Show and Film Pictorial* of July 1945 illustrates the point perfectly. Inside the cover page is publicity blurb for George's film, *I Didn't Do It*, released that same month. On the cover is a close-up still of a passionate moment between Lauren Bacall and Humphrey Bogart from *To Have and Have Not*. But even George's film career was not totally immune from the current trend – *I Didn't Do It* was given an 'A' certificate by the censors because the murder scene, of an acrobat in a boarding house, was so grimly realistic.

Since 1943 George had been expressing a desire to go to Burma, known as he was, according to contemporary news reports, as 'Johnny Formby the banjo wallah'. He probably wanted to be 'with the boys when they go into Mandalay'. He liked to be first. No doubt his particular wish to entertain those who were isolated in remote areas was also part of the appeal for him. After finishing *He Snoops to Conquer* and as soon as the monsoon was over, George and Beryl went off to Burma via India and Sri Lanka in January 1945, to entertain the Indian Division of the 14th Army. The show was big news because it was headlined 'At Last England Remembers the Forgotten Army' – the Formbys being among the first group of entertainers to go there. The soldiers' favourites were listed by Basil Dean as being Will Fyffe, Gracie Fields and George. One man remembered meeting George at the Marine airport at Karachi. 'When he stepped off the plane he was in ENSA uniform sweating profusely. Someone had told him it would be cold when he arrived. Anyway he immediately threw off his overcoat and disappeared among the crowd signing autographs. We were chasing around after him to go for his injections.' A temporary stage was set up on the tennis courts, with two rows of chairs in the front marked 'reserved'. George asked about them and was told they were for the officers. He replied that there were no officers in his show and told the men to move down. At Korangi Creek, about fifteen miles outside Karachi, George played to RAF Catalina Flying

Boat airmen on a stage made of oil drums with wood set across them, at the back of the men's billets.

On the last day of January the Formbys flew to Bombay. 'In the evening George gave the opening performance of his tour on the football ground, in the presence of the Supreme Commander and Lady Mountbatten, Sir John and Lady Colville, numerous military and civil dignitaries and over 5,000 troops', wrote Basil Dean.

> The portable stage was to be erected in front of the grandstand immediately after the Indians had finished football, but the game was nearly two hours late... Shortly after the show began some one or something severed the main cable, cutting out the microphone and throwing the stage into darkness. With the aid of motor-car lamps Formby carried on for thirty-five minutes. When the microphone was finally restored he resang many of the songs he had sung in darkness, without any sign of audience impatience: a genuine triumph of personality. George, indefatigably strumming on his uke, did more to sustain morale in the war years than many performers of less restricted talent.

From Bombay George and Beryl visited the British Army base in Deolali, 100 miles to the north-east. It was a departure centre for men going back to England after a tour of duty, its name the origin of the word 'doolally'. Men supposedly went a bit 'stir-crazy' while waiting there. It was also the setting of the first four series of the BBC comedy *It Ain't Half Hot, Mum!* made in the late 1970s and set in 1945. George gave a two-hour show – his largest in the Far East – on the football pitch, to 12,000 men in the afternoon and another 7,000 in the evening. At about midnight he was packed up and ready to leave. At the exit gates he happened to ask the sergeant on duty if he had enjoyed the show. He got the very grumpy reply that he hadn't seen it as he had been on guard – well, somebody had to be. A few at the other gate had missed it as well. 'Ooh,' said George, 'we'll have to do something about that,' and the Camp Commandant was phoned. The guard was reorganized and the twenty-five or thirty men who had missed the show arrived in trucks. George realised that if their headlights pointed to one spot he would have a 'stage' and quickly organized the trucks himself. He and Beryl sang together and performed a sketch, then George played and sang for three quarters of an hour. Of course the Formbys missed the train back to Bombay — not that George was in the least concerned.

But not everyone was beguiled by the Formby humour. When the TV producer Daniel Wiles asked soldiers to write to him with their wartime memories of George for the *South Bank Show* all but one recounted happy occasions, with much laughter, and expressed admiration of George's courage, stamina and generosity of spirit. But he encountered blistering criticism from one soldier of a show in Assam in early 1945. He described it as 'the most nauseating and distasteful [show] I had till that moment ever experienced. It would not have been so bad had his wife not taken part'. Which shows that you can't please all the people all the time.

The Formbys were in India and Burma for three months. Both of them learned to fire a machine gun, though after Beryl hit a cow her training came to an abrupt end. In Burma George once again performed in the oversized khaki shorts which looked funny in themselves. Then he did the 'looking down the trousers' routine, this time wordlessly. With the Formbys were a pianist, Gerald Benson, and Tony Heaton, a female impersonator. Benson recalled that they had flown from Cairo to India, flying the length of the sub-continent from north to south, from Karachi via Bombay to Bangalore. From there they went to Colombo, Assam and Burma. Benson got on very well with George, who bought him a gold-coloured fountain pen in Calcutta. He remembered that the plane had to fly low, at under 8,000 feet because of George's heart condition. Considering that he was not yet forty-one it was a bleak omen.

The conditions of the trip were punishing. The Formbys found themselves trying to sleep under mosquito nets in jungle clearings, the heat intense, the shrieks and cries of baboons and jackals making the night unearthly. Gurkhas guarded them from prowling leopards. They had to look out for the deadly shoelace snakes themselves. George reported that they would go away if he stamped his feet. The next night, many miles away, it would be the intense cold that kept them awake. One soldier, recovering in a tented hospital in Shwebo, central Burma, was sufficiently grateful to George for his effort to visit that he wrote to the local newspaper more than half a century later. 'What made George come to such a God-forsaken place? There was no running water, no W.C. There was heat and disease and Japs. There was cornbeef stew and insects in the biscuits.' He recalled that an airstrip was constructed to let in Dakotas and that George did a two-hour show. 'What a tonic! It was better than medicine.' Another soldier was serving near Maungdaw on the Burmese border, in the extreme south of modern Bangladesh. He wondered how they managed to get a piano to such an inhospitable area and remembered that as they were very near the front line the concert was interrupted several times by the firing of the Division's guns.

A young Richard Howard, whilst working at the veterinary practice of McLintock and Partners in Norwich in 1962, went out on a visit with one of the partners, Jimmy Phillips. Jimmy recalled his time in the Royal Army Veterinary Corps when he met George and Beryl in Burma. At the time he was operating to remove the vocal chords of mules – the only effective beast of burden in that theatre of war – so that their braying could not give away the troops' position to the enemy. With George's interest in all things equine he had wandered into the temporary stabling and operating theatres. Jimmy, with typical Scottish humour, offered George a transplant, years ahead of its time, saying it would improve his range! Needless to say George left rather rapidly.

By the beginning of March 1945 the Formbys had reached Ramree Island in the Bay of Bengal, where George and Beryl visited an RAF Mobile Signals Unit. The soldiers built a makeshift theatre from material salvaged from a damaged pagoda, and by the time George and Beryl arrived the RAF Coconut Grove Theatre was complete. Two ambulances served as dressing rooms. A soldier obtained George's autograph through Beryl's good offices, written on a Japanese note, but had to 'wait for it until George woke up. He was exhausted!' Some relaxation was essential and George got out his camera, taking a series of photos of Beryl posing in her swimsuit, sitting on a rock in the sea, signing autographs, washing her hair outside their tent, and

Ramree Island, Burma, March 1945

so on. Slimmed down by wartime rationing and their gruelling schedule she looks much younger than her forty-three years and was still clearly a very attractive subject to her husband.

It took six days' hard air travel to get home. They had had many uncomfortable hours in a jeep before that, and George had got malaria. Beryl had also been ill and, unsurprisingly, George confessed later, 'we were just all in'. But once again they returned to controversy. Basil Dean, speaking in a press conference broadcast on All India Radio, criticized 'this business of favoured artistes coming out under special privilege, and when they get here rushing about all over the place like scalded cats in special aircraft, thus providing less entertainment for the men than if they were not too snobbish to accept ENSA's directions'. George and Wee Georgie Wood took this personally and riposted with an indignant letter printed in *The Times* on 3 April. They pointed out some home truths. Again George was not prepared to sit back in the face of apparent criticism. There was nothing 'simple' or 'gormless' about him in these situations.

Left: Beryl relaxing, Ramree Island

Below: Beryl and soldiers. Note her ever-present mascot

He says that three stars with parties made things very difficult for Ensa by their behaviour in the Far East while he was there. His further complaints are that 'the stars seem to have expected the order of battle should be altered to suit their convenience. It is plumb crazy for such people to come home and suggest their services are not wanted because they cannot be accepted in the front line at a particular moment. There are thousands and thousands of chaps in the back areas lacking the excitement of active operation who need entertainment just as badly'. Quite so, but when the undersigned arrived at these places with their respective parties they found these very men in the back areas felt it was the duty of the stars to play the forward areas first and work their way back. This view is subscribed to by Army Welfare.

There is much criticism directed at the stars that they prefer to work comfortably the large base areas instead of going forward. The fact is, of course, that we have to go where Ensa sends us... General Leese made it possible for Mr Formby to get to Burma. Air Marshal Joubert arranged for Mr Wood to go there. It is nonsense to suggest that they would pander to artists by making it possible for them to have special aircraft unless they saw good reasons for giving the actors such valuable transport... The suggestion that stars expected the order of battle should be changed is childish. We certainly have not suggested that our services were not wanted because we could not be accepted in the front line at a particular moment. We did suggest that our services were wanted in the forward areas and Ensa seemingly did not realise this. Mr Dean complains about the stars who do not go oversea and Mr Dean complains about us who do go oversea. We venture to suggest that we never asked for such special privileges as Mr Basil Dean had on his tour. It seems to us to be, to say the least, a little unkind of him to talk like this about us when our only fault was the desire to do a maximum job for the troops.

Dean maintained that he could not understand why they had written the letter as 'there were no stars in the ENSA firmament to whom my remarks applied with less reason'. Presumably the two men wanted to make it clear to the widest possible audience that they did not accept without comment this view of what appeared to be *their* behaviour.

Perhaps dreaming of life in the slow lane, George had bought, in January 1945, a farm in Sullom End, near Preston, complete with its herd of four pedigree cattle. The house itself has been described as a mansion, standing on a hill and overlooking an extensive estate of over a hundred acres. The family, Beryl taking her parents to live there with them, moved on 23 April and the Formbys took two weeks off to recover from their travels. But the venture did not suit George long term and he left after only eight months. It appears that he wanted to convert at least some of the property, including the dairy, into flats, but this didn't happen. His nephew Jeffrey recalled a holiday there.

> In the evening George would sit on the settee… and he would sing songs, play his uke and we as children would sit in front – George liked an audience, he always liked an audience, and one of the things we had to do was – Beryl would say – 'Now don't forget, you must clap, you must applaud.' Right, fair enough, so we would applaud when George had finished, and one of the humorous parts was George had a new song that he was probably trying out, and we weren't quite sure when it had finished, we just sat there and George said, 'Well, it wasn't that bloody bad, surely.'

Jeffrey went on:

> My Aunty Beryl was very warm. Relating back [to] when we forgot to clap, George immediately said, 'Beryl, it's time that the children were put to bed,' and Beryl would take us and tuck us up in bed and she'd say, 'It's all right, he'll have forgotten about it in the morning.'

But much of the time George was simply not able to be the gentleman farmer. Between July and October he was filming *George in Civvy Street*. Meanwhile, in August he put Sullom End up for sale and bought a house at Mere.

The recognition of George's wartime contribution meant that the accolades began to arrive, not least his appearance in wax at Madame Tussaud's. By the end of the war he had also been awarded seven campaign medals and Beryl five. They visited every battle front but the Russian, advancing into Italy and occupied Europe with Montgomery's spearheads. In June 1946 George was awarded the OBE (along with Elsie and Doris Waters and Wee Georgie Wood) in the King's Birthday Honours List. He had been ENSA's top performer, entertaining over three million troops. His great disappointment was that Beryl was not credited, which he felt was unfair, not only because she had shown great personal bravery and made a significant contribution to the war effort, but also because some of her schemes, taken up by other women who had remained at home, had won *them* the public recognition *she* had been denied.

George's hand being modelled for his waxwork.
With kind permission of Madame Tussauds

But George had paid a heavy price for his success. He acknowledged it himself in an interview in 1960. 'I think I drove myself too hard at times, during the war especially.' After his death John Carter wrote that he had 'worked himself into the sickbed with sad regularity… One-night stands in the tropics, shows on top of NAAFI tables in the Arctic cold took their toll. Back home at Lytham George was put to bed for weeks at a stretch. '"Stay there, George," said his doctor, "or you'll never see the war out." Beryl saw to it that he did as he was told.'

CHAPTER FOURTEEN

Why Should I Work for Tanners?

Compared with his previous films *George in Civvy Street*, released in June 1946, was a box office failure. He was not the only one of the comic greats to suffer declining popularity in the cinema – the same was true of Will Hay and Frank Randle. Audiences had stayed with the Gainsborough melodramas. George's writers were Ted Kavanagh of *ITMA* (*It's That Man Again*) fame and Gale Pedrick, later the comedy script editor at the BBC. This was a high-powered team and they produced a brand of homely, reassuring humour which had been so popular during the war. Lines like 'You want to start on milk stout with a teat on the end of a bottle' or 'What's love? It's a very funny feeling that goes right through you and buttons up at the back' and 'Nothing like whisky to make you feel frisky' were designed to appeal to a young and unsophisticated audience. The social historian of popular culture and film expert Jeffrey Richards sees 'symbolic significance' in *Civvy Street*. As George, the owner of the Unicorn pub, marries the landlady of the rival Lion, so 'the two sides of the British national persona – character and imagination' were also united. Richards has written, 'So George bowed out of films unifying the nation mythically, communally and matrimonially.'

Beryl was in negotiations with British Lion Studios at the time but no contract emerged. Nothing came of the film script *Talkie Mad*, which they'd bought, perhaps with a view to using it post-Columbia. George himself may not have been very enthusiastic about prolonging his film career as he always preferred playing to a live audience. He liked the immediate feedback as to how his act was going down. It is easy with hindsight to see his last film as marking the beginning of a slippery slope for George's career as a whole, but that can't have been obvious at the time. Indeed, on 24 June George received the letter awarding him his OBE for his 'contribution as comedian for services to the Forces'.

What was clear, though, was that this *was* a turning point. What next for George? He could have retired. From a purely financial point of view work was not very rewarding. The return of a Labour government in 1946 was a financial disaster for him, paying as he did surtax, or supertax, of 19s. 6d. in the pound. For the tax year 1946/7 this amounted to £12,000. In almost every interview of the post-war period he complained about the Chancellor of the Exchequer, Stafford Cripps. In 1949 he asked 'why should I work for tanners?' – a fair question. It was said that Beryl negotiated with theatre managers to give him carpets and household items instead of a fee. He had received notice from the Revenue that he owed nearly £9,000 for 1947/8 – but Beryl hadn't paid, as she was claiming nearly a third of it in tax relief. In 1952 George estimated that he had given the taxman nearly £300,000 during the war years, although he had spent most of the time on the ENSA wage of £10 a week. But he was also making two films a year and appearing in pantomime, and these were big earners. BBC broadcasts and commercial radio also contributed, as of course did record sales. All in all his income at that time had amounted to over £84,000 (£258,000) a year.

The Sullom End experiment had showed him very clearly that he was not ready to retire. March 1946 found him back in a studio with the pianist and bandleader Harry Bidgood conducting. He recorded 'You Don't Need a Licence for That', 'The Mad March Hare', 'We've Been a Long Time Gone' and 'It Could Be'. His contract with Regal-Zonophone had come to an end in 1945 and the songs were recorded on the Columbia label. George was often backed by high-quality orchestras and excellent musicians. A case in point is 'You Don't Need a Licence for That', one of the high points of *Civvy Street*. He was accompanied by the Johnny Gray Orchestra with Ronnie Scott on the saxophone, himself producing a superb ukulele solo. But shortly afterwards he found himself in trouble with the BBC on account of another of his 'daft little songs'. 'With My Little Stick of Blackpool Rock', recorded in 1937, was belatedly causing offence. A manager wrote to the producer of George's proposed live show, 'We have no record that "With

My Little Stick of Blackpool Rock" is banned. We do however know and so does Formby, that certain lines in the lyric must not be broadcast.' Another manager commented, 'There is a long and tangled history of the BBC's standards and Formby's reluctance to accept them… all artists are very selfish as I well know, but George Formby is a thoroughly intractable kind of person.' An irritable memo later that year commented, 'When we were discussing George Formby in Head Office at the end of last month, you said that you had given instructions that he was never again to be permitted to broadcast from the North Region. You can imagine therefore that I was rather surprised when I saw his name prominently billed in the *Radio Times* for the following week and I heard part of this performance from Blackpool, which was evidently a great success… What however was more surprising still was the fact that one of the items was our old friend, "With My Little Stick of Blackpool Rock", over which there has been so much trouble when I permitted him to sing it in Belfast during the war and which was subsequently barred.' Obviously you can't keep an intractable person down.

When George's youngest brother Ted was demobbed he got a job with Odeon Theatres as a cinema manager. He was very short of suitable clothes after nearly seven years in the army, and he'd just got married. He phoned Beryl to ask her if she had any ideas about what he could do and she invited him to Beryldene. As they went upstairs George asked what was going on. 'Nothing to do with you,' said Beryl, 'I'm going to give him some of your clothes.'

'Well, you'll have to be careful what you give him, because I might want to wear it,' was George's not unreasonable response. But that didn't deter Beryl. She took Ted to George's huge wardrobe and began to take out items she thought he might like. A blazer and slacks, sweaters and shirts all came his way. He was concerned that George wouldn't be pleased.

'He won't even notice,' said Beryl. Perhaps not…

Another of George's responses to the question of what he should do next was to travel. A restless soul, he had much enjoyed his wartime adventures and felt he could still do good for a Britain suffering from rationing. His first postwar shows abroad were in Stockholm and Copenhagen in May 1946, which were tremendous successes. But he also wanted to tour the Commonwealth, starting with South Africa, and to return to his roots on the live stage.

George opened the Gem Club in 1947 when Ted was working for Odeon cinemas
From left to right: Ted, Frank, Eliza and Win Formby

The Star claimed that the couple had been trying to get to South Africa for twenty-three years. Only George's courtship of Beryl stood in his way in the early days. Another interview referred to an invitation in 1931 but Beryl had decided that 'a straight course in home waters' till he was established was the best policy. He dared not risk a long absence from the British stage. George had finally been booked to come to the Union in 1939 but war stopped him. The Formbys explained that after a traumatic time getting out of Burma, during which they had come to within 100 miles of the Chinese border and contracted malaria, George had taken to his bed with exhaustion and Beryl was 'pretty done up' too. Earlier in 1946 they couldn't get a flight because of a contingent of brides rushing to meet their waiting grooms, so, they said, they went to Scandinavia instead. They could stay for only five weeks because, although George had no contract, 'Tom [Arnold] and I have had an understanding for years that I appear in his Christmas pantos, and I wouldn't dream of letting him down'.

George finished at the Opera House, Blackpool, on 12 October 1946, and a few days later the *Cape Mercury* previewed his visit, referring to him

George being silly in Stockholm

as the 'darling of the lowbrows'. 'We are', said the reviewer, 'in many ways an extremely green and innocent kind of a theatre-going public, with a "don't-shoot-the-pianist-he's-doing-his-best" attitude towards performers.' But George didn't need that sort of kindly patronage. The defensive tone was perhaps because his tour was seen in South Africa as being in the nature of a costly experiment, as he was to receive the highest fee paid to any artist visiting the country and the cost of air travel added to the expense. His performances were to be worked into cinema programmes, with some tickets dearer than usual, but some, particularly the afternoon ones, held at normal levels to enable children to go to see their idol.

A carefully lit and heavily retouched photo showing Beryl dressed and made up as a glamorous movie star advertised her arrival in the South African magazine *Spotlight*. She looked nearer twenty-five than forty-five. The headline was 'Best-dressed actress to visit us'. After the austerity of war the luxury of feathers and velvet and the name of Norman Hartnell,

202

couturier to the queen, Vivien Leigh and Marlene Dietrich as well as to Beryl, lent alluring sophistication. More advance publicity appeared in the local newspaper *Onsland*, Port Elizabeth, on 18 October, translated from Afrikaans. 'Formby's charm lies in his natural simplicity for no one would really admire his singing capabilities.' But 'the manner in which he renders his songs... with a liveliness and enthusiasm all his own – literally compels one to listen'. The reporter expressed his hope that the Mother City would not be treated in a 'step-motherly' manner.

The two aspects of George's life aired over and over again in newspaper reports were his remarkable career during the war and his popularity with the Royal Family. 'George always sings ten songs... always "Our Sergeant Major" for Princess Margaret and "In the Air" for Princess Elizabeth.' He carried with him the photo showing, from left to right, himself, Queen Mary and Beryl. (Coincidentally, George and Queen Mary shared a birthday, 26 May.) The South African public was also hungry for titbits about the private George Formby. His right forefinger nail, it was said, was worn away by playing the ukulele. He was reported to be crazy about cars, fond of horseracing and liked riding to hounds whenever he got the chance.

George and Beryl flew from England on 19 October into Johannesburg. The tour was originally to be five weeks at £1,000 a week, (£30,700) far outdistancing the Prime Minister's pay. But after the Revenue and the Union took their share Beryl estimated that they would have a total of £250 to bank. George was well used to the taxman's cut, of course, but never tired of complaining about it. With George and Beryl were Harry Scott and five ukuleles (one a spare). They flew in a Douglas DC4 Skymaster to Palmietfontein airport and George opened at the Colosseum on Monday, 21 October. He was scheduled to appear for a fortnight and the house was sold out for every performance, his welcome being compared with that of Harry Lauder and Will Fyffe many years before. George was unable to start his first song for several minutes because of the cheers and applause. A significant number in the audience were ex-servicemen who had heard him in the Middle East, and his repertoire was adjusted accordingly. 'Out in the Middle East' and 'Our Sergeant Major' were loudly requested and sung. The programme also comprised songs from his films interspersed with stories, the South African press noting approvingly that George was generous with encores. Ian Cunningham, a South African by birth, was feted in the press as he had written 'Up in the Air and Down in the Dumps', which featured in the programme, and had composed the lyrics of 'Unconditional Surrender', performed in *He Snoops to Conquer*. *The Star* described George, approvingly, as 'exactly the same, on and off the stage'. The audience liked being referred to as 'boys and girls'. But the high point of the evening was the singing of 'Sarie Marais' in Afrikaans which was 'received with tremendous applause and gales of mirth' at his 'Afrikaanshire' accent.

The South African press struggled to analyse George's appeal and come to terms with his brand of humour. *The Star* commented on the 'primitive ambiguity' of the songs, presumably a reference to the *double entendres*, but the *Daily News* of Durban spoke of his 'genuine bonhomie… [He hypnotises] them [the audience] with the regular twang of his ukulele and completes the conquest with a peculiarly tuneful voice'. *The Forum* of Johannesburg felt that George's films 'bring out the mother-instinct in people, while others say they merely arouse homicidal urges'. *Eendrag* described George as differing 'vastly from the George who appears on the screen', having 'lovely black hair, a nice set of teeth and through and through a very efficient person'. His voice, however, sounded very much the same as expected. 'George Formby is not one for art and culture – he is a comedian and an entirely successful one. From the moment he appears on the stage he has the theatre-goers in his grip.' George was genial to the last – 'If you can stand 'em I'll sing 'em,' he assured his audiences. The more strait-laced aspect of South African opinion got Beryl wrong, though. 'His wife, Beryl, was also introduced to the public – after George had told all his jokes, to some of which she may have objected.'

Beryl gave numerous interviews, often recounting her routine. Between the hours of nine and twelve each day she answered fan mail and sent off autographed photos. As she proudly pointed out, she was business manager, secretary and songwriter. She estimated that she dealt with over a hundred letters a day. On a more personal note she revealed to her more than receptive audience that at that time they owned six cars and that they had owned 170 during their marriage. She also boasted that for six years George topped the *Motion Picture Herald* poll of high-earning British stars – a record. Their personal connection with Montgomery always aroused interest, and she spoke of his not wanting her to go with George to the front line in Normandy. She explained her insistence on accompanying him, revealing how much she depended on her husband, and how much her life was bound up in his. 'We've got no children. If anything was going to happen to one of us it would be better if the other was in on it too. I know wives will understand how I felt about it.' They had, she said, their own caravan, but ate with the boys, emphasising their specialness and yet their capacity for 'down-to-earth mucking-in' in the same breath.

The Formbys were besieged by invitations and alive to the need for diplomacy. At a cocktail party in his honour, George drank a 'funeral tea' – with a drop of Scotch in it. He marvelled more than once at the availability of fruit and meat, on one occasion remarking that the only country not to be liberated was Britain. The day he arrived in South Africa, he said, he had his first steak for five years. Beryl was reportedly delighted to buy nylon stockings for 9s. 5d. compared with the £4 outlay she had had to make at home. George wanted to let his hosts know that he had missed some special occasions to be with them – another command performance, for instance. He was also unable to be at the Alamein reunion in the Albert Hall to which he had been invited by Montgomery to help build up the atmosphere. But, as George remarked, there were two superb showmen in Churchill and Monty already present.

Off stage Beryl and George were in constant demand for a variety of visits, photo opportunities and leisure activities, along, of course, with their considerable charitable work. *The Spotlight* published an article about a boy who had become deaf because of meningitis but could hear George's music. He met Formby at the Colosseum in the dressing room, much to the boy's delight. George played some songs for him. Beryl explained that this had happened before – 'George had a very high and penetrating voice and the pitch of the ukulele was also exceptionally high.' George was made Mayor for a day in Johannesburg, and Beryl made history by being the only woman to go down a gold mine wearing bedroom slippers. She was warned that she would ruin her shoes and was offered a pair of miner's boots. One look at them – 'I knew they were likely to cripple me!' – and she dived into her bag for some soft shoes. George was invited to go tunny fishing off Cape Point, but turned this down flat. 'That's one thing I can't take – I get as sick as a dog.' The couple even visited Mrs Smuts, the wife of the South African Prime Minister and a friend of Lord Derby, George autographing a ukulele for one of her grandchildren.

Cliff Green, a pilot who had served in the Far East, was in Baragwanath Military Hospital, Johannesburg, suffering from tuberculosis. He remembered over forty years later the occasion when George arrived to perform for the men who were ill.

In the hospital complex there was a large YMCA Hall with stage, and from time to time there was entertainment for patients allowed out of bed. We had films or stage entertainment by amateurs, hospital staff and occasionally professionals who were appearing in Johannesburg... George Formby... took time out to entertain the patients in Baragwanath. Beryl came with him (complete with hat!). He joked and played to a packed audience for hours and nobody who was there could fail to have lasting admiration for this man who gave such pleasure to men who were ill and had not seen England and home for many years. After the performance he visited the men in the wards who were too ill to leave their beds. That day he gave so much of his energy and talent that he became ill and was unable to perform at the theatre for a few nights afterwards... I count myself lucky to have had the wonderful experience of being there.

On the 30 and 31 October George certainly *was* ill, with gastric flu, and for the first time in twenty-three years (he claimed) he had to cancel a performance because of illness. Belittling his indisposition afterwards, he claimed that his 'apricot sickness' was traceable to theatrical superstition. Deanna Durbin sang Tosti's 'Goodbye' in the film *Because of Him* which was shown before George's performance, and the story was that when it was played something bad would happen to someone on the same programme. Another superstition, told by Beryl, was that no one should whistle in a dressing room. If a chorus girl should do so she would be sent into the

Baragwanath Military Hospital, South Africa, 1946

corridor regardless of her state of dress and there must turn round three times or the girl nearest the door would be sacked by the end of the week. However, there was more to George's illness than superstitions…

The Formbys' visit to Johannesburg was extended to three weeks, as, in George's words, the audiences were 'unbelievably appreciative'. From there they flew to Cape Town where George was to play the Alhambra Theatre from Monday, 11 November. Through the city they travelled in a Lindbergh Shower of paper and streamers. In Adderley-street 15,000 people 'went hysterical'. George himself described the scene, though his words seem rather stilted: 'The newspapers said it was the biggest reception Cape Town had known. The next day the post office was busy reissuing new telephone books for those torn up by the paper-throwing crowds, and the civic authorities were hard at it repairing the lamp-posts damaged by enthusiastic youngsters who had used them as grandstands.' The open car was filled with paper, not showered, but filled, to the extent that George and Beryl almost disappeared from sight as if in an avalanche. By the time the car reached Darling-street, having covered only half the journey, it was so full of rubbish that only the driver's head was visible. The Formbys continually had to battle to give themselves enough room to return the welcome by waving their hands. The couple was mobbed by the 'unruly' crowd both there and when they finally got out of the car. It took the efforts of six policemen to get them into the building and a long time to get them out again to go to City Hall to meet the Mayor. Members of the crowd fared less well – shoppers were trampled underfoot and their cars damaged by fans climbing on them to get a view of the visitors. After all that George was asked to speak from a balcony, which he did. The city council sent African Consolidated Theatres Ltd a bill for £12 for clearing the streets. It was a bargain, given that it took twenty-three sweepers four hours to clear the debris.

George gave two shows daily and three on Saturday. The top-price tickets were ten shillings while the cheapest seats were at a matinee for 2s. 1d. If a fan wanted to buy a Regal record, that would cost 2s. 11d. The format was of a Personality Show Plus – at the Alhambra George had a forty-five-minute slot during which he performed nine songs. He started with 'In My Little Snapshot Album' and between songs told his chatty/ wisecracking parrot stories. The audience liked his old songs such as 'With My Little Ukulele in My Hand' and 'When I'm Cleaning Windows' and called for Beryl to appear. Unusually, the reporter of the *Cape Argus* referred to her as 'a dear' and thought she had almost as much stage personality as George! In one report 'When I'm Cleaning Windows' was said to be written by Beryl, and in another George claimed it himself, though it is normally attributed to Formby, Gifford and Cliffe. Elsewhere George continued to fan the smokescreen by saying that he had 'forgotten' how he came to write the song – or 'Chinese Laundry Blues' either!

Once again George announced a change to the programme. He was going to sing something 'in a very strong Lancashire accent' – 'Sarie Marais'. His Afrikaans was described as 'recognisable', getting a big laugh and tremendous applause. 'Ee, I bet you've never heard Afrikaans sung like that before,' was his only comment. The audience loved him, his essay into local culture winning him 'his passport to the freedom of South Africa'. But all was not so easy. He later recalled the one occasion on the tour when he had been truly scared. 'We had a request from a group of coloured Africans to play at a theatre in the non-white quarter of Cape Town. I thought nothing of it. My agent had told me Formby pictures were popular with the Africans. So I immediately offered to give a free show. But unknown to me that offer made history. Next afternoon the hotel porter phoned my room. "Your car is waiting, sir," he said. So Beryl put on her best sable and I blossomed out in a dinner jacket. Outside we found that the car was a Black Maria!' Judging by a contemporary photograph his memory was not quite accurate. George is shown getting out of a vehicle described as a 'police pick up van' wearing his trilby, an overcoat and light-coloured trousers.

He was giving his performance at a 'coloured' cinema in District Six, Cape Town, in an area where black gangs fought each other, it was said, with razors and bicycle chains. Two armed policemen shared the van with George and Beryl while fifteen motorcycle outriders, also armed, roared alongside them as the 'crowds threatened to sweep Formby off his feet'. His audience gave him 'a terrific reception', clapping their hands, singing along with him, stamping their feet and shouting, 'Dis 'n goele ou, daai.' (He's a good fellow.) Beryl was greeted warmly when she appeared on stage and, George recounted, 'Just before the final curtain a sweet little African girl came on stage with a bouquet [newspaper reports said a box of chocolates] for Beryl. A great silence came over the audience – I couldn't think why. And it was at that moment that Beryl leaned down and kissed the little girl on the cheeks. The audience gasped – a white woman kissing a coloured girl! Perhaps you can't understand why a gesture like that should cause a sensation and nor can I. It startled a few Blimps in Cape Town, but we didn't care. Neither did the audience. They stood on their feet after a moment's astonished hush, and literally howled with applause.' George and Beryl showed very clearly what they thought of apartheid. The following day they visited the Princess Alice Home for Crippled Children, where they were photographed with two black children, Beryl with her arm around the girl.

Between 18 and 23 November the Formbys were in Pretoria, at the Capitol. There were queues from 7.30 a.m. till the box office opened at 8.45 a.m. The management allowed people to stand in the foyer so that they could keep out of the sun. For the *Pretoria News* Beryl described their regimen: 'We never go out after an evening show – we believe in going straight home to bed.

209

Beryl with an African child

We'll do anything for people during the day, but it's no use their asking us to parties and entertainments after the evening show. We simply can't do it, though it's nice of them to ask us. We consider it our duty to the public to start each day fit and fresh. Would you believe it, but neither George nor I have ever been to a nightclub in our lives.' She claimed that both of them were practically teetotal. 'George usually finishes the party with the same drink in his hand that he had when he started.' They liked a very little wine before dinner and a tot of whisky in milk before retiring – their experience in war having taught them that this is the best way of 'dropping off'. George, she said, occasionally played some light tennis and golf. 'We used to ride a lot before the war but we dropped it when war broke out. It seemed to us ostentatious and out of place to be out riding while the boys were away fighting.' George spoke of their future plans – nine weeks of panto after South Africa then a holiday in Switzerland, their first for seven years. An article in the *Pretoria News* referring to George and Beryl seeing 'some of the native life' outside Pretoria where the reporter got 'pictures of George entertaining some piccanins' shows how much attitudes have changed in the last sixty years.

On Sunday, 24 November George and Beryl arrived in Durban. Beryl, once again recalling her war memories, spoke of a sandstorm at El Adem where their 'only dwelling was a room in which a shell had passed clean through two opposite sides' and where she was amazed to find a refrigerator. She was told it was 'the only one in captivity', and she set to with the help of the troops to make ice cream. Despite some enthusiastic billing, 'The most eagerly awaited thrill of the year!', there were clearly some worries about the first matinee on the Monday afternoon. To bring the punters in, free souvenir autographed photographs were offered to all patrons of that show. The following day, 'One of the most enthusiastic ovations ever to greet a visiting artist was given to George Formby when he made his first appearance on a Durban stage.' He gave a twenty-minute act with five encores. The secret of his great success in South Africa was deemed to be that 'he draws his audience into the fun and makes them feel a part of the show'.

In his free time, George, a keen photographer, tried to get some shots of monkeys but failed. He and Beryl went to a war dance in the Valley of a Thousand Hills where they were presented with a shield and an assegai, a photograph of the ceremony occupying the top half of the front page of the local newspaper. George told a reporter that what had impressed him most about South Africa was the climate – the guarantee of sunshine almost every day. He also liked Durban's low position, at only twenty-six feet above sea level, commenting that he couldn't cope with the altitude of the Rand, the ridge on which Johannesburg is built. At over 6,000 feet it has significantly thinner air. He had told *The Star* reporter that, 'It's far warmer here than back home; I'm fair puffed!' He confided that he would love to come back when his contracts had been fulfilled in England to spend six weeks incognito in the Kruger National Park. Beryl's comment that they had been 'smothered' in kindness and hospitality was revealing. The couple, both still only in their forties, were nonetheless feeling the pace. And it was straight home to the rigours of the pantomime season...

CHAPTER FIFTEEN

The Call of Norfolk

The daylight fades, swift scudding cloud
Swathing the waters as a shroud –
Sweeping far o'er the Broadland high
Rings many a mournful eerie cry.

Across the sky-line's bar of grey
Pass flighting wildfowl on their way,
To plunder, where deep dikes are free,
With provender and sanctuary.

Downward on graceful speeding wing,
Grey geese in level skein outswing
To distant space; and the echoes die
Away in a doleful lullaby.

Tense silence falls! Naught but the hoot
Of a lonely owl or straying coot
Seeking its mate 'neath the sedges hide
Abounding the osier beds divide.

A blinding sleet and a grip that stings;
Again the flap of myriad wings –
Weathering the storm inland to seek
Shelter of some neighbouring creek.

Black night! The blizzard in fury rolls
O'er Broadland deeps, shallows and pools.
No sound astir – save guns of war,
Grim sentinels of the North Sea shore.

Towards the end of the war, two friends from Norfolk had given the Formbys a book entitled *Broadland and other Verses* by Clarissa Alcock. Over the years some of these poems had been printed in the *Shooting Times,* the *Eastern Daily Press,* the *Girl Guide Gazette* and *The Landswoman.* Inside the front cover they wrote: 'To George and Beryl "A taste of the Broads".' The poem above, 'Broadland', evoked the Norfolk landscape of the 1940s. Whether or not this sowed the seed that germinated into the love the Formbys had for the Broads is impossible to say, but in early 1947 George and Beryl came to Norfolk in that notoriously hard winter, looking for a property and for a boat of their own, after finishing the pantomime season. A craving for quiet, fresh air and anonymity took them there more and more often. Their love affair with the county, and the Broads in particular, had started in the mid-1930s. 'These few hundred square miles of enchanted country' (C. A. Hannaford) with 'delectable' air became for them a home from home. They had at first rented a boat which moved from Oulton Broad to Wroxham and all stops in-between. Her name was *Doris.* They were in good company – Edward and Mrs Simpson also hired *Doris* to 'get away from it all'. (Local schoolchildren were aware that they were around, and at Christmas 1936 were singing 'Hark the Herald Angels sing, Mrs Simpson's pinched our King'!)

The Formbys had been renting boats for their holidays for the previous few years, but by this time George's fame was proving a nuisance. He was recognized everywhere he went and his regular mooring was very prominent. Worse was that the skippers of the water buses would pick him out to their passengers and they would shout greetings to him. However friendly the intentions, this invasion of his privacy sent him rapidly off deck to his refuge inside the boat. It was rumoured that he wrote to a local tour operator threatening him with legal action if this practice was not stopped. This was probably why he wanted a property with a more private mooring. Another

Top: *Doris*
Above: *The last word in 1930s luxury*
With kind permission of Jamie Campbell, O.G.

consideration was that Beryl was not well and had to be admitted to hospital for tests and observation for two weeks. George wanted somewhere for her to recuperate in quiet and fresh air. But for the moment they couldn't find what they were looking for.

By the end of February George was back in variety (still described as music hall) for a two-week stint at the London Palladium. The following day *The Times* reviewer wrote:

Herbert Woods' boatyard, Potter Heigham, Norfolk
With kind permission of Margaret Bird

At the top of this not very exciting bill is Mr George Formby, more than ever the mechanised perfection of naïve jollity. His smile, though fixed, is winning, and his songs, though four out of five of them follow the same rhythm, are catchy. Even if voice and ukulele appear to have been wound up, and a sudden aside to the audience has almost the effect of a technical hitch, there is no gainsaying that the human gramophone puts itself across and creates a very jolly impression.

Perhaps he had been at this game too long; the excitement and challenge dulled. Certainly the names of his fellow entertainers have not stood the test of time. More likely this was a typically cool review from a London paper. George signed a lucrative contract for *Starry Way*, a season in revue at Blackpool's New Opera House, but it was not long before he and Beryl set out on their travels again – this time to New Zealand and Australia.

215

They went to New York and across America by train to Los Angeles and Hollywood on the way to New Zealand. From Vancouver they flew to Hawaii and Fiji then on to Auckland, New Zealand, for two weeks at the Queen's Theatre. There was a family link in that George's sister Ethel was married to a New Zealander, Johnny Gibson, a wartime air ace, and was on her way there to introduce their baby son to his Gibson grandparents. But much more important for George was the opportunity to meet some old acquaintances again. Having entertained the New Zealand troops in Mahdi in 1943, he said they had to go there to meet everyone else. By performing to some of his wartime audiences in a peacetime setting, George was able to recapture the elation he had felt when singing to the troops. One of the many such people George and Beryl met was a former Lieutenant-Commander in the navy who had arrived at Akyab in early 1945.

> George Formby had been entertaining the troops in that dirty, hot, dreary little Burman town, and as soon as I heard I went ashore to see if I could get him to do something for our chaps, who had been having a boring, monotonous time. George and Beryl were both worn out with the long air trips they had been making, with the heat and the humidity – they had been on the go all day. But they came out to the ship without a word of protest, gave a rousing show and proved a real tonic to the men.

As in South Africa, Beryl gave a series of interviews. She described George's hobbies as horse racing, motorcycle racing and cruising. On the subject of clothes she was patriotic. 'England holds the sway for fashions,' she asserted, and hats, mainly trimmed with feathers, a trend popularised by the queen, were also smarter there. George later cracked that the feathers in her hats came from the Oozlum bird, many of which could be found at Stretton (near Warrington). Beryl asked him, 'What's an Oozlum bird, George?' He replied, 'They bury their heads in the sand and whistle through the whole of the afternoon.'

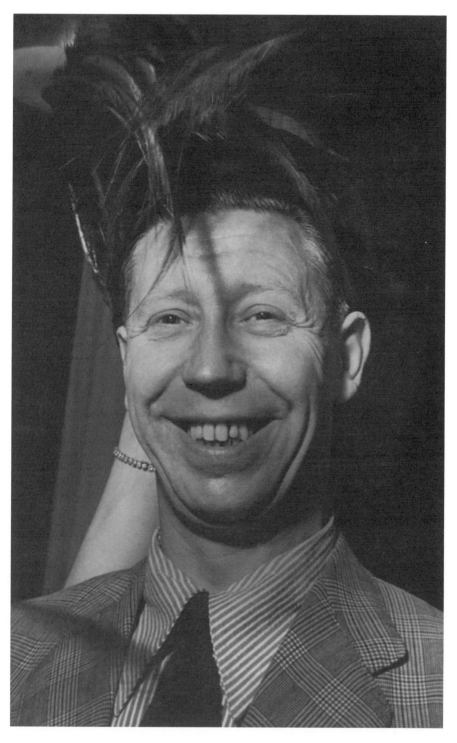

George with Beryl's hat of Oozlum bird feathers

Britain was, said Beryl, short of lard and tinned meat, as well, of course, as chocolates and sweets for children. She and George, she said, arrived at the theatre for 'twice nightly' performances at 6 p.m. and left at 11 p.m. This arrangement was foreign to New Zealanders. She explained that George was working on his own because they did not know her there. George would usually sing ten songs then a further six. Then he took a meal or tea. It was reported that he received eighty or ninety letters a day, and, George added, 'nearly all from children. Around ten years old is just the age for a Formby fan'. The *Auckland Star* reported George trying to do his bit for the Food For Britain fund. Nine hundred children made George's speech something of an uphill struggle. 'Well, girls and boys...' (roars of laughter). 'I'm not supposed to be funny...' (more laughter). 'What I would like to say...' (screams of laughter). 'I must look as daft as I do on the screen...' (prolonged laughter). After two weeks they moved on for a projected five-week season in Sydney which in fact stretched to eleven weeks.

Their arrival in Sydney was marked by a crowd of about three hundred, including a large number of excited children. Standing in an Austin with a slide-back roof which was loaned to him for his entire visit and escorted by six police motorcyclists George was driven to the city, receiving 'a terrific greeting' as he went. Once there he was protected from overenthusiastic fans by Bill Willis, a seventeen-stone Bondi Beach inspector. His first performance was to 1,500 patients at the Yaralla Repatriation Hospital, Concord. On stage for nearly an hour, a performance extended because of the big demand for encores, he reprised many favourite songs, introduced Beryl and then went round the theatre to shake hands with patients in beds and wheelchairs. Percy Crawford, the Tivoli Theatre's director of publicity, remarked, predictably, that George was doing bigger business in Sydney than had ever before been experienced and was a 'sensational success'. It was just as well: George was receiving the biggest salary ever paid up to that time to an entertainer in Australia.

The couple then departed for six weeks in Melbourne, arriving to a tumultuous reception on 18 December 1947. While George had been 'knocked off his perch' in Britain, in the Commonwealth countries he was still extremely popular. Here, the traffic was held up while the 3,000-strong

Top Left: *George receiving his North Bondi Surf Club badge from Bill Willis, Bondi Beach lifesaver*

Top Right: *Kerwin Maegraith's caricature given to George by the artist on leaving Australia*

Bottom: *George taking part in the Sydney Sports Ground Carnival to raise funds for the Boys' Town*

crowd mobbed the car, George at one point being carried shoulder high. Only four 'perplexed' policemen had been assigned to look after George and Beryl, and they weren't equal to the task. It was reported the following day that it took George half an hour to get upstairs in the Tivoli Theatre. Despite describing the crush as 'oppressive' and George being marooned on a buffet counter while Beryl cowered behind it, the reporter was happy to repeat George's somewhat desperate assertion that 'he liked it'. Bathed in perspiration by the time he reached the upstairs office and with Beryl visibly shaken, he had received 'a violent jab in the midriff' from a minder who was trying to clear a course for him through the crowd. His insistence that 'the day that people don't want to see me and say "Hullo George," is the day I want to put off as long as I can' didn't seem quite to cover it. But he was able to summon up a humorous comment – 'What they'd have done to me if they didn't like me!' Reports the following day admitted that his ribs had been bruised and that he and Beryl had needed to recuperate with a strong cup of tea. Even then the boisterous reception wasn't over. A group declaring themselves to

George arriving in Melbourne

be the George Formby Fan Club of Victoria burst into the office where he and Beryl had taken refuge. The fact that neither of them was aware of such a club's existence made it the more laudable that they allowed themselves to be photographed for the members.

In Melbourne he met an old friend, Jenny Howard, who had appeared with him as long ago as 1926 in *Formby Seeing Life*. She was starring in the pantomime *Babes in the Wood* which was running at the Tivoli during the daytime slots while George was appearing twice nightly in *It's Turned Out Nice Again* at 5.50 and 8.30 p.m. At the lunchtime reception held for them at the Town Hall on 19 December George replied to the Mayor's speech of welcome with 'pleasant anecdotal and somewhat hesitant thanks'. George said that he felt all right on the stage but always 'made a muck' of speeches. The Minister for Housing raised a laugh when he suggested that the Formbys might stay in Australia as immigrants, but it was nothing to the laugh when Beryl, quick as a flash, asked if he could get them a house. The press were impressed that Beryl also quickly repaired George's failure to mention his support for the Lord Mayor's camp for country children at Portsea. *The Sun* report described her as 'an alert and charming woman and bright as a button. She made a bigger hit with the Lord Mayor's guests than George'.

Helen Seager interviewed the 'sparkling pair', George telling her about his sinus trouble. She reported that for every waking moment for the last twenty years he had had a buzzing in his left ear that gave him 'fits' and that had led to his having sixty-six injections since his arrival in Australia. It was the dry Melbourne weather that he looked forward to as in New Zealand Beryl had had to buy a raincoat, and the wet weather in Sydney – only four fine days in eleven weeks – had 'played havoc with him'. He told one audience that he had had a very fine view of Sydney from his umbrella. Hence his first question on arrival – 'Hey, where's all your rain?' It was soon to appear. As for Beryl, her sharp wit once again found an admirer. Introduced to the Taxation Commissioner she pointed out, 'He's the man who'll see me last in Victoria. I can't get out without his OK.' When he graciously mentioned 'refunds', she called for witnesses.

On 22 December George opened at the Tivoli, kicking off with a specially written Fred Godfrey number, 'The Other Side of the World'.

George casting an appreciative eye over a racehorse, Sydney, Australia

'Smash Hit', 'Triumph' and 'Ovation' were all headlines the following morning. He dedicated 'Out in the Middle East' to a soldier killed near Tobruk and then, after several more numbers, asked the audience what they wanted to hear. 'Cleaning Windows', 'Mr Wu' and 'Bless 'Em All' were top of the pops as George promised to sing them all 'but one at a time' and 'led the audience in community singing and community whistling in a way that few artists would attempt'. One paper called it a near riot; another described the 'thunderous applause'. Beryl, ever vigilant and critical, was seen creeping to the back of the dress circle to watch him shortly before George came on.

More than a hundred migrant children en route to Sydney on board the liner *Largs Bay* berthed at South Wharf were the next recipients of George's charity work. On Christmas Day they were given, along with the adults, a festive dinner with fruit and ice cream. Balloons, streamers and a real Christmas tree entranced those who were too young to remember pre-war celebrations. Santa Claus arrived with presents, George following him up the gangway. He sang, played the ukulele, cracked jokes and signed autographs on a variety of available surfaces.

As ever, the critics felt that they had to try to analyse the secret of the Formby success. One commented that, 'One of the greatest charms of this notable comedian is that he enjoys his jokes with the audience.' Another wrote, 'his grin is the passport which takes the audience on tour'. 'They liked his stories – just a bit spicy, but saved from being vulgar by guffaws of laughter from Formby himself, as the audience caught on. Formby has the gift of making others happy.' 'He is one of the living naturals of the music hall… This seemingly artless familiarity with the audience is a quality laboured for by most public entertainers and achieved by very few… That place of honour (the top of the bill) is reserved for the Formbys, who can just walk on the stage, grin across the footlights, sing ordinary songs in ordinary voices and make everybody feel that they haven't a care in the world.' George himself confirmed that live theatre was his first love and film work a strain. 'In the film you don't know whether your stuff is going over, or otherwise.' Rapport with the audience was still his lifeblood.

Meanwhile, 'England's Ambassador of Mirth' was heard on Australia's *Shell Show* on Wednesday evenings throughout January. He was thought to be very successful, his performances contrasting favourably with the previous year's offering from Tommy Trinder and the lacklustre Gracie Fields show. His wartime experiences were, as they'd been in South Africa, a major part of his appeal and the 'last civilian out of Dunkirk and first in Normandy with Montgomery's forces' story was repeated again and again, as were his royal command performances at Windsor Castle. Arthur Askey maintained that the Australians laughed at Beryl's airs and graces. Certainly she laid it on pretty thickly when describing their relationship with the king and queen. As they were leaving Windsor Castle on one occasion Beryl tripped, and the queen steadied her. Apparently Beryl said, 'They say in the theatre that if you trip over the mat you're asked back.'

'Well,' replied the queen, 'you know where we live.'

Beryl again decided that she must be an ambassador for British couturiers and turned up at a Boxing Day race meeting in sables and diamonds. George's expense account for the year from April 1947 to April 1948 confirms that Beryl wasn't herself experiencing the austerity she talked about in her radio interviews. One item was a fox fur coat for which she paid £499. (£14,500) Australians were, apparently, impressed by her peaches and cream complexion, her graceful dancer's carriage, her sense of humour and her business sense. They perceived George as 'the typical comedian offstage... quiet, retiring, almost aesthetic, definitely shy'. In Ballarat on New Year's Day he opened the Motor Cycle Grand Prix in Victoria Park and acted as starter for the first race, an event which attracted a huge crowd. Responding to the Mayor's welcome he gave three reasons for coming to Ballarat: he liked to have a day out; he wanted to help the Food for Britain Appeal; and he loved motorbikes. He raised £100 through giving autographs alone. As he rode a motorcycle slowly round, boy scouts followed him carrying blankets into which money could be thrown. The race meeting, based on the one at Northolt, raised £31,000. (£900,000)

George appeared at the Geelong Theatre with Jenny Howard on 18 January to raise money for the George Formby Geelong Food for Britain Appeal, explaining that small families with few ration books were often the most vulnerable. The money – at a minimum of a guinea a ticket – went to people

Ballarat Motor Cycle Grand Prix

in Manchester, Newcastle and Glasgow in 700 food parcels. He explained how much families in Britain appreciated the parcels, adding that he was looking forward to opening the ones he had sent himself when he got home.

A week later nearly 3,000 people crowded into Melbourne Town Hall to hear *George in Concert for the Mayor's Holiday Camp Fund* for charity. Donations of between ten shillings and £5 secured invitations. George himself gave £50 for fifty invitations 'so that there'll be at least fifty in the audience'. All were given to ex-servicemen in hospitals. The occasion raised a record £3,025, exceeding – just – the total raised the previous year when Tommy Trinder had starred. The Formbys had to leave Melbourne on 31 January, officially because they had been away for six months, but privately Beryl had received news that her mother was seriously ill. Widowed a couple of years before, she had kept house for George and Beryl for years and lived

225

with them at their home in Mere, in a thirteenth-century house previously known as The Spinney. Harry Scott, George's pianist, and the two dogs, a Manchester terrier and a golden retriever, completed the household. Beryl had hoped, she said in an interview, to spend Christmas with her, 'but you Australians wouldn't let George go'. Three weeks after their return she died.

After the winter of 1946–7 George and Beryl had started making regular trips to Norfolk. Most of July 1948 was spent on the Norfolk Broads, on a six-berth 44-foot boat named *Priscilla* while awaiting delivery of the boat they had just bought, which was to be renamed *Lady Beryl*. George told a newspaper reporter in Australia that the dinghy would be *Baby Beryl* and the speedboat *Crazy Beryl*, explaining, 'We like to keep it in the family.' The speedboat seems never to have materialised. The boat he had settled on after a long search was a large motor cruiser, for sale at Herbert Woods' boatyard at Potter Heigham. Surveyed by the Board of Trade in July 1940 (perhaps to assess its possible usefulness for war purposes), it was called *Moudou*. The ownership was transferred on 30 August 1948, and the change of name registered on 9 September, Beryl's birthday. George loved the opportunity which sailing offered to be 'a scruffy deck-hand... When I go sailing my trousers are baggy and dirty; my hair goes all anarchist; and you wouldn't recognize the Formby chin for bristles. That's what I call enjoying myself, taking it nice and easy'. Beryl and George would spend weeks simply moored up at Broads-Haven. Jennifer Woods, Herbert's daughter, recalls that as a girl she was very keen on tap-dancing and that Beryl used to run through the routines with her.

They also finally found a house to buy, Heronby, Beech Road, Wroxham. They bought it for about £2,000 in the name of Beryl Booth and promptly rechristened it Beryldene. It was a thatched riverside house which had stood empty and neglected during the war years and was in a very poor state of repair. George paid Nat Bircham to quayhead the river frontage, quayhead the dykes and repair or replace the footbridges. Bircham explained to George the legal restrictions and submitted an invoice for £98 for the quayheading and the rest for 'dredging and soil lighterage'. George then hired a builder to install a bathroom and an electrician to make good the wiring. It is said that the couple were prosecuted under the 1939 Defence Regulation for

Above: Lady Beryl

Right: Heaven at Broads-
Haven

*With kind permission of
Margaret Bird*

spending too much on the house at a time of rationing, though it's surprising that there was nothing in the local paper, the *Eastern Daily Press*, at the time. They were, apparently, fined £100 with ten guineas costs and the two contractors £50 each. As the house seems to have remained uninhabitable and uninsurable, George gave up the idea of living there.

Back home in the North West, Bill Innes remembered a chance encounter with George and Beryl.

> In 1948 as a very new policeman in Warrington I was on night duty and was sent to find and remove a horse reported in the road. It was very dark and the time of old gas lamps (at 50 yards apart). I found this big black horse standing in the road – no reins or halter. I am petrified of horses and every time I went towards it it would turn its back end towards me. There were few cars in those days but I saw headlights coming from the Wigan direction. I managed to stop the car and told them to drive carefully as there was a horse on the road. The man could see I was worried and said 'Can't you get hold of it?' I told him I hated horses, he laughed, got out, took a toffee from his pocket and the horse went to him and took the toffee. He then shouted 'Fetch the dog lead, Beryl.' Beryl came out and gave George the lead which he put round the horse's neck and handed the horse to me. He told me he was appearing in Blackpool, told me the name of a local address where I could leave the lead, then gave me a handful of toffees and told me to keep giving it one if it played up. They both had a good laugh before driving off. Lovely people.

In April 1949 Beryl paid into her own personal Dublin bank account 'monies brought over from South Africa' – nearly £20,000, (£541,000) in preparation for another move. That July the Formbys sold their house in Mere. As they were away on tour for much of the time it was felt to be too remote, so they returned to Poulton-le-Fylde, buying a house at Ansdell, Fairhaven, Lytham St Anne's.

On one of their trips to Norfolk they had pulled into the filling station at Middleton on the A47 just outside King's Lynn to fill up their Mark 6 Bentley. The garage was owned by Jack Talbot and his wife. This chance meeting became a friendship which would last for the rest of their lives. George got chatting to Jack and discovered he was a huge motorcycle speedway fan and had ridden on many occasions. He also still had his bike. George, of course, also had a passion for motorbikes. In July 1947 he had been given a Norton International when he appeared in *Workers' Playtime* from the works canteen in Birmingham. Nortons were much sought after, and HVU 111 fully satisfied George's hunger not only for a great bike but also his superstition about number plates. He always insisted that his vehicles ended in double, or if possible, triple numerals. The conversation with Talbot suggested an idea which took about eighteen months to come to fruition. In June 1949 the Middleton and District branch of the British Legion ran a huge Garden Fete and Grasstrack Speedway Meeting in the grounds of Middleton Tower with the billing 'Official opening by George Formby and Beryl (famous stage, screen, and radio stars)'. In the post-war era speedway racing was very popular for its exciting and dramatic appeal to spectators. Bus and train loads of people – the crowd was nearly 5,000 strong – descended on Middleton. An official programme cost sixpence. The film rights were reserved for Messrs Davis and Co (Cambridgeshire) Ltd of Wisbech who recorded the day's events for posterity on 16-mm sound film, a film subsequently shown in schools and village halls all over Norfolk.

George and Beryl had agreed to work for nothing because of Jack's influence and because of George's support for the work of the British Legion. Said to be 'in his finest form', George referred in his opening speech to: 'A lot of people all going different ways, pushing on and inclined to forget those who did so much during the last war. And there are a lot of chaps from the war before who still need our help.' He ended with the comment, 'What's life if you don't laugh?' George, with Ted Williams of Wisbech, happily started the racing, showing off his expertise in riding a Rudge belonging to his Lancashire friend Bill Kitchen, who was not able to get to the event. The day went extremely well, with George affable, warm and obliging, notwithstanding the odd parrot joke here and there. Beryl, resplendent in a New Look red

Middleton Tower, Norfolk, the gatehouse
G E Chambers, FSA (1930)

George in his element on Bill Kitchen's Rudge J.A.P. Grasstrack bike
With kind permission of EDP

gored coat and black dress, a hat with her trademark feather, and jewels, was alongside her husband as he told of their courtship, to much laughter. 'I did my courting on a motorbike, well, not exactly on the bike. We used to stop now and again.' She was presented with a large bouquet of carnations, and charmingly broke off a stem for the giver, to the mutual pleasure of all parties. The British Legion benefited from the £600 profit, (£15,800) an astounding sum considering this was really only a rural village fete. With it they were able to buy the Shepherd Hall in Middleton as their headquarters.

The following month George's mother Eliza was seventy. She celebrated in some style. George, she said:

> Flew from Blackpool to Liverpool and then went back to Southport the same night to play at the Garrick Theatre. He entertained three hundred and forty old-age pensioners of mine in my back garden here. About fifty people came to my private party, a lot of people from Warrington, and then provided out of his own pocket – no free passes with Georgie, took me and twenty-five friends to the Garrick at his invitation to go and see the show at night, and I was taken on the stage each house.

231

Eliza's seventieth birthday, July 1949

There is a photograph from that summer of George, Beryl and Eliza inscribed on the back '25th wedding anniversary'. The three of them are standing beside a light plane, perhaps for a trip to the Isle of Man. The usual belief is that George saw little of his mother, but at that time, as so often, they were in close touch.

In September and October the Formbys toured Canada. George was once again a big draw for the ex-servicemen and -women as he had been in other parts of the Commonwealth. The Canadian press also emphasised his wartime bravery in being last to leave before Dunkirk and first into Normandy, mentioning his commendation by Montgomery. The other popular theme was his connection with the Royal Family through '7 Royal Command Performances at the Albert Hall and 10 at Windsor Castle', something of an exaggeration. *Celebrity News* of Edmonton revealed that George 'broke all attendance records wherever he played'. George gave several radio broadcasts, in one replying to a question about the authorship of his songs. 'Beryl writes a lot of them – the old woman – we have to tone them down a bit when she's finished with them. Some of them we've forgotten to tone down.'

CHAPTER SIXTEEN

Ordinary People

That winter George appeared in *Cinderella,* this time at the Grand Theatre, Leeds. He was ill with an attack of dysentery, which he had first suffered in North Africa in 1943. But despite having to have morphine injections to combat the pain he carried on. At the beginning of 1950 he made his first records for four years, including 'When I'm Cleaning Windows', 'Leaning on a Lamp Post', 'Auntie Maggie's Remedy' and 'Come Hither with Your Zither'. The last named was the only new song among them. The long gap between recording sessions is in sharp contrast to his career in the Thirties and early Forties, when he was in the studio every few months. The reason for this session is revealed in a letter from Leslie Grade to Columbia. George's tour of Canada had created a big demand and Decca wanted to distribute some of his old songs on record there, as Columbia had no organisation that could do it. 'I would like to tell you that these recordings would be of very little financial benefit to George Formby owing to tax restrictions etc., but it would be very good for this country as it would bring in a good deal of dollars and this is the main reason Mr Formby wants to record for Decca. After all, everyone is trying to do their best to bring dollars into England.' But George was still grumbling. He maintained that after his tour of Canada, having earned $100,000 for Britain, he took home only £800 after tax and expenses. He complained that he had to earn £7 before he could buy a packet of fags. The begging letters from 'fans', their demands sometimes amounting to thousands of pounds a week, were loathsome to him. One of his methods of outsmarting the man from the revenue was revealed years after George's death. He used to have his Allard sports cars delivered half-finished so that he didn't have to pay purchase tax on them.

In March he suffered a bout of severe stomach pain, a return, he thought, of the dysentery that had plagued him a few months before. But this time he had to have a 'complicated' operation for appendicitis. He was delighted when on his next visit to Windsor Castle for the Lifeguards' show the following month the king wished him a good recovery. He then went off to Scandinavia, giving a charity concert in Copenhagen in the presence of the Danish and Swedish royal families on the fifth anniversary of Denmark's liberation, the proceeds going to the widows and orphans of the Danish resistance movement. In a move that was becoming something of a trademark – singing in the language of the country – George essayed a little Danish to amuse his audience. To the tune of 'She'll Be Coming Round the Mountain' and with English words apparently composed by him, the last verse of 'Hello Denmark' was a tribute to Anglo–Danish friendship. By 7 May he was in Stockholm for a single show. The media were not so interested as they had been in 1946 but the theatre was still packed to capacity with an audience of 7,000. As his pianist Bert Halliday pointed out, few of them could have understood his songs, but 'his personality made him a success in any language'.

Winnipeg, Canada, suffered a flood in the spring of 1950. Only one person had lost his life in the disaster but over 100,000 people had been evacuated from their homes and their distress – and the damage – were immense. Beryl received a request for George to visit Canada again, this time at his own expense, to headline the Flood Relief rally. The concert was to be at the Maple Leaf Gardens, Toronto's largest auditorium and usually an ice hockey stadium – on George's birthday, as it happened. The broadcast of the show set a new radio record by being carried by 729 stations of the major American and Canadian networks – an indication of the revolution in communications technology at the time. In effect he was playing to tens of millions of listeners. He travelled 20,000 miles and visited 21 cities, earning nearly $27,000 net for the tour. Beryl's rewards to herself were 'Fur Coat, cape &c. £1,400'. (£35,700) While he was there George was pressed to accept an invitation to tour six US cities, culminating in a show at Carnegie Hall, one of the most prestigious venues in the whole of the United States. He turned down this opportunity even though he was offered the chance to set his own date and fee: his films had never had much of an airing there and it seemed a challenge too far.

In June 1950 George's accountant was writing that he hoped his present rest would 'enable Mr Formby to fully recover from his recent journeys'. George was still far from well, and he and Beryl spent most of the summer in Norfolk. By August he was appearing at the Regal, Great Yarmouth, in a summer special. At the end of the month he and Beryl went on the *Empress of France* to Montreal for a seven-week tour which in the event was extended to ten weeks. During the winter the Formbys planned a move to Ireland, to escape the taxman's clutches, from the seclusion of the out-of-season Norfolk Broads. In February 1951 George and Beryl withdrew £8,000 for the Irish house and put it into their account in Dublin, which at the time showed a balance of over £73,000. (£1,710,000) In April, Beryl got another handy injection of cash – nearly £5,000 from Associated Talking Pictures, the annual royalties from *Come On George!* which had been released twelve years before. Letters flew between George's accountant, Beryl and the taxman about the amount of tax George should have to pay. The Inspector of Taxes and Beryl remained locked in dispute for some time. A series of queries was raised which revealed her tactics:

George and Beryl at the launch party of Her Majesty *at Broads Tours*
With kind permission of Herbert Woods

9. What relevance to professional earnings have the items of travelling to the houseboat?

10. The fur coats &c. appear to call for special consideration as it may be the normal three-quarters is justifiable for professional purposes.

11. The home travelling expenses in the year to March 1948 seem remarkably high, as there were only apparently three home engagements in this year. What is the explanation? What purely personal expenses are included?

Whenever George began thinking of a quieter regime, he conjured up childhood memories of an outdoor life with horses, and no doubt that was part of the attraction of Ireland. It was when the Formbys were looking around for a house in Dublin that they heard of the new project which would delay their plans. They were approached by the impresario Emile Littler, probably the most powerful figure in the theatre world, with an offer of the leading role in the London stage show which came to be known as *Zip Goes a Million*. This new version of the 1907 play *Brewster's Millions* had George playing the hero Percy Piggott, a window cleaner from Newton-le-Willows, the man left £8m on condition that he spends – not gives away – a million in one year. Of course all his efforts to spend the money actually increase his fortune. Perhaps George had a hankering to conquer the West End, perhaps Beryl encouraged him or perhaps his hunger for the adulation of a live audience overcame his feeling that he wasn't well – at any rate he accepted the offer, perhaps in the private belief that it would be a flop and have only a short run. In the peace of Broads-Haven, taking things as easily as he could, he polished up the details of his role. His sister Mary wrote to Louie in June 1951 that, 'Mother is down on the Norfolk Broads with our Georgie and Beryl on their boat and I believe they are going to take her back to Blackpool for a while with them, so I am glad she is enjoying herself.'

The 'world premiere' of the show was at the Coventry Hippodrome on 4 September, followed by a month's pre-season showing in Manchester, George senior's favourite city. A special preview of *Zip Goes a Million* was given at the Palace Theatre in aid of the Royal London Society for Teaching and Training the Blind on 19 October 1951. *Zip* then opened at the Palace Theatre, London – George's first West End hit. He was reputed to be on a salary of £1,500 a week, though Beryl's paying-in stubs show sums of only around £450. George had never lost his anxiety about playing London venues. 'Fancy me and my ukulele on the stage where Ivor Novello knelt before the altar with a rose in his teeth,' he said in January 1952. 'Audiences wept on his first nights and the wise boys of the West End thought they would weep on mine too.' Far from it: the ukulele was not meant to be part of the show but the screams of the audience that evening forced its inclusion and a performance of 'When I'm Cleaning Windows'. George's mother, then aged seventy-two, was there, afterwards saying, 'I should have liked his father to have seen him. He would have been so proud of the way he's kept up his name.' Not all the family were pleased with George, though. Years later Louie expressed the view that he could have engineered a role for their brother Frank as a dancer. He was never going to do that. Eddie Latta was quite clear about George's point of view. 'There could only be one at the top. So naturally George didn't want Frank...'

The *Daily Express* reviewer who saw the Manchester show called it 'a musical play which blends corny gags with transatlantic zip'. Emile Littler himself, interviewed some years later, said that to begin with George was a bit provincial, but soon became the toast of the West End. In February 1952, *Theatre World* reviewed *Zip*, calling it 'a big personal triumph' and 'A first rate English musical'. *The Times* critic described it in a much less straightforward way.

> Flattened into a conventional musical comedy plot by the weight of a huge spectacular show, there is not a breath of humour left in it after the first impact. That is a matter of no moment. If the idea is flattened it is flattened triumphantly... The audience on Saturday night gave every sign of having found the singing, the dancing (especially, perhaps, the dancing) and the simple friendliness of Mr George Formby much to their taste... the verdict at curtain-fall was not in doubt. Mr Formby, whose fame has, of course, preceded him to the West End stage,

is a comedian whose talents are not easily definable. He is extraordinary only in his ordinariness. He has a deft way with a song or a banjo, but little or no finesse in his handling of a comic situation. His whole art seems to consist in projecting an engagingly simple stage personality.

Barbara Perry, an American dancer who played Lilac Delaney, thought much the same. 'He really was a shy man, but he had magnetism and charm that never stopped. His greatness was his relaxation.' Barbara was unwittingly the cause of a strike, over her membership of Equity, or the lack of it. Naively she had asked Emile Littler if she should join and he advised against it. The fee of £50 eventually paid on her behalf, the show went on. Barbara struck up a friendship with Beryl, based, Barbara felt, on the fact that they were both dancers. On one occasion, Beryl told Barbara about her prize-winning clog dancing days. The judges of the competition stood inside 'a sort of oversized phone booth, while each competitor danced on top. They were judged by the sound alone'. The friendship between Barbara and the Formbys is indicated by a note sent by Beryl which she kept.

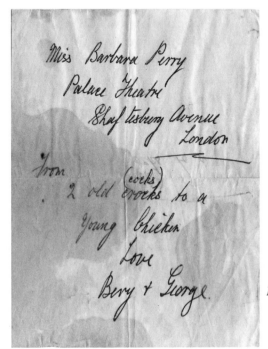

Beryl to her friend Barbara Perry, 1951

George gradually gained the confidence to make the show his own. On one occasion he invited some of the workers from Herbert Woods' boatyard and ad-libbed so much trying to get all their names in that he completely lost the rest of the cast. As Sam Cooke remembered, 'Two coachloads of people from Norfolk just rolled about whilst the rest of the audience hadn't a clue about what was going on.' By April 1952 *Zip* had earned George over £16,000. Despite this large new cash injection he sold the Rolls as an economy measure. Cumbersome as it was in West End traffic, he decided he would be better saving the 4*s*. 6*d*. a night garage fees! *Zip* revived his popularity in more ways than one. Film profits soared up again and George was back in the limelight. No doubt because of this current exposure in *Zip,* on 21 November 1951 George featured on *Desert Island Discs*, just a couple of weeks after his old film colleague Ronald Shiner. His choices included songs by Bing Crosby, his friend the Irish tenor Josef Locke and his wartime colleague Vera Lynn. Irish music may have recalled his time at the Curragh as a boy, but his last record was the most personal – his father singing 'I Was Standing at the Corner of the Street'. He chose as his luxury – and not everyone chose one at the time – his first ukulele.

Six months into the run, on 10 April, the day before Good Friday, George collapsed at the wheel of his car about twenty miles from London when travelling with Beryl to the Norfolk Broads for an Easter weekend rest. He was forty-seven years old. The strain of the show was immense and he had been feeling ill in London. He had suffered from laryngitis for the whole month in Manchester. In his words, 'I was in terrible pain. I told Beryl I felt limp and could not lift my hand on the steering wheel. I conked out. We were in the heart of the country. It was pouring with rain. There was no garage for miles around. Beryl ran up and down the road.' Eventually a driver pulled up and turned the car round. When George felt a little better Beryl drove him back to London and called a doctor. At first it wasn't clear what was wrong with him – a duodenal ulcer was suspected – and he was not admitted to hospital until five days after the attack.

Once in his London clinic, treated by Sir John Weir and Sir Horace Evans, physicians to Queen Mary, he was in excellent hands. He told a newspaper reporter in early 1953, 'Three famous doctors, among them Sir

Horace Evans, Queen Mary's physician, stood at my bedside, looked at me solemnly and said, "You have coronary thrombosis." I sat up. The doctors rushed towards me. "Please lie down, you mustn't move."' Eddie Latta said that George, predictably, focused on the financial angle.

The king's physician treated him – costing him £100 a visit. He said, 'Do you know, Eddie, he comes in, takes a sample of blood, they put it in a tuppenny medicine bottle and shake it up and down. If it goes down the sides it means the blood isn't congealing. If it sticks on the side – you've got to keep quiet and still and all the rest of it. £100 for a medicine bottle!'

Queen Mary regularly sent him messages to have courage and not to work so hard. A week after the onset of his illness his condition was publicly stated to be 'not so very good' and his replacement, Reg Dixon, announced. George's West End run was over. Dixon said that when George was feeling better he came to see him in the show more than once, giving him 'encouragement and kindly words'. He described this role of deputising for him as the highlight of his career.

It was not until 18 May, nearly six weeks after the coronary, that George was allowed to return home – under strict instructions to get up for only fifteen minutes a day. In early June he gave a statement to the press that when he was well enough to leave Lytham he would live quietly on the Norfolk Broads. Beryl wrote: 'His illness was very serious but I am pleased to say he is coming along quite nicely now, although he needs a great deal of rest'. George himself added: 'It will be about a year before I am right.' In 1959 George recalled this part of his life. 'I'd started feeling ill at Easter 1951. I laid off work. Early in 1952 I had a thrombosis. The doctors told me that was the finish so far as treading the boards was concerned. Frankly, I was too ill to bother whether they were right or not.'

George and Beryl went to Norfolk for an eight-week holiday, visited often by Norman Evans, another Lancashire comedian, whose *Over the Garden Wall* character was the inspiration for Les Dawson's Ada. Born in Rochdale and about the same age as George, he was cheerful company. Max Miller also turned up at George's boat in the early Fifties. They had first met when George was playing a northern music hall. Miller was the juvenile lead in the show across the road. He 'borrowed' the 'baby' sketch 'Easy Going Chap' which George had recorded in 1937. Pooh Curtis remembers as a little girl of about nine spending the summer at Potter Heigham and seeing George and Max at Broads-Haven sitting in deckchairs with a group of friends on the deck of a very opulent boat, singing and drinking. Her brother Anthony Benthall, three years her senior, recalls another incident, this time at Coldham Hall, a riverside pub on the Yare, where the family boat, *Forester*, was moored just a few away from *Lady Beryl*. As the evening grew late Mrs Benthall became increasingly annoyed by the singing and party noise coming from the nearby boat, which was preventing her from getting to sleep. She persuaded her husband, Tony, a Norwich gynaecologist, to go to ask them to keep the noise down. In the words of his son he 'failed to return'. The party was too good to leave. There was none of the aloofness of modern celebrity about George – he was friendly to everyone. He also liked to go fishing and joined in the local regatta, though his pennant of crossed ukuleles and assorted underwear (as in *Bell-Bottom George*) bedecking the boat didn't impress some of the other, more serious, sailors.

Towards the end of September George had another setback – an attack of gastro-enteritis. While he was recovering, the house that he and Beryl had been planning to buy in Ireland was finally acquired – a twenty-four-roomed mansion in an expensive residential area, for which they paid £18,000 with another £5,000 spent on redecoration. From 1 October 1952 the Formbys' new address was to be Beryldene, Knocksinna, Foxrock, Dublin. Tempted by the prospect of quiet, good food and horse breeding – the Leopardstown racecourse is at Foxrock – George felt this move was a good one, but in the event it was as short-lived an experiment as his previous move to country life had been. Eddie Latta recounted a story about this time in George's life, which perhaps had some bearing on his decision to return to Lancashire.

> Billy Barr [a friend of George's] went over to Ireland with him. George went there to avoid tax and while he was there he bought a chain of grocery stores. Then he rang up Bill Barr. 'Ee, Bill, will you come over? I don't know what I've done here!'

So Billy said, 'OK, I'll come over' – got on a plane within an hour. Flew over to Ireland and he said, 'Let's see the shops, George.' George said, 'Well, there's two here and two somewhere else or other.'

So they go in and Billy says, 'Let's see the books.' Looked at them.

'How much have you put down?'

'£5,000.'

'Forget it.'

'I can't forget it.'

'Write it off – tell him you're finished.'

So he took Billy's advice and saved God knows how much. But he never looked after Bill; it wasn't that he wasn't grateful, [it] never occurred to him.

Beryl made an intriguing remark to Barbara Perry around this time. After George's coronary Barbara and her mother used to go for tea with George and Beryl. Barbara's mother asked Beryl's advice about a problem she was having with some employees at a rehearsal hall she owned in the States, who, she believed, were cheating her. Beryl agreed that they certainly would be, but told her not to worry. 'George and I open businesses in every place we play, and we give the managers a chance. If they steal a little, OK. As long as you don't bother them and they just take a little you have an income.' Yet again George was looking for a business opportunity. He hadn't gone to Ireland purely to take it easy.

Despite an episode in which he swallowed a chicken bone which lodged in his gullet, necessitating another operation, after only three months George felt well enough to return home permanently. But work was still out. There was a gap in his career from Good Friday 1952 to spring 1953. In that summer the last Beryldene was bought, and bought cheaply, from Josef Locke, who found himself in difficult financial negotiations with the Inland Revenue and needed to raise money quickly. It is not clear how much they paid: one account says only £6,000 for a house Locke had bought seven months before for £7,000. Another estimate, more widely

243

accepted, is £15,000. (312,000) What is certain is that £9,400 left their Dublin account in mid-April. With it they got a substantial double-fronted house with a Westmoreland green slate roof on the Inner Promenade, Lytham St Anne's.

After his heart attack George cut down on his work considerably. There's no doubt that his confidence had been knocked – he said as much in several interviews in the early Fifties. In April 1953 he was asked to come out of retirement to appear at the Rhodesia Centenary Celebrations. On 30 May he and Beryl were in Bulawayo, George performing at the Theatre Royal before an audience of 3,000 and topping the bill. Given his recent medical history it's astonishing that he undertook such a long flight. Why did he go back to work at all? He confessed that he had 'never been so scared in all my life', yet he took on the challenge. One reason could have been that he was offered the immense salary of £6,000 (£125,000) for two weeks' work. Beryl always liked to take her cut and their expenses would easily cover the £300 she spent on 'dresses and hats etc.'. On his return George spoke to the journalist Graham Stanford who asked him what his motives had been. Revealingly he answered that, 'There's more in show business than money. It's true it gets into the blood. And I'm going back to it.' He realised he was most himself in front of an audience. 'The longer you're away the longer you want to stay away, but once you are back and you hear the applause then you feel you could go on for ever. You feel you're really part of things again, not broken down and finished… Getting back your confidence is half the battle. At one time I was a proper worry-guts…'

In September, returning to home territory, George switched on the lights at Blackpool Illuminations. Val Parnell, the Managing Director of Moss Empires, offered him a season at the London Palladium, running until pantomime began. This was in the revue *Fun and the Fair*, at 'The World's No.1 Music Hall' as it called itself, with Terry-Thomas and the Billy Cotton Band. He signed a nine-week agreement that from 5 October he would give thirteen performances a week for £1,250 per week – still a large salary. It was also agreed that if weekly receipts exceeded £10,000 he would receive 40 per cent of the box office. Clause 6, that the copyright of songs, gags, etc.

became the property of the company, was deleted. Instead all the material remained the sole property of George Formby. 'It is understood that the Artiste's name shall go right across the top of the billing over the title and no other Artiste's name shall be billed in larger or more prominent type.' Beryl had done well. The press were still interested in the state of George's health. He told them that the doctors had prescribed whisky to assist his convalescence. 'I am inclined to think it helped. But I had none yesterday until after the show. Then I had a couple of pips.'

The *London Evening Standard* critic reported that George – looking somewhat slimmer, was nonetheless every bit his old self as far as the humour was concerned. 'The applause when he first came on stage stopped the show.' George commented, 'I hope you're like that when we finish.' This was to be his last Palladium appearance. His act closed the first half while the up-and-coming Terry-Thomas had the top slot. After Thomas had not gone well, feeling his act was something of an anticlimax after George, he asked the producer, Charles Henry, why Formby had not gone on last. 'What, with all those fucking stories?' was the reply. Henry didn't like the 'old-hat' parrot jokes but the audience still loved them. The gags themselves weren't the point. George's way of telling them was. *The Times* reviewer focused on a different aspect of George's act, writing words that would appear eventually in his obituary: that the pointing of his songs was 'artlessly exact' and the rhythm of the ukulele playing 'flawless'.

Whenever they could the Formbys escaped to Norfolk. The next boat they bought, in 1953, was originally named *Traumerei* (Daydreaming). Alan Kennaugh of the George Formby Society told the story that shortly after George took delivery of this second luxury yacht he wandered down to the yard and spoke to Donald Hagenbach, who had built it. He asked if a man could be spared to polish the brasses on the boat for him. Teasing him, Hagenbach replied that it was 'no use being a boatman if you can't do your own metalwork. Go to a store and buy some polish and dusters and do it yourself'. So George did – and enjoyed it! The boat had been built by Graham Bunn (Wroxham) Ltd and launched on 8 September 1950. For the Formbys it became their second *Lady Beryl*.

George with the men of Graham Bunn's Windboats, the builders of Lady Beryl II
By kind permission of EDP

David Boag remembers George's hospitality. When on holiday with some of his school chums at Potter Heigham they moored up for the night and saw this huge (at least to them) luxury cruiser complete with all mod cons. As they looked in through one of the windows, curious, they were greeted with 'Hello lads' and after a few minutes invited on board to meet Beryl, who produced large quantities of coffee and biscuits. The next year three of the same group were back on the Broads with three other friends and moored up in the evening at about the same place. As they were cleaning up before they returned their boat the next day they heard a voice behind them. 'Oh, it's you lot again. Beryl'll be pleased to see you. Come aboard. Beryl's got some food on the go.' Again David remembered a happy time, giving the lie to the later stories that by this time there were deep tensions in the Formby marriage.

Neighbours at Potter Heigham were Margaret Bird and her parents. She recalls that whenever the Broads Tours boat *Her Majesty* came past George used to go on deck and start cleaning the windows! While they were waiting for their new boat to be built George played about in his little runabout

246

Baby Beryl, about ten feet long, made for him by Sam Cooke of Herbert Woods' boatyard. He built the entire boat in four weeks, apparently for George to go off on his own, sailing and fishing on Hickling Broad. Sam remembers George getting off his boat one morning to go to get his papers and groceries. 'The sun was shining very brightly, casting large shadows. George stepped off his boat and walked straight into the water.' His excuse was that his eyes had suffered from so many years of theatre limelight that he had been temporarily blinded. He took the whole incident as a great joke though he had confessed in Australia in 1947 that he couldn't swim – 'three strokes and I'm under!' Later the same morning the young lad who looked after the petrol pump at Herbert Woods turned up on a spanking new motorcycle. George saw it and went over to ask if he could have a look at his new pride and joy. Seconds later he was in the saddle and, despite his age and ill health, tearing up over Potter Heigham bridge towards Yarmouth. The poor lad, knowing nothing of George's obsession with motorbikes, feared he would never see his prized possession again. Needless to say, a short while later the broadest grin in Norfolk reappeared – on the bike, much to the young man's relief.

Clive Manson, who spent most of his working life in and around Yarmouth and knew the impresarios and theatre owners Jack and Peter Jay, remembers George standing at the bar in the Bridge Hotel at Potter Heigham when he was approached by a woman who asked him if anyone had ever told him that he looked exactly like George Formby. 'No,' said George. She then said, 'Would you mind if my husband took a photograph of us standing together as my friends at home will never believe the similarity?' George never let on, and to this day she probably believes that he was a very good double.

In February 1954 George was involved in an accident with two other vehicles on the Great North Road (A1) near Peterborough. Beryl was also in the car but neither of them was injured. In March the insurers' letter concerning the recent accident arrived. Of the Bentley it said 'the offside front tyre is cut badly' and 'the whole of the front suspension assembly has been returned to Bentley Motors for complete examination and rebuilding'. The accident may have been another sign that George was far from well. By now, though, there are hints that George's health was under attack from another source.

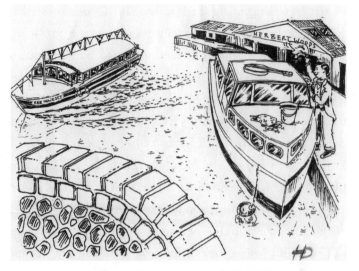

By Hazel Dormer, after 'Film Fun'

Cheque stubs in Beryl's writing show three visits to Joseph Steele, grocers, in Fairhaven during February. While she probably bought other goods – the stubs are marked, 'whiskey etc.' – the form of words suggests that the main part of the purchase was the spirits. A bottle of whisky cost about £1 15s. in 1952 and these bills varied from about £7 to about £20 (£408).

Jessie Bailey said that the Formbys started drinking after their return from the Far East. Beryl had confided to her Australian audience in a radio interview in 1947 that she and George had acquired the habit of drinking a tot of whisky with milk to help get them off to sleep during the war years. But much more whisky than that was being consumed in the Formby household in the spring and summer of 1954, though of course it comprised three (or four) people, including Harry, and presumably his wife Cis, as well. Most of May seems to have been spent on the Norfolk Broads, with Beryl frequently – every few days – shopping at Roys of Wroxham for 'whiskey etc.'. The Formbys were very hospitable, and it may be that they were entertaining on a lavish scale. They were either partying hard or drowning their sorrows. But for George, who had suffered a major heart attack, this consumption of alcohol, as well as a heavy smoking habit – Woodbines and Player's – was potentially disastrous. It has been said, no doubt with some truth, that Beryl was drinking heavily towards the end of her life to help dull the pain of her cancer. Previous biographers have estimated her liquor bill at '£20 a week'. In fact her cheque stubs show that in October 1959, by which time she was too ill to appear on stage with George any longer, she spent £71 on 'whiskey etc.' and in November, only £54 (£936). Five years before though, in July, the bill had been over £175 (£3,570). However that sum is analysed, it's a massive amount for food and drink (or drink and food) for a month.

From June 1954 George was performing in *Turned Out Nice Again* in Blackpool at the Hippodrome when, six weeks later, he fell ill again. Back on the Broads to recuperate, on August Bank Holiday Monday he and Beryl entertained the Howsons with their daughter Pat to tea on board the boat. Pat was an attractive brunette of twenty-nine, a school teacher, straightforward and a devout Catholic. George had known her since she was a little girl, as her father, Fred, was his car dealer. Years later George pinpointed this meeting as the moment when he fell in love with her. The road accident, the heavy drinking and his renewed illness suggest that George was in some mental turmoil and that at this unhappy time he sought comfort in the fantasy of a new life. On 21 September it was reported that George had pulled out of the forthcoming pantomime *Dick Whittington* at the Palace Theatre, Manchester – a most unusual move for him – on medical advice. He was clearly cutting back on the alcohol too. Beryl recorded only one visit to Roys of Wroxham, for under £13.

CHAPTER SEVENTEEN

Got to Get Your Photo in the Press

The coronation of Elizabeth II in June 1953 prompted thousands of Britons to buy a television to watch the historic spectacle in their own homes. Neighbours crowded into the living rooms of more affluent friends, gathering around an eleven-inch screen to see the black and white images. Of course, the infant had to find its feet, and early TV programmes were a mixture of old and new. Variety rubbed shoulders with sitcoms, soap operas, *Six-Five Special* – a rock and roll show – and imported American westerns. So there was a place for George and soon he was using the new medium. At this time George was taking up a mixture of offers – some, like the Blackpool shows, comfortably familiar, others on television much less so. One false start followed his appearance as a mystery guest on *What's My Line* in December 1953, signing his name slowly. His identity was quickly guessed, despite his using a falsetto voice, by Isobel Barnett. Later he took Gilbert Harding's place when he was ill for a few weeks. 'People said that George was out of place in this role... but he gave a breath of fresh air to a panel of highbrow experts.' On the other hand the actor Gerry George said 'he died the death' and described him as 'painfully unsuccessful. Backstage gossip told how this lovely man appeared utterly clueless when he was plunged into a show that he didn't understand and couldn't get to grips with. Despite Beryl's energetic and audible offstage prompting poor George just couldn't handle it'. But on New Year's Eve 1954 he made a much more successful TV appearance, on *Ask Pickles*, an early version of *Jim'll Fix It*. This radio request show, hosted by Wilfred Pickles, a well-known personality, had transferred to TV. George was the guest star, back on well-trodden territory and singing four songs.

In the following January in *Top of the Town* George sang and appeared in two sketches. His television work continued, but it was patchy, with a 'hand-to-mouth' feel, and it didn't pay particularly well. In September 1955 he got work with Associated Rediffusion Ltd – two weeks at £200 a week. On the same day he signed up for a cabaret appearance at the Mayfair Hotel, only eight minutes long, to be shown on television on 22 September for a special fee of £100, to be paid by cheque after the performance. The occasion was the opening night of the Independent Television Authority, and the novelty of the adverts stole the show for some reviewers. Sir John Gielgud and Dame Edith Evans were strong challengers though, as was Alec Guinness, but obviously it was thought that George's contribution would be popular. So it was: one commentator wrote that he performed 'some of his familiar songs with a devil-may-care bonhomie that certainly brightened the picture'.

Eventually, in June 1957 George got his own TV programme, *The George Formby Show*. *Val Parnell's Saturday Spectacular* was broadcast by ABC, an independent TV company focusing on the North and the Midlands. The chorus girls danced and George appeared sliding down a short helter-skelter in a lounge suit and holding his Gibson ukulele. When he stood up he was so out of breath that the band had to repeat the introduction. David Nixon, the magician and friend of the Formbys, was on the bill, as was Petula Clark, with whom George sang a duet, 'Ordinary People', from *Zip Goes a Million*. He finished with 'Leaning on a Lamp Post' and a ukulele solo. In January 1958 he was the guest star on *The Frankie Vaughan Show*. He had been billed to appear on the *Billy Cotton Band Show* three weeks previously but had been ill. And the following month he was part of *Many Happy Returns,* the two-year anniversary celebration for ABC. In August the demands of television to be up to date forced a change in George's style. In *George Formby Presents: Formby Favourites*, his own show, he joined the Deep River Boys in a rock and roll medley of 'Rock Around the Clock', 'Some of these Days', 'Dinah' and 'Sweet Georgia Brown'. Jazz violinist Stephane Grappelli and singer Des O'Connor were among other artists on the bill. The show ran for sixty minutes, and in it he sang nine songs, including, of course, 'Leaning on a Lamp Post'.

Atlantic Showboat was shown on ABC TV in January 1959. Filmed on the *Empress of Britain*, a cruise ship recently launched as Britain's first fully air-conditioned liner, it was hosted by Hughie Green, very popular at the time as the presenter of *Double Your Money*, a quiz show with cash prizes. The destination was Canada, which was Green's homeland. Green was a friend of George's but hadn't included him in the line-up. When George asked why, Hughie told him he couldn't afford his fee, but George agreed to do the show for the price of his ticket. A young Shirley Bassey appeared. George sang two songs, 'The Pleasure Cruise' and a specially written, but unrecorded, song for his first Canadian visit, 'Hello Canada'. In April, on a Saturday evening at 7.30 p.m., prime time, *Steppin' Out with Formby* was broadcast. George performed seven songs, wearing a tuxedo and looking well. Beryl was annoyed that the ending of the programme was 'hijacked' by Eamonn Andrews who wanted to surprise Tommy Trinder for *This is Your Life*, and forced the BBC to announce at the start of the tribute, 'We are very grateful to Mr Formby for allowing us to encroach on his programme.'

With the compère of Atlantic Showboat, Hughie Green

But between these small jobs George always returned to the live stage, where he was happiest, and in particular to pantomime. In early spring 1955 he signed up for the coming winter season again. At this stage in his career his usual salary was a guaranteed £500 a week and a percentage of net admission receipts. While not nearly so much as he'd earned in his heyday, it was still a good income. The usual clauses about his top billing were included, but more unusually the subject of the pantomime was to be agreed with him and it was to be a completely new production. Perhaps significantly, the printed clause about illness was altered to George's benefit. Only five days later, on 14 February, he signed with Emile Littler for the male lead in *Too Young to Marry*, George's first straight play, the show to begin on 26 September. Top billing was agreed, as was the right of George to do broadcasts and/or films while the engagement proceeded.

George was the star of *Babes in the Wood* at the Royal Court, Liverpool, that Christmas season. Jane Bottone (Fairy Stardust) thought George old, but 'absolutely superb'. Very professional, but 'rather a remote sort of gentleman… we always called him Mr Formby'. She remembered Beryl's unpleasantness to her following a schoolroom sketch. A boy stood up and said: 'My name's Dan. When I grow up to be a man I want to be a missionary in Japan, if I can. And I think I can.' Jane's feed line to George was: 'My name's Sadie. When I grow up to be a lady, I'd like to marry and have a baby, if I can, and I think I can.' George's line, looking at Jane, was: 'My name's Sam, I don't want to be a missionary in Japan, I'd rather help Sadie with her plan, if I can, and I think I can.' This got a big laugh from the boys in the pit, to Beryl's fury. Apparently she used to hiss at Jane from the wings to try to put her off. Jane thought it was because she seemed to be sharing the laugh with George, but there was plenty for Beryl to dislike in the exchange apart from that! On his home ground, Lancashire, Jane saw no fading of George's reputation. 'The audiences adored him – we were there for fourteen weeks and we played to packed houses.'

Most of 1956 was devoted to the live stage with engagements between 9 July and 12 November in a variety of theatres from Eastbourne to Aberdeen. He played Idle Jack in *Dick Whittington* during the Christmas season of 1956–7 at the Palace Theatre, Shaftesbury Avenue, under the auspices of Emile Littler, a familiar role in an unfamiliar venue. The show was another London success for George. It is said that this was the first pantomime Charles, Prince of Wales and Princess Anne were taken to see. The royal party went backstage so that George could be introduced to another generation of the family. It was a sign of the times that an excerpt was broadcast by BBC TV in January. But he was still dogged by ill health. Attacks of laryngitis in January recurred the following month forcing his withdrawal or, according to one source, sacking.

Despite his heart attack George remained a restless soul, and in March 1955 he had accepted an invitation to undertake another South African tour for a month. Considering his state of health it is perhaps surprising the Formbys were so keen to go, but they liked the country, which may have been associated in George's mind with health. That was where his father's doctors had recommended *he* should go to prolong his life. These shows, in aid of the National Cancer Fund, were given free and raised £12,000. A South African theatre programme described how 'after his convalescence he has given unstintingly of his time and talents in the war against disease'. George's comment was, 'We get a lot more fun out of doing this kind of work. I don't want to die the richest man in the cemetery.' In the Great Hall of Witwatersrand University he played to a large audience of 'Non-Europeans' and was given a gold half-sovereign as a tribute for being the first internationally known artist to perform to such an audience in that city. George in his acceptance speech was overwhelmed with emotion and his voice faltered as he said, 'It is truly the nicest present I have ever received in my life. I shall have it engraved: From the Non-Europeans...' and broke off. In the silence the sympathetic and appreciative applause began while George and Beryl hurried off the stage.

George was back by 13 April when a royal variety show was given at the Opera House, Blackpool, the first in Elizabeth II's reign to be outside London. He was one of twenty northern performers of a total of thirty-five, the show to coincide with the queen's tour of North Lancashire. Gracie Fields came back from the United States to take part and Arthur Askey, Wilfred Pickles, Geraldo, and Morecambe and Wise were also there, with Alma

Cogan and a host of others. George's modest comment on the evening was, 'The Queen looked lovely in a white dress; she went better than anybody!' But his stay in England was a short interlude before he went abroad again, this time to Canada – his fourth visit. Working for expenses only, his warm friendliness got a great reception from the audiences he sang and joked with. A newsreel from Toronto Variety Village shows George being presented with a Gold Lifetime Variety Card on 13 May from the Variety Club of Toronto to certify that he had donated his services for eight performances to raise funds for a vocational training school for physically disabled boys – a school that he visited while he was there.

As soon as there was a break from work and travel the Formbys made straight for the Norfolk Broads, and in the summer of 1958 they were taking delivery of a new boat. This time they had commissioned it from Graham Bunn, the proprietor of Windboats, Wroxham. With a reputation locally as an eccentric, and a minor poet, he was also a perfectionist, and his boats were beautifully built, well equipped and fitted with very powerful engines. *Lady Beryl II*, a seagoing boat, was built by him and was bespoke for George. She was the last word in luxury, with writing desk and cocktail cabinet in the owner's cabin, a refrigerator and full-sized cooker in the galley and a double bedroom forward. 'With a range of 280 miles the canals of Holland – a favourite holiday ground for the Formbys – are in easy reach of the Broads', commented the *Eastern Daily Press* reporter. There's no evidence that they sailed there, though. When the water level at the medieval Potter Heigham bridge – notoriously the most difficult to navigate on the Broads – was too high and George could not get under it with this majestic boat, he used to hire a twelve-foot day boat, by coincidence also named *Beryl*, from Applegate's Boatyard. A postcard of the Norfolk Broads shows *Lady Beryl II* moored up beside the Swan Hotel at Horning with bunting fluttering in the breeze. It had been placed there to celebrate Beryl's birthday. The gesture says a great deal about George's feelings for his wife.

The following spring George saw a gleaming new Jaguar in Woodhead's garage in Blackpool and promptly bought it. It was a Mark 1 3.4 litre model, mist grey, with lovely red leather upholstery. This was a considerably smaller

Pennant from Lady Beryl II

car than he had been used to but it was fitted with the new Dunlop 'disc brakes' which were to prove an asset later on in the year. He transferred his personalised plate GF 2 onto it. It seems he managed to acquire both GF 1 and GF 2 sometime during 1956. It is interesting to theorise as to how George got these numbers as all the 'GF' records – a London registration authority – were lost during the wartime Blitz.

Over the previous twelve years the Formbys' friendship with the Talbots had blossomed. They often spent time together on the Broads, Jack no doubt enjoying himself by tinkering with *Lady Beryl II*'s engines, keeping them in peak condition for George. Whenever the Formbys were coming to Norfolk they tried to stop off at one or other of the hostelries owned by the Talbots for a meal to break the journey and to catch up with each other's news. Bank Holiday Monday, 3 August 1959 was one of those occasions. George was appearing at the Windmill Theatre, Great Yarmouth, for impresario Jack Jay. Jay had noticed that in previous years, when George had been holidaying in Wroxham and popped in to see some of the shows, he had got a 'tremendous reception' from the public, and later claimed he had written to George inviting him to appear there for the last ten years. When George finally agreed, Jay had asked him why he wanted to go to a small theatre like the Windmill which only seated 900 when he could go to theatres in other seaside towns which would seat 2–3000. His reply was, 'Well, if I go to a big theatre and there's empty seats, people will say old George has had it and he's past it and everything else. If I go to a small theatre and it's packed out everybody will say I'm a great success.' He regarded the short summer season as 'a try-out for my future'. That was the way it happened. To the surprise of many – perhaps of him too – he packed the theatre every night. 'People', according to Jay, 'really thought I was crackers.' One of them, a colleague, had told him in no uncertain terms: 'This is 1959, not 1938!'

It was a dry and sunny day with a light west to north-westerly breeze, unusually pleasant for a bank holiday. George and Beryl were driving to Yarmouth along the A47 from King's Lynn, having spent the weekend at home in St Anne's. They had stopped at the Woolpack, Terrington St John, for lunch to visit Jack and his wife. Mrs Talbot always put on 'a good spread' and as Beryl was by this time not at all well they may have lingered longer than they intended. They had got as far as East Winch in west Norfolk when George's car collided with an Austin A30 driven by a local man as it turned right

An advertisement for the Windmill Theatre Great Yarmouth, displaying George's publicity

The Woolpack, Terrington St John
With kind permission of Roger Talbot

to go into a cricket field opposite East Winch Hall and rolled it into some road works. Twenty-six-year-old shop manager Maurice Bunting of Stoke Ferry, the driver and only occupant of the Austin, was a little shaken up but not injured. Beryl had apparently been asleep in the back of George's new Jaguar with Punch, their terrier dog, beside her. She and George were both taken to the King's Lynn hospital suffering from shock. Beryl was quickly discharged but George was kept in a private ward for observation. The doctor who attended at the crash site took George to hospital in his own car, rather than waiting for the ambulance to arrive, so concerned was he about George's state of health and the possibility of his having a heart attack. He had a private room, which one nurse remembered was smoky. Angela Sims, a student nurse at that time, said in a newspaper article, 'He was quite poorly. He was bed-nursed for the first few days. Beryl was there with him and sat by his bed. She was always very quiet – well, they both were until George felt a bit better.' Children from the nearby eye unit, the Fermoy Ward, came to visit and George signed autographs for them. Hughie Green and Tommy Trinder were among a number of visitors. Mrs Sims recalled, 'He had quite a bad heart, and about two years later died of a heart attack, not unexpected from the medical side.' On the Monday following the accident George was finally released from hospital and went to meet Beryl at the Globe Hotel, where they and Punch the dog were presented with a huge basket of fruit from the Lynn Players. They then went to the Broads for a further week for George to convalesce. Beryl told a reporter from *The Star* that he ordered a new Jaguar 'on the spot. He won't get into any car that's been in a smash. He's superstitious, you know'.

The accident created something of a sensation, such was George's fame. Geoff Allen, Bunting's boss, who had lent him his wife's car to get to the cricket match, rang the *Daily Mirror* with the news and was rewarded with a guinea. Coincidentally he had seen George on the beach at Arromanches. Meanwhile the management of the Windmill in Yarmouth was plunged into crisis. Beryl called Jack Jay, the owner, from King's Lynn to tell him what had happened and that George was being kept in hospital. Tommy Trinder was the obvious choice to stand in for him, having starred at the Windmill in what Jay remembered as 'a bumper season' two years previously. Jay phoned Trinder's Surrey home to be told he was playing a charity cricket match at Walton-on-Thames. The *Emergency News Bulletin of the Norfolk News Company* (there was a newspaper strike) reported on Wednesday that the Metropolitan Police had whisked Tommy Trinder from the match to deputise for George. The police had turned up to find Trinder at square leg, and going on to the pitch asked him to phone Jack Jay. He thought it was a joke and asked them if they would like to bowl a few overs. Eventually Trinder agreed to cover for a week and dashed home to get his stage clothes. Despite his best efforts – and the benefit of a Rolls – he couldn't get there for the first house. Luckily the circus was in town and helped out with a few acts. Trinder arrived just in time for the second house. His opening words won the audience's approval – 'What do I do here?' In Jay's words, 'After that TT just ran riot, ad-libbing like mad. The bedroom sketch which normally runs for eight minutes went on for nearly three-quarters of an hour.'

At Grimston Magistrates' Court, where his case was subsequently heard, George was the chief prosecution witness. He sat on a bench alongside Bunting and 'a few poachers' before being called to the witness box. Beryl, sitting in the public benches, was there to support him as he gave his account of events. He described the scene very clearly. Driving at about forty-five miles an hour, he had 'seen a car ahead on an otherwise clear road near road improvements at the Swaffham end of the village. He began to overtake and suddenly when he was about 75 feet away the driver in front put out his indicator and almost immediately turned to the right...' he braked as hard as he could but could not avoid a collision. 'I hadn't an earthly chance of avoiding him... It's lucky I have a car with terrific braking power.' His wife, he added, was asleep in the car and the impact was not sufficient to wake her up. George said that Bunting had told him that he had no idea there had been any vehicle behind him. He stressed that he had not been 'hurrying' to Yarmouth and was strongly supported by a motorcyclist, Peter Plant of Norwich, who had been travelling behind the Formbys' car for about the last ten miles. He gave evidence that George had pulled out after giving a proper signal then he had seen the indicator of Bunting's car flash and the car turn almost immediately. He saw George 'step on everything' and he himself had swerved to avoid going into the back of the Jaguar, according to the *Eastern Daily Press* report. It was his opinion that George could have done nothing more to avoid an accident, and he had heard him sound his horn as he began to overtake. Bunting had told Sanderson, the local policeman who had come from about half a mile away on his bike (these were the days of the village bobby), that he had been driving at about ten miles per hour at the time of the accident. He claimed to have looked in his mirror before turning but had seen no vehicle behind, nor had he heard a car horn.

Bunting said in 2004 he found it very strange that Beryl hadn't woken up, as there were, of course, no seatbelts at that time and George had braked very sharply. He was disappointed that George had reacted by wanting to call the police immediately, not even asking Bunting if he was all right. Bunting insinuated that George might have been the worse for drink, pointing out that these were pre-breathalyser days, and was convinced that he had been speeding. As he said, to get from King's Lynn to Great Yarmouth on the old A47 in an hour and a half was pushing it in those days, and George had repeatedly told Bunting that he would be late for the show at the Windmill. It is tempting to wonder if George had put his foot down to try out his new car. However, at the time Bunting's 'not guilty' plea to the charge of careless

driving was not accepted. He was fined £10 with £3 8s. costs and disqualified from driving for six months. But in this the Grimston Magistrates had
overplayed their hand. Bunting appealed, his counsel pointing out that he
had driven for five years with a clean record and as this was a first offence
the most the magistrates were empowered to impose was a one month ban.
As the appeal was heard on 12 October a month had already gone by, and
Bunting was able to drive away from the court there and then.

George also needed to think about driving, of course. His mist grey
Jaguar, acquired only months before, needed replacing. In August Michael
McKee, General Manager of Mann Egerton in Norwich, wrote to the
Formbys discussing a new Jaguar Mark IX, in Sherwood green with green
upholstery, an automatic with power-assisted steering which George had
indicated that he wanted. McKee quoted an allowance of £1,425 for the
grey 3.4 Jaguar, most generously adding 'and when this car is repaired
and we sell it that anything made above this figure will be divided in half
between yourself and ourselves'. McKee got to know the Formbys quite
well. He had a keen interest in fine paintings, and George bought a number
of pictures from him. He remembers spending time on *Lady Beryl II* and
what fun it was.

After his two weeks off work, George had returned to a huge welcome at
the Windmill. At one of the return performances Clive Manson recalls that
not only did George overrun on time, by popular request, but, a little over-
weight, he perspired profusely throughout the evening, presumably a side
effect of his heart condition. 'A fabulous season, in which every Windmill
house record was broken,' was how Jack Jay summed up that period as the
show closed in September. George for his part said that for the thirty-eight
years he had been in the business he did not think that 'he and Beryl had
ever had a more comfortable season… they had really enjoyed themselves
in Yarmouth'. The first of the many bouquets distributed went to Beryl.
On the Formbys' return to the show she did not go on stage with George.
She allowed Bettina Richman to take her place – without any instructions,
which was quite out of character. Later on in a newspaper article, however,
Beryl was quoted at her tough and triumphant best. 'For years now I've

Above: George was feted on his arrival back after his road accident

Right: George with Jack Jay

Below: The Windmill - final curtain, September 1959

All photos on this page by kind permission of EDP

263

read every clause in a contract ten times over and if it doesn't make sense to me and George out it goes... He reaps while he sleeps – that's what I can always say about George.' The Formbys stayed in Norfolk to recover quietly from the stresses of the accident and the show, agreeing as on-the-spot celebrities to open a new Food Hall at Roy's of Wroxham. Neither of them was feeling well. George was having trouble with his teeth and was paying Gerald Sambrook-Sturgess to stop the pain he was experiencing, while Beryl's cheque book stubs show frequent trips to Doctor Shields in Norwich. Nonetheless she held a big birthday party at the Bure Court Hotel for her Norfolk friends, and is remembered fifty years on by one of the staff members there as a generous tipper. George, for his part, good-naturedly entertained the guests to a few of his songs.

In November he was the guest star on his friend David Nixon's BBC TV programme *Showtime*. The following day, one critic confessed that there was a lump in his throat when he heard 'those dear old songs with their outrageous double meanings... to me – and to millions like me – he recalled a sadder and happier, lost and unforgettable world'. George and Beryl then set

George and Beryl at the opening of the Food Hall at Roy's of Wroxham
By kind permission of EDP

off for a cruise to New York and the West Indies. When the ship returned to New York the Formbys stayed on and sailed the Caribbean for three months. One reason for this was that George loved it, but the second was that Beryl's health was deteriorating rapidly. About twelve months before, she had had her first consultation with Dr J. F. Wilkinson, a pioneer in his field and a director of the relatively new department of clinical investigation at the Manchester Royal Infirmary. His speciality was the treatment of pernicious anaemia and chronic leukaemia. She paid him four guineas as a private patient. She had got the best possible doctor but the news for her was not good. She was to see Wilkinson on numerous occasions as her illness progressed, and by 1959 she was visiting him in Manchester every month. She told her brother-in-law Ted that the steroid injections she was prescribed at £25 each were keeping her going, but outsiders did not know how ill she was.

CHAPTER EIGHTEEN

Oh, You Have No Idea

On New Year's Day 1960 Harry Gifford, the survivor of George's famous songwriting duo, died aged eighty-two. He had composed the tunes of some of George's most famous songs – 'Fanlight Fanny' and 'The Window Cleaner' amongst them – during a career which began before the First World War, writing songs for Marie Lloyd and other music hall stars. His songwriting partner Fred Cliffe had died in September 1957 aged seventy-two. At the time Beryl wrote to his son:

> It was with deep regret that we heard about your father. Both George and I are more than sorry for there is no doubt that your father was a clever man and he will be missed by many. I know that George and I will miss him very much.

It was not only a personal loss. As George's other favourite songwriter, Fred Godfrey, himself a one-time collaborator with Gifford, had died in 1953, the loss of all his old composers made it the more difficult for George to find suitable new material. Eddie Latta had a theory which suggests that maybe George wasn't looking very hard anyway.

When you get on a bit he couldn't be bothered with a new one, because very often with a song, you put it in and it's good, but there's little things that need altering or strengthening and when you're young and you're fighting – you'll do it. But when you're getting on you think, Oh well, let's go back to the others.

And by this time George was a very sick man. It was eight years since his heart attack, and, remembering his father's lingering illness, it haunted him. Both he and Beryl referred to his coronary thrombosis respectfully, if not laughingly, as 'Mr C.T.'. He suffered from recurrent stomach problems. He also knew that Beryl had terminal cancer. Wee Georgie Wood remembered George telling him that Beryl was ill when they were in Australia as early as 1947. In that year a benign uterine tumour was discovered, and in February Beryl had been admitted to a Norwich hospital for observation and tests, remaining there for two weeks. It is not clear if the two illnesses were related – Stan Evans estimated that Beryl had been seriously ill for three years rather than thirteen – or how much *she* knew of her prognosis.

In May George cut his last disc, on the Pye label, the ironically titled 'Happy Go Lucky Me'. It was eight and a half years since George had been in a recording studio. He told Peter Evans that it had been a hard decision to go back. 'You get to the point where you get scared. I don't want to sound big-headed or anything, but when you've been at the top as long as I have you have a sort of standard and reputation to keep up. I would rather never work again and let people remember me the way I was then than disappoint them now.' The record was made in one take. He was asked if he wanted to hear the playback. 'No,' he said as he was leaving, 'it'll be all right.' This, the only 45 rpm of his career, entered the pop charts in July, reaching number forty. The following month he opened at the Queen's Theatre, Blackpool, for his summer show *The Time of Your Life*, at £1,500 a week (£25,700), a big salary for a man who could still pull in the holiday crowds into the late autumn. He had not done a Blackpool season since 1954 and was aware that some people might think this one was a mistake. As he himself put it, 'Why dig that old corpse out of his grave?' The answer was, apparently, to prove to himself that he was still a box office draw. A BBC TV programme of the show was broadcast in July with George singing four songs including, as ever, 'Leaning on a Lamp Post'.

He also began negotiations with Tommy Steele, who was playing at the Opera House, Blackpool, to see if he was interested in portraying the young performer George in a film of his life. The idea was that an unspecified child actor would be George as a boy, George himself would appear in the latter stages and Steele would do the bit in-between. George felt Tommy had the right 'toothy' look and with his hair slicked back would be just right. Tommy was keen to do it and filming was scheduled for the following year, but nothing came of it.

Beryl by this time had become very difficult. According to Arthur Askey's memoir, George would 'pop into his room for a quick drink if he could shake Beryl off for a few seconds. What a life he had with her! There was no doubt as to who was the boss'. Jimmy Clitheroe, who had played George's young brother in the 1942 film *Much Too Shy* and had been with him in Australia in 1947, was on the same bill. He recalled Beryl berating him for

Jimmy Clitheroe with George and Beryl in Australia, 1947.
They had worked together on Much Too Shy

getting the biggest laughs. She complained about him to Jimmy Brennan, the manager of the Queen's Theatre, who was so annoyed by her rudeness and her drinking that he threatened to cancel George's contract if she didn't leave immediately. This time she did as she was told and went home. In reality she was too ill to stay. George, too, was feeling ill. Billy Winsor, a comedian on the same bill, claimed he had a heart attack during the show's run but was able to fulfil all his performance obligations with the precaution of a doctor standing by. The whole business was hushed up and not reported in the papers as he wanted to carry on with the show. Perhaps he also wanted to 'carry on' with another of his colleagues, the blonde, buxom and glamorous singer Yana, a former hairdresser whose real name was Pamela Guard. He had been a friend of hers for two or three years, according to Harry Scott. Given George's state of health it's not clear quite what the nature of this 'friendship' was. He told Askey that these were the happiest eight weeks of his life. Yana would visit George in his dressing room, if Beryl was not around, to 'cheer him up', and George would accompany her back to her rented flat after the evening show.

George invited Jack Jay to come to Blackpool to discuss a play that he wanted Jack to put on at the Windmill. Beryl had been taken into hospital for tests and he suggested a meal cooked by Harry at his home in St Anne's. Yana – who had been given a little boxer puppy by George – and her manager were also there. 'We had a fantastic meal, wine was flowing and we all got a bit tipsy. Harry Scott said to me, I've never seen anything like it, we've never had parties like this... old George, he's like a schoolboy isn't he?' George seems to have told Beryl about Yana, her response being, 'Let him play, he's only like a big boy really.' Her tolerance was an insult in itself.

His mother Eliza later spoke of this period of his life:

> The last time I saw him work on stage was the last night of the Queen's, Blackpool 1960, and the opening. I went to all the openings, unbeknown to him some of the times. And then I would go round to the back of the stage and then surprise him. And he always used to say, 'Well, what did I do that I shouldn't have done, and what should I have done that I didn't?' Lots of

friends used to take me over to see him, thinking I had influence to [take] them backstage to meet him, they liked it you know – but he was a very bashful man really about anything like that; he liked the public, he used to say if it wasn't for his public he wouldn't be where he was. But he was rather a bashful man if any strangers went in, for the first few minutes, until he had got over it. His family's always idolised him and I adored him. My children knew I did, I was so proud of him, very proud of him – I admired him, and he knew I did.

George's last television programme, *The Friday Show*, broadcast on 16 December 1960, was a gripping thirty-five minutes. George said beforehand that he was terrified of this one-man show, but he worked the newer medium almost as well as he had live theatre. Facing camera and establishing the same connection with each and every viewer as he had on stage and in his films, he told his audience about his upbringing, confessing that he could not read or write very well and was a bad speller. A film clip from the set of *George in Civvy Street* shows George, with Beryl alongside him, reading somewhat hesitantly from his script. Beryl listens, then explains and interprets the sentence for him. No doubt the fact that George received little formal schooling after the age of seven, at which point he left home, hadn't helped. Many people would struggle to achieve adult reading fluency in similar circumstances. He may also have been too modest: his handwriting was mature and accurate, though it was the careful, studied hand of the occasional writer. He probably got no pleasure from writing. But he read well enough – just – to function in the world, and by modern standards wrote legibly, if not neatly. His business correspondence, of course, was the province of his willing wife. He was not, as has been said, illiterate.

It was of Beryl he spoke next, obviously moved, and of his gratefulness to her. He regretted, he said, not having children. He expressed deep affection for his father's memory and satisfaction that he had died the way he would have wanted to. Tears came as a recording of George senior singing 'Standing at the Corner of the Street', made fifty-three years before, was played. During the song, George seemed unaware that the cameras were on him and looked deeply sad. Back to performing mode, the familiar smiles were a little forced and tired. Singing songs associated with different phases of his career between the chat, his performance was a tour de force. Afterwards the BBC had the largest number of telephone calls about a programme they had had for years, the viewers wanting to congratulate him.

Harry Scott, who with the help of his wife, Cis, was nursing Beryl at home, described the scene at Beryldene. As she could no longer take solid food Beryl was very weak, but rallied before the broadcast, making up her face, doing her hair and putting on a pink satin bed jacket with a careful selection of accompanying jewellery. Though excited, she 'tapped her eiderdown in irritation at some remark she didn't exactly appreciate. She was always George's severest critic'. The day after the *Friday Show*, in the evening, journalist Gerry Nicholas phoned Beryldene, hoping to speak to Beryl. 'Instead what I thought was a child's voice answered, a little voice, and it said "Hallo," and I thought it was somebody joking. "Who is that? May I speak to Mrs Formby?" and this voice said, "I am Mrs Formby," and I said, "What's the matter?" and she said, "You won't keep me long, love, will you, I'm very, very ill," and I said "I'm sorry Mrs Formby, is Mr Formby there?" she said "No." I said, "Do you know where he is?" She said, "I don't know and I don't care." I think that she was forlorn… she sounded to me like a woman who had abandoned the very last thing she believed in.'

The strain of Beryl's illness was wearing George down and her visible decline was utterly depressing. He needed distance and an escape. Despite the fact that he had said in 1958 that he could no longer do a panto season, as two performances a day was too much, he asked his doctor's advice and was given the go-ahead. On 19 December, just before the pantomime run began, and with Beryl fading fast, they made their wills, each leaving everything to the other. Then George opened in what was to be his last pantomime, a special version of *Aladdin*, in Bristol, in which he played Mr Wu. Harry Scott recalled that there had been some discussion about the venue, which was two hundred miles from St Anne's. Nottingham would have been much nearer if George had had to drive home in an emergency. But he had played

Nottingham a few times and thought a new region might be better. Despite the lavish sets and costumes the reviews were muted. The high spot of the show was George's sole turn with the ukulele.

From Bristol George phoned home several times a day, trying to encourage Beryl with talk of the cruise he had booked for them after the pantomime was over, but on about 21 December she lapsed into a coma. George was told that the end was near during the interval of the show on Christmas Eve. He carried on with the second half before he drove north, stopping for a break, as he frequently did, at the home of Fred and Jessie Bailey in Warrington. He had just arrived when the phone rang at about 2.10 a.m. 'I know, Harry,' he said before Scott could tell him the news. Beryl had died at about 1.30 a.m. on Christmas Day 1960, of uraemia, heart failure and pernicious anaemia. His younger brother Ted described George's behaviour in continuing to perform right to the end as 'heartless. She gave all her time and her life for him'.

Eddie Latta remembered George's comments the following day.

> George told me, 'They've all been on to me, the whole shower.'
> That's true, they're his actual words.
>
> So I said, 'Well, I've rung up, George, about your mother.' (This was on Boxing Day.) 'Your mother is talking about coming through, do you want her to come through?'
>
> 'Oh yes,' he said, 'I'd love to see Mother.'
>
> I said, 'Well, you don't want her to come down on the train at half past seven on a Boxing Morning?'
>
> 'Oh no,' he said. 'Look after Mother, send her.'

Eddie organized for her to go in a friend's car. Two days after her death Beryl's body was cremated. 'There were just 15 mourners at Beryl's funeral. Her ashes were scattered, and there is no plaque, no statement anywhere that she was George's wife', Stan Evans has written. Clearly he thought this was a sad state of affairs, but it may have been her wish. In the crematorium George sat next to his mother. According to a *Daily Express* report, at one point during the service he buried his head in his hands and wept. 'Goodbye, pal' was the inscription on his flowers, a phrase which has been criticized for its apparent lukewarmness, but such an understated, laconic expression is typical of a northerner. It was also the way his father, with great affection, had often addressed his much-loved Eliza, George's mother. George must have heard it from childhood and it may have had special meaning for him. An hour after the funeral he set off with Harry Scott for Bristol, to prepare for a matinee the following day, 28 December. George told him: 'I am going to do lots of work. It's all I can do.' On stage again, he nonetheless had a doctor in attendance in the wings, a sad reminder of the role long ago played by George's mother in looking after her terminally ill husband.

Much ink has been spilt in discussing Beryl Formby's character and most of it has been aimed at showing that she was a snob, a shrew, a bully, and towards the end of her life, an alcoholic. She has been accused of controlling George to the point of locking him up, forcing him to exist on five shillings a day 'pocket money' and of forbidding him to have anything to do with his leading ladies, or indeed any woman except her. Not only Arthur Askey believed that she gave George a terrible life. Even George, after she had died, admitted that they had not 'lived together as man and wife' for the past fifteen years. Beryl has been portrayed as so ghastly that she has become a caricature, a figure of folklore: 'Wasn't he the one with the dreadful wife?' The only positive comments most of her critics have allowed are to do with her management skills. Yet some men were entranced by her. Harry Scott, George's manservant for thirty years, was one of them. In his memoir *The Fabulous Formby* he commented that 'she was more of a friend of mine than George was' and that she called him her brother. Despite their rows they were quickly reconciled. 'A marvellous woman was Beryl Formby. She was the best.'

No one in George's immediate family criticized Beryl. Ella thought that she and George were 'really ideal together. They were very happy, they had a lot of fun, they used to laugh a lot. They were inseparable really and I think they were very much in love for years'. Beryl's young brother-in-law Ted particularly had a soft spot for her. She was also very fond of him and often gave him money and presents. When she married George, 'Teddy' was only five years old and Beryl must have seemed a glamorous and affectionate big sister to him. He remembered sitting on her knee as a little boy. When he spoke of her towards the end of his long life he sounded half in love with her, and his fierce comments about Pat Howson reflect the loyalty he felt for Beryl in what he saw as her ultimate 'betrayal'. She was, he said, 'a lovely lady, an intelligent woman', and recalled her generosity, contrasted by him and by Harry Scott with George's 'tightness' with money. Beryl sparkled when she was with Ted, and it's hardly surprising that sometimes George seemed grumpy when he was there – 'something had upset his applecart' as Ted put it.

Like George, but for different reasons, Beryl lacked much of a formal education. Her clog dancing talent had meant that she left school aged about eleven or twelve to 'hoof' the circuit of music halls with her sister. Blond, slim and athletic, she was deeply desirable to her husband who was still taking pictures of her in her swimsuit when she was in her early forties. She was very successful as a dancer, but that career didn't fulfil her ambitions. In George she found her life's work, and quickly made herself of maximum use to him. Highly organized, toughened by her teenage years in the halls, intelligent and confident, she learned to type and took elocution lessons. The Lancashire dialect was not part of *her* stock-in-trade, and she would let no one despise her for her provincial roots. She recognized early the value of Received Pronunciation when dealing with men of business.

It's difficult to recapture in the early twenty-first century the shock effect of Beryl's management of George's career. Women's roles were strictly compartmentalised, and there was no stereotypical slot for a hard-headed female manager in the imaginations of most of the men with whom she cut her lucrative deals. It must have been a challenge to them to know how to respond to her, and when she showed her ruthless determination it was greatly resented. Most reacted with extreme dislike. Beryl, for her part, seems to have relished the battle. She was unswerving in her determination to draw all criticism away from George and onto herself, and she absorbed an awful lot of it. Ted recalled: 'She used to laugh, she used to say, "They say some wicked things about me." I said, do you really mind, Beryl? She said, "Not at all – have another drink."'

The price she extracted was staying very close to George indeed. There are numerous reports of George's standoffishness on film sets, of how he and

Beryl ate separately from everyone else in the canteen or even in their dressing room, Beryl cooking on a small gas ring, or even in a specially appointed kitchen. No doubt these were times when Beryl could run through George's lines with him, away from the critical glances of others. When the rushes were shown they sat together away from everyone else. They took holidays, rubbing shoulders in the isolation of their cruiser on the Norfolk Broads, every summer from 1947, 'a grand way,' in Beryl's words, 'of discovering whether you like each other or not.' Shortly after her death George spoke of her refusal to allow him to accept five boxes of records at the Queen's Theatre in summer 1960. 'Beryl was full of tricks like that – she lost me a lot of friends because she wouldn't let me speak to people, and the public thought it was me but it wasn't me. But you know, poor love, that was Beryl. She wanted to keep me to herself, that's all.'

Beryl has been accused of causing George great sadness in several important ways. An atheist herself, she was apparently unsympathetic to his Catholicism. Their childlessness has been attributed to her lack of desire for him and to her ambition for his career. After his heart attack in the early Fifties she is said to have forced him back to work when he, naturally indolent and having achieved so many remarkable goals already, would have much preferred to holiday on the Broads or potter about at home. Most of these allegations do not ring true. 'I shall always be grateful to Beryl,' were George's words only days before her death, broadcast on *The Friday Show*. The fact that, as late as 19 December 1960, when in making their wills each left everything to the other suggests that the marriage had not turned irreparably sour.

Nonetheless, Beryl's death has been widely seen as a psychological release for George. He himself said in a letter sent from the Grand Hotel, Bristol, dated 10 January 1961, to Beryl's old friend Hilda, 'She had been ill a long time and I knew it had to come but could not tell her, or anybody else. It will feel very strange trying to start again on my own but I shall just have to put up with it.' He thought that Beryl may have accepted that she was dying only in the last few weeks. The following day he also replied to a letter from Don Harvey, the manager of the Windmill Theatre, Great Yarmouth.

PRIVATE TELEPHONE EXCHANGE
BRISTOL 21645

TELEGRAMS
GRAND BRISTOL

GRAND HOTEL
BRISTOL

Don Harvey Esq.,
The Gordon Private Hotel,
73 Marine Parade,
Great Yarmouth.

11th January 1961.

Dear Don,

Very many thanks for your kind letter.
It is going to be 'tough' on my own for a while,
but I shall just have to make the best of it.
There is not much I can say to you about Beryl,
as you knew her, probably more than 90% of the
people we came into contact with, but for all
that it was a sad blow. You say you thought
the world of her, and I should think you are
the only one that Beryl really 'got on' with,
she was very fond of you.

Anyway, I shall be in Yarmouth after
Pantomime and will pop down and have a drink
with you. Yes, it is just Harry, Punch and
me now.

Once again, Don, thanks very much
and all the best,

Yours sincerely,

George .

George's last letter? January 1961

In the first days after Beryl's death the press knew nothing of any difficulties in the relationship and was immensely sympathetic. James Hartley in *Lines from Lancs* wrote, 'He will never cease to mourn the woman he so greatly loved, his constant companion and helpmate...' But it was not long before another version of George's marriage hit the headlines.

CHAPTER NINETEEN

Remember Me

In the immediate aftermath of Beryl's death George's brother Ted phoned him. Ted felt that this was a difficult and vulnerable moment for George, and he offered to come to stay with him for a couple of weeks. It was a time, he said, to have someone who loved him with him, to protect him from the likely onslaught from those attracted by his money. George turned him down. Instead he went straight back to performing in Bristol – missing only four shows between Beryl's death and her funeral. But he was driving himself too hard. He developed a serious cold which threatened to become pneumonia and went home on 5 January. Harry Scott claimed he had had another heart attack and Eliza seems to suggest something similar in an interview of the 1960s.

> I was going to see him in pantomime in Bristol in 1960 when Beryl died. He rang me up to tell me he was coming home – he had a seizure in the street you see. People thought he was pulling their leg but he wasn't. He was coming from the Grand Hotel to the Hippodrome and this seizure took all the use of his arms away.

On 15 January he was admitted to the Victoria Hospital, Blackpool. Fans sent him 200 get well letters and cards a day. Now that he couldn't bury himself in work his thoughts turned to Beryl. According to Harry Scott, George said to him, 'If only we had Beryl back. She could have what she wanted and do what she liked. Oh, just to have her back with us again.' Scott added, 'For without Beryl at his side he always appeared to be lost.'

Yana maintained that George decided to get rid of Beryldene as soon as possible, discharging himself from hospital on 31 January to organize its sale. The house was full of memories, some difficult and sad, but others, of course, happy and proud. In the attic were 120 pairs of his stage shoes, in the lounge were his ukuleles and his framed personal letter from Field Marshal Montgomery. A signed photo of King George VI stood on the piano.

Patricia Howson, whom George and Beryl had entertained to tea in Wroxham in August 1954, had sent him a get well card and then visited him in hospital. She was by now thirty-six years old. He rang her father from hospital to ask if she had married. When he learned that she hadn't, he said, 'Tell her I'm a single lad now.' He told Fred he was hoping to marry again, saying, 'I'll not ask ten years of anyone.' Pat and her father were phoned by Harry Scott and invited for a drink with George, an offer they accepted for 3 February. Having gained her father's approval of his proposal, he got into his Bentley S.2 two days later and went to see her, as she was off work that day with flu. According to the newspaper reports of later court proceedings, Pat took some persuading to accept his offer of marriage. On 9 February George took her with him to a doctor's appointment so that she could hear the doctor's opinion that if she accepted she would not be marrying an invalid.

Seven weeks after Beryl's death, and after an eight-day courtship, they announced their engagement on Valentine's Day, 1961, Pat's birthday. He clearly foresaw that some would disapprove, saying he 'hoped his friends would not begrudge him his happiness'. One seems to have done. Scott recalled that George received a phone call from Yana when the news broke and replied, 'Well, you had your chance. Now you've had your chips.' Perhaps he had actually proposed to her and been turned down. To a reporter he justified his engagement by saying that his doctor had advised him, 'It is the finest thing you can do to settle down with someone who will take care of you.' Still on the theme of being looked after, he commented, 'Put me on a ukulele or at the wheel of a car and I'd get along – but not in a kitchen!' Harry Scott recounted that George had told him, 'I have no wish to be hypocritical. There is certainly no disrespect to Beryl, as you know. I don't want anyone to put any sordid interpretation on what I have just done. I hate loneliness. I am still a sick man and Pat is a wonderful doctor in her own way, and that's just the sort of doctoring I need.'

In the rather jerky news film of their engagement interview it's possible to begin to see how the relationship worked. For once, at long last, George was in control of the situation. He did most of the talking, though it's clear that he sometimes found it difficult to express himself. Pat sat quietly and smiled for the most part, but her spirit and humour came through now and then. When George commented that she'd 'got something on her plate' in taking him on she laughingly replied, 'So have you, but you don't know it!' George described Pat's diamond solitaire engagement ring as one which had been in the family. He said it belonged once to his maternal grandmother. He also gave her a ukulele-shaped brooch in diamonds as an engagement present and a Rover saloon as a birthday present. Both of them made a point of telling reporters that they had not seen each other romantically while Beryl was alive. George commented, 'When I saw her eight days ago it was our first meeting since 1954 when the family had tea with me while we were holidaying on the Norfolk Broads.' That, of course, was the summer when the Formbys' whisky drinking had apparently got out of hand. According to a *Daily Mail* article published the day after his death, he disclosed that he had loved her since then but refused to see her because of his Roman Catholic faith, which of course ruled out divorce. Pat told reporters, 'We met recently after a gap of seven years and it all happened with shattering suddenness.' She had tried for a week to keep the engagement secret and, surprisingly in view of Yana's comment, said they intended to live at Beryldene. '"Pat shall choose a new name," said Formby. "It really doesn't bother me at all," said Miss Howson.' Later, George joked, 'I've been trying to telephone you all morning. I thought you had run off already!' He told a reporter that the doctor had told him he must not work for nine months at least and remarked that his fiancée didn't know what an old man she'd got. Despite the fact that he was still very weak and on a regime of pills, George drove Pat, her mother and two friends to the Moorcock Inn, on the fells overlooking the Ribble Valley, for a celebratory lunch.

Marjorie Proops, a famous agony aunt of the time, lent him her support the following day under the headline 'Good for you, George!' Her argument was that when a man has been happily married he pays his wife a compliment if he marries again after her death. She quoted George on his engagement day as saying, 'Beryl knew I'd never survive on my own. I'm such a helpless chap. I honestly believe that what I'm doing is a tribute to Beryl and all the happy years we spent together. And I know she'd approve.' Perhaps. Ted Formby took a different line. 'Personally I thought it was disgusting. I don't think he was in love with Howson at all; she just made a beeline for him. He had just lost Beryl and he was a naïve, vulnerable man out in the world on his own at the age of 56.' Ella put it more charitably. 'I think he really was lost when she went. Absolutely lost.' Eddie Latta also had a view. 'George… was very happy with Pat. Within five minutes it was Pat this, Pat that. You see George wanted someone to hold his hand.'

Certainly a very different picture of the Formby marriage began to emerge. 'A close friend' said it was true that Beryl 'drank considerably and that they had not lived together as man and wife for fifteen years'. According to this 'friend', George 'regarded her behaviour as being due to illness. He was tremendously patient and understanding under somewhat trying circumstances'. Then George himself, in a confessional interview to the *Daily Express*'s theatre critic Michael Walsh which may have been cathartic at the time, revealed to the world that:

> Drink got the better of her. Nothing we could do would stop her. We locked the stuff in the garage. We hid the key. We even tried not having a drop on the premises. Towards the end she would not eat. We lost all our friends because she could be so rude to them. We used to sit on each side of the fire looking at each other, Beryl in a world of her own. When we used to go on cruises people thought it was for the benefit of my health. But it was really for Beryl's. After living on your nerves for so long something is bound to go.

What he didn't admit was that he had been drinking too. Loyally, Harry Scott tried to put the best spin on the situation. 'Although neither of them at any time could be classed as alcoholics, both George and Beryl were drinking heavily in the last stages of their lives. Beryl, when the end was near, would try to keep pace with George with their favourite drink, whisky. In those days Beryl was not eating anything. The effect of the alcohol she was consuming was rather noticeable at times.' But in fact they had been drinking heavily for years.

Unfortunately the revelations in the newspaper about the unravelling of his marriage appeared only a few days after his engagement announcement, and he quickly came to regret his frankness. According to Harry Scott, 'He sat in his pyjamas in an armchair facing the sea stunned and silent. Then he said, "This shouldn't have been done to me, Harry. This should have been one of the happiest days of my life. Instead I am hurt and upset. I was married to Beryl for 36 years. I owe so much to her and now this report that she became an alcoholic and even tried to turn me against religion is simply baring my private life with her to the whole world."' The words sound unnatural, even stilted, but it's noticeable that George didn't question the truth of the reports. He merely regretted that they had been made public.

George and Pat booked their wedding, planned for May, at a small Roman Catholic country church, St Francis, Hill Chapel, Goosnargh, seven miles north of Preston. On 22 February, only eight days later, after dining at the Howsons' home, George was sitting in his car in their drive when he had a heart attack so severe that when he got to hospital he was given the last rites. In the previous few days he had had plenty to concern him apart from the negative press. He was apparently still preoccupied with the selling of Beryldene, even at a loss. Earlier on the same day that he fell ill he had paid a 'five figure price', probably £10,000, for White Lodge, a modernised Georgian farmhouse at Little Lea, near Preston, where he planned to live with Pat.

During the next few days George's mother and sister Louie visited him in St Joseph's, a hospital run by a Catholic religious order. According to Ted, one of the first things George said to Eliza was, 'There's five hundred pounds in that cupboard – you'd better have it.' His mother retorted that she hadn't come for his money but to ask him what was going on. 'What's all this bloody nonsense about? What the hell are you doing?' she wanted to know. George was uncomfortable. 'Don't go on, Mother, don't go on.'

Sheepishly, he told her not to worry; that 'something was said' and 'things had got out of hand. Word had got out' and he didn't know how to get out of the situation without embarrassment. He assured her that he would not marry Pat: he had just got rather carried away.

Eliza's memory was a little different, but the main point was the same:

> I said, 'George, you be careful.' I said, 'You know, there are always people out hunting, you know.' I said, 'You would be able to pick up anybody.'
>
> 'Oh,' he says. 'Don't worry, Mother,' he says, 'I've no intentions to get married.' He said, 'This one's got her head screwed on right.'
>
> I said, 'Well, you have yours screwed on right, never mind her.'
>
> He said, 'Don't worry, I shan't marry.'

Nevertheless the plans for the wedding went forward, just as they had done in the teeth of his mother's disapproval in 1924. On Monday, 6 March, as George and Pat were sitting hand in hand, and, just minutes after she had shown him the wedding ring she had bought that day, George suffered another heart attack. She saw the sudden change in his condition and called for help. A doctor was called and the matron, a priest and a nun also came in, but, 'with a dreadful hacking cough', George died. He had survived Beryl by ten weeks.

★★★

The hours after the death were extraordinary. According to Eliza, she was not told and had to hear of it in the evening on the radio. She told Kevin Daly in 1962 that she learned later that her son had died at about quarter past four. She arranged to go to the hospital at ten o'clock that night to bring the body home to her house.

Harry went, that was his manservant, he should have sent for me... And by quarter to five that body was out of that hospital, taken to the parlour and being embalmed without my permission... She was having him embalmed and was going to have him buried in Preston without my permission. And without me knowing.

Comment on the wretched period after George's death has focused on Eliza's fight for some of the money. But her words were at least as much about the emotional hurt she had suffered. 'Nobody was allowed to go near him when she met him... She broke my heart.' The day before George died Pat Howson didn't visit him. Eliza wanted to know, 'Why didn't she say "I'm out playing golf today, would you like to come and sit with your son?"'

George's sister Ethel turned up at Beryldene within hours of the death amid rumours that money was in the house. It was said that George had a stash of £60,000 in 'the suitcase' under his bed. If he had, it was never found. According to his brother Ted, this was because Ethel got drunk with Harry Scott and they shared the money between them. But perhaps that wasn't quite what happened...

The *Daily Mirror* of 8 March announced 'Mix up over Formby funeral'. Pat had assumed that she would be organising it and contacted a local firm. This was extremely high-handed given that Eliza was George's next of kin. She said in 1970 that it had meant a lot to her that George had re-found his Catholic faith with her and the service was planned to be at St Wilfred's Roman Catholic Church, Preston. But Eliza was a Roman Catholic too, and, understandably, had other ideas. On the Tuesday she personally registered his death in Preston, then had George's body taken to Liverpool. She rearranged the funeral to be at her own parish church, the undertaker being Bruce Williams (George's one-time songwriter Eddie Latta). The paper blandly commented 'Everything has now been sorted out in an amicable way'. It was a deeply ironic remark.

By coincidence, two famous 'Lancashire lads' were buried on Friday, 10 March 1961. Sir Thomas Beecham, the popular conductor and impresario, born in St Helens, was laid to rest in Surrey. George's funeral was at eleven o'clock, a Requiem Mass said at St Charles' Roman Catholic Church, Aigburth Road, Sefton Park. Some of the crowd were at the church two and a half hours before the service was due to begin. The entire two miles from the chapel of rest was lined with people. Eliza, by now eighty-two and almost blind, leant on Frank's arm as she approached, carrying her white stick and crying quietly. Some women also burst into tears as the coffin was carried into the church. The crowd surged forward and police had difficulty in keeping a clear way for the mourners. A sergeant had even to warn people to beware of crushing children. Pat, described as 'pale but composed', walked into the church behind the family group. She sat on the other side of the aisle from them. The cortège of fourteen cars then drove the seventeen miles to Warrington, to arrive at the cemetery at 12.30 p.m., a hearse filled with flowers leading the way. In a sombre echo of his father, the number of people lining the route of the funeral procession was immense – perhaps as many as 150,000 – and was controlled by mounted police. 'At Market Gate the lunchtime traffic was almost brought to a standstill by the crowds.'

The pressing crowd at George's funeral, Liverpool, March 1961

They stood, most of them women, some straining at the crash barriers and pressing up to the hearse, hushed in the cold, dry wind.

Jimmy Clitheroe, who described George's death as 'a huge personal loss', and Ronnie Hilton represented the world of entertainment. Clitheroe had worked with George on *Much Too Shy* and was also with him on the bill in summer 1960 at the Queen's, Blackpool. Among the wreaths from show business friends and colleagues was a cross of lilies, tulips and carnations sent by Gracie Fields and her husband Boris. Beside a crucifix the family's white and pink carnations and red roses for 'Our Georgie' lay on the light-oak coffin with Pat's flowers – a large cross entirely of deep red roses. Her simple card read: 'Now and always'. At the side of the grave where her husband had been buried forty years before, Eliza, dressed in black, was supported by Frank and Ted. The family came forward in turn to sprinkle holy water on George's coffin. Pat, dressed in a grey suit, a white blouse and a black hat, was one of the last, afterwards returning with her parents to their Preston home. Harry Scott carried in his arms Punch, nicknamed Willie Waterbucket, George's much-loved Lakeland terrier, his companion for sixteen years and now to be in Harry's care.

The Formby family at George's funeral

The funeral has been depicted as something of a battleground, with George's mother openly hostile to Pat. She is said to have referred to Pat as 'George's floozie' and on another occasion 'that fucking floozie', a slur fiercely, and reasonably, rebutted by George's brother Ted. It's highly unlikely that a woman of Eliza's generation would use that adjective, though Ted's rendering of her speech suggests that she did swear now and then. Eliza herself said that Pat spoke to her at the graveside 'to offer her condolence to me. I said, "Why? Why? After he's dead?"' Ted remembered it differently. He said that after the funeral Pat approached the car with George's mother – and Ted – in it and asked to speak to her. Eliza declined, but politely and with dignity. Newspaper reports revealed that less than an hour after the interment the family gathered at a Warrington café to hear the contents of George's will. It had been drawn up and signed only a fortnight before, on 23 February, the day after his coronary thrombosis at Pat's house, while George was in hospital. It was his third will in three months. Harry Scott was left £5,000. George left everything else – declared at probate in August as £135,142 5s. 9d. (£2,240,000) – to Pat, to the outrage of his family.

Ted was very bitter about Pat's inheritance because he felt that George should have provided for his mother. The day after George's funeral the *Daily Mirror* quoted him as saying:

> It is a terrible shock to know mother has been left out of the will. I got the impression that she would have been looked after and I can't think how my brother could have done this thing… The family will contest the will and I shall begin legal proceedings. What we want to know is whether the drugs given to George in hospital as part of his heart treatment could have affected him. We don't want to start a squabble – George's memory is good enough for us. But I am a working man with three children. Then there are my sisters, Ella, Ethel, Louie and Mary, and my brother Frank.

Ella maintained that George was mean. 'George was very tight-fisted and we did wonder why he didn't ever help us.' From the perspective of the family, the 'gold-digger' that Beryl had always feared would ensnare George had appeared as soon as she was unable to protect him. In Pat's defence, no one could have been less like the stereotype.

Predictably, there was an avalanche of comment following George's death, largely centring on the sensational last few weeks. Stan Evans took the view that George was perhaps hoping for children with Pat, but, 'The switch was too quick. He was grabbing at straws.' *The Times* obituary described his stage persona. He was 'a good-natured, foolish (but not witless) chap' and 'a music hall professional of genius'. The *Daily Mail* guessed that George's fortune might amount to £250,000, including the almost £20,000 left by Beryl to him. Reporters managed to get a statement from Ethel, now Mrs Corless and the wife of a publican in Liverpool. 'We certainly don't want any squabble over money matters so soon after George's death, but if there has been a change in the will to our disadvantage we shall certainly contest it seriously.' She revealed that she had seen George at his home about a month before and he had told her that his mother and sisters would receive bequests in his will. 'Four days before he died I saw him again and he made no mention of any alteration to the will.' It was said later in court that George had discussed with Ethel the possibility of his going into business with her and her husband on his retirement. It would be reasonable to think, however, that Mr and Mrs Howson might have asked, on the engagement of their daughter, what provision George was planning to make for her, given the state of his health.

As George's will was in dispute, an auction of George's and Beryl's home and effects was inevitable. Pat began to arrange it, and the sale lasted three days, from Tuesday to Thursday, 20 to 22 June 1961. At the last minute £30,000-worth of furs and jewellery were withdrawn from sale 'by the joint agreement between Formby's fiancée Miss Pat Howson, his mother, Mrs. Eliza Booth, and his three sisters'. Pat maintained that they were gifts to her, but a later report said that they would remain in the custody of John Crowther, the executor, until 'the final details of ownership' were decided.

Thousands of people queued and police were drafted in to control the crowd. Entrance was strictly by catalogue. Gerry Nicholas found the whole business extremely depressing. 'It was almost like the *Marie Céleste*... everything had a look of abandonment about it. The curious were there in their hundreds... and everything, but everything, was exposed, right down to his socks and his underwear.' Eliza had asked if Ted could have George's clothes and shoes as they would fit him perfectly, but her request was turned down. In a marquee set up in the garden, at noon on the first day, the smoke-green Bentley, with only 2,200 miles on the clock, was sold. Peter Suckling was despatched by his employers, a garage in Mayfair, to Lancashire to 'not come back without the registration number GF 1'. He secured the plate for £250.

George and Beryl had kept an extremely comfortable household, laden with china, glass, silver and plate, linens and blankets. It was furnished with expensive Chinese carpets, silk and brocade curtains and heavy carved furniture in oak, walnut and mahogany. Among many items utterly typical of a middle-class home in the mid-twentieth century were some exceptional lots: the embroidered mandarin's robe worn in *South American George*, for example, went for £17 10s. Then there were the 'framed personal letter from Tactical Headquarters, Eighth Army, to the deceased, by direction of General Montgomery'; as well as 'a pair of tall cut tumblers etched "G.R. 1918", and a star cut wine glass etched "G.R."'

George said more than once that he made the money and Beryl spent it. The list of her jewellery shows that when she did she spent lavishly. 'An exquisite diamond bracelet' of 284 stones, and a 'fabulously beautiful set of diamond and ruby jewellery comprising bracelet, spray brooch and pair of earrings' were but two of nineteen lots described in capital letters in the catalogue. Beryl's platinum wedding ring was there, as well as a 'platinum eternity ring with eighteen matched diamonds each of approx. a quarter carat'. One of the most sensational items was a 'superb heart-shaped single stone diamond ring, the stone in excess of 5cts, set in platinum and with ruby-set shoulders'. A list of ten fur coats and jackets; mink, ocelot, Persian lamb and Russian ermine completed Beryl's personal estate.

For a man 'allowed to spend only five bob a day' George had also managed to acquire a lot of material goods. His cigar cupboard contained five caskets of cigars, many from Havana and Jamaica. His clothing, 'Much of which is new and unworn', comprised over 150 shirts, 16 pairs of pyjamas, 84 pairs

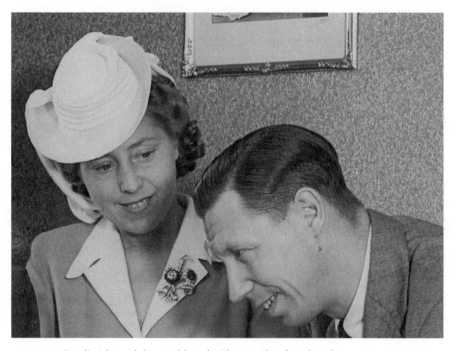

Beryl's ruby and diamond brooch. Photographs often show her wearing it

of new socks, 227 ties and 19 pairs of trousers. Among over forty-five pairs of shoes were eight in brown suede. Lot 788 was '8 various ladies' feather-trimmed hats and a gents. trilby hat'. Nineteen ukuleles were listed, among them the named instruments which George had played on the recordings of his most famous songs. There were two so-called Golden Banjoleles, the one which George had used on 'The Window Cleaner' record reaching the highest price – £145. To the applause of the crowd as she gave her name, Joy Formby, the wife of George's brother Frank bought the second, the 'Chinese Laundry Blues' banjolele, for £110. Her comment to reporters was that she bought it 'for Frank for sentimental reasons… He will use the banjolele in his act. He's always wanted to sing George's old songs, especially 'Leaning on a Lamp Post'. George's sister Ethel Corless paid £380 for a maple wood bedroom suite and a Jacobean-style dining suite designed and made especially for George. She had, she said, to borrow some of the money from friends, but she said wanted to keep some of George's possessions in the family. Despite the bitterness over the will sentimental ties were still important. At noon on the second day the house itself was auctioned. In the event, the sale of Beryldene was an anticlimax. It made only £9,000, much less than the guide price of £11,500 that George had wanted. The sale total was £22,379, with *Lady Beryl II* going to a private buyer.

In May 1961 Pat seems to have made an offer of £5,000 to Eliza, the amount she would have received from the will of 18 January. When the three months stipulated for the family's consideration of the offer elapsed, the offer was withdrawn. The ensuing legal battle between Pat and the Formby women over George's will lasted for over four years. His family argued that he had not been of testamentary capacity when the last will was made and didn't know of or approve its contents. Ted wanted to throw in undue influence on Pat's part for good measure. They counter-claimed for a will of January 1961 in which Harry Scott and George's mother received £5,000 each. In that will £1,000 had been left to the nurse who looked after Beryl and the residue was to go equally to three of George's sisters, who thus had lost by far the most in the redrafting of the will. Ella, living in America, was not part of the legal action.

Their case was weak. On 14 May 1963 Eliza settled for the £5,000 payout that Pat maintained she had always offered her, and on that day the action was declared to be over. The sisters, with much more at stake, wanted to carry on their fight. But by the end of the day and after an adjournment for an hour's discussion they too had conceded, accepting payments of £2,000 each. Some of the issues raised in court showed what the family thought of Pat and how their counsel sought to depict her. Her solicitor, John Crowther, was asked about gifts of jewels and furs received by her from George to the value of £6,540, (£108,000) these in addition to a payment to her of £1,000 and the gift of a Rover. The jewels and furs had been Beryl's, while the money was to cover Pat's living expenses before the wedding, as she had given up her teaching job at George's request. Crowther, who had drawn up Beryl's will as well as George's, denied all knowledge that George had been given a shot of morphine that morning and another, to alleviate a paroxysm of pain, just an hour before he signed the third will. He did not know that a doctor had instructed that George should have no visitors or telephone calls that day. He was unsurprised by the change in the provisions of the will because a month earlier George had left the residuary bequests to his sisters 'with reluctance', describing his family as 'a set of scroungers' to explain why he had left them nothing in his final will.

Crowther had asked George if he wished to make provision for his mother, but was told that he had already bought her a block of flats. This remark was used by the family to suggest that George was confused and incapable of making a will, as in fact it was his father who had bought the flats for his mother, and she had drawn income of £4 a week from them over the last forty years. Crowther had also wanted to establish whether George wished it be a condition under the will that Pat should receive the bequest only if they were married. 'His reply was most emphatic. If he were to die tomorrow, he said, he wanted Pat to have everything – she had brought him more happiness than he had ever known before.' Reference was made to letters found in George's possession from members of his family asking for financial help. 'I am not suggesting for one moment that these letters show that the description of scroungers is applicable to members of his family. What they [do] show is that some members sought help from him and that he had a certain resentment that greater demands were made upon him than ought to have been.'

The solicitor said that when he went to see George that February evening he was watching *Sea Hunt* on television. He saw no sign of special circumstances which would call for a doctor's attendance – 'he was only interested in Mr Formby's mental capacity'. He said, 'There is no doubt in my mind he knew what he was doing. His attitude on all the occasions I saw him was consistent – bright, cheerful and alert.' On 15 May the *Daily Mirror* was stating that Pat would be 'richer by £60,000' after all the costs of the court case and death duties on George's estate were paid. It was also said that the marriage was to have taken place in 'a few days' – in March, not May. Tantalizingly, the *Daily Express* reported: 'Certain articles, Mr Crowther agreed, were removed by Miss Howson from Formby's house Beryldene the morning after Formby's death. He added: I was more concerned with a suitcase taken from the house containing money.' Ah, the suitcase. But what *did* Pat remove from Beryldene on 7 March? Eliza told Rex Blaker in 1967 that her husband had 'started to write his own life and it was among Pat

Howson's stuff'. Was that one of the things she took away?

By 1965 Pat was feeling very low. She described her brief time with George as 'a lifetime in a few weeks', but her troubles dragged on. George's family had decided to appeal against the decision of May 1963. Twenty thousand pounds had been spent on legal charges and she approached her MP for help. She spoke of desperate unhappiness and the 'intolerable mental strain' she was under. She had not been able to work for two years after George's death and had then returned to part-time teaching, so, she said, she needed the money. This prostration doesn't ring true. Why did she feel such incapacitating grief for a man she had known well for only a few weeks? Part of the delay was actually her responsibility. As she had changed solicitors 'a number of times' this had contributed significantly. At last, in September 1965, the family's appeal having been rejected, the case was over.

Five years after George's death his mother was said to be 'flat broke'. Mrs Booth variously said that most of her money went in legal fees or that she spent it to buy the semi-detached house in Stechford, Birmingham, where she and Louisa were living. Louie, aged nearly sixty, was working as a shop assistant in Birmingham for £7 14s. 6d. (£99) a week. They had also hoped to make money from two racehorses but, having spent over £2,000 on training and stabling, they 'never won a penny'. Eliza reflected that she had raised large sums of money for charity in the past but she now was facing hard times. The hard truth was that, as Ted said, 'She always thought she was a very good businesswoman, but of course that wasn't true.' Pat showed them no sympathy. 'George never had any time for them.'

★ ★ ★

Who were the men behind the myths? George junior's personality is as elusive as his father's was obvious. Formby senior took on the world with relish and unshakeable self-confidence. He was not intimidated by his hard beginnings or the illness that would kill him. He brazened out the consequences of his secret crime all his life, changing his family name and adopting a stage name to bury his tracks, creating his own life story to protect himself and his family. The myths around his son were quite different. Behind the onstage matey manner and broad grin was a shy man, who didn't mind or even positively welcomed, for most of the time, the elaborate shield constructed and maintained by Beryl between himself and the rest of the world. Not only his brother Ted thought that he was introverted and taciturn – unable to express himself confidently or fluently. Gerry Nicholas described him as an 'almost monosyllabic man, easily frightened by questions'. It has been said that as a child at the stables he was solitary, even lonely, and he may never have overcome the experience of being cast out from the family to face the world on his own at the age of seven. His inner loneliness of the soul was always there, but Beryl ensured that he would never have to be on his own again. Until her death, of course… His bereavement may have involved complicated feelings, but it could not possibly have been over when his deep need for companionship – and nursing – drove him to contemplate a hasty second marriage with all the stresses of will-changing, house-buying and wedding preparations which would have tested a much stronger man.

It would be easy to characterise George as the clichéd 'man of simple tastes'. In fact some of his tastes were expensive and luxurious, if conventional. His material possessions were the visible reminders of his success and served to buttress his fragile ego. It has been said that his audiences thought they knew him, but his friends were certain that *they* didn't. Too many people in his own lifetime and since have confused his gormless stage persona with the man himself. He may not have been the world's greatest actor, but he did his job almost too well. Those who lived and worked closely with him knew at least that *that* was not the truth. He was quite capable of sticking up for himself. His sister Ella, writing to Stan Evans in 1990, had clear memories of her elder brother as a young man. 'When I think of George I realise he was an artist. He was not a bit funny off stage, he was not meek, and he had to be top dog. Sunday nights we would all play cards for halfpennies. He'd get mad if he lost.' During the war he didn't shirk controversy, publicly criticising his fellow artistes more than once as well as the 'top brass' for hogging the best seats at his shows. Eddie Latta thought him 'a hard-headed Lancashire lad'; quite capable of using his friends to his advantage if it suited him, and ready to buy businesses and property for profit. Harry Scott, who saw more of him than most, was convinced that George was every bit as ambitious for himself as Beryl was for him. 'There has never been a shrewder professional in his own line than Formby,' he maintained.

George was well able to take command of a situation and of his wife. Scott recalled him saying, angrily, 'I'm the comic in this business. My job is to make the brass by going out there on the stage. Beryl's job is looking after the contracts and the engagements. Your business, Harry, is to look after my clothes and get the music, the ukes, and the banjos out before I go on the stage.' He kept his end up in rows with Beryl and was quite prepared to tell her what to do. Once, a star-struck fan at the stage door heard him say, coldly, 'Take the dog and get into the car.' Beryl went without a word. But the golden leashes, which had kept him free to do his job and indulge himself with his expensive 'toys', were eventually drawn too tightly even for him. By the time of Beryl's death, her illness and its consequences had worn him out and depressed him. Conversations by the fire had degenerated into silent drinking sessions, both downing more whisky than was good for them.

What was George's appeal? Those who knew him believed that it was his unchanging nature in the face of success and wealth. His film persona gave encouragement to the plain, shy and/or accident-prone underdogs among his audiences. His popularity in the Thirties reminded them during the war of the 'British' values of honesty and bravery. Max Bygraves described him as 'a really lovely guy' who 'did as much for morale in this country during the war as any of the great leaders. He was born a man of the people and stayed that way all his life. The people themselves loved him for it'. Bob Monkhouse's view was that 'he was cheeky but totally inoffensive, with a permanent air of innocence about him'. Gerry Nicholas said of him, 'He was optimism personified.'

EPILOGUE

We've Been a Long Time Gone

'Wherever ukuleles and banjoleles are played it will always be George Formby's name that is fondly and affectionately remembered.' The words of Bill Logan, a founder member of the George Formby Society and its first president, spoken at the end of the first meeting, provide the perfect answer to George's anxious question. 'If I'm not there in the limelight do you know if people will remember George Formby?' The answer has been a very clear 'yes'. Shortly after his death four of his ardent fans founded the George Formby Appreciation Society (to become the George Formby Society within months), a friendly, enthusiastic and down-to-earth club. William Logan, George Wilson, Kevin Daly and Gerald Nicholas worked hard in the weeks following George's death to structure the Society and form an archive. According to Wilson, he and Daly bore all the early costs, though in his nomination of Bill Logan as first President he spoke of his 'invaluable help… both intrinsically and financially'. It was decided that the subscription fee should be one guinea. George Wilson was the Secretary and Kevin Daly the Custodian of the Sound Archive. Ray Bernard was Custodian of the Sheet Music. During the summer they made contact with Harry Scott, Pat Howson and Frank and Joy Formby, all of whom showed positive interest. So did John Crowther and Donald Hagenbach. Wilson and Logan attended the Beryldene sale, acquiring six ukuleles for the Society, as well as some of George's souvenirs.

The first meeting was on 16 September 1961, at Blackpool's Imperial Hotel. Frank and Joy Formby were there, as were their sons Michael and Christopher. The group hired 16-mm films, some of which had not been screened for twenty years, and showed two at each meeting. They displayed the ukuleles Bill Logan had bought, and sometimes these were played. His fans listened to George's 78 rpm records and staged members' concerts. It took eight years to compile an accurate list of his recorded songs and nine months to sort out his films. They bought his wartime newsreels. The Society is flourishing today, fifty years on, and regular conventions in Blackpool keep the Formby music and the Formby memory alive.

Pat Howson's early enthusiasm quickly cooled. Kevin Daly described her in November 1962 as not wanting to 'have anything to do with the society at all'. But she seems to have changed her mind again, as in 1969 she visited Blackpool for the March meeting, with her mother, and gave the society a large photograph of herself and George celebrating their engagement. Five years after George's death she was still living with her parents and teaching. She hoped to enter a convent, the Carmelite Monastery, Stoney Brow, Up Holland, near Wigan, but died of ovarian cancer, aged only forty-six, in the Rossendale Nursing Home, Lytham in November 1971. On one of her visits to the convent she gave the sisters a gift of a cassette player – a novelty to them at that time. Apart from a few bequests to friends and a sum of £100 for masses for the repose of her soul, she left £2,000 (£21,000) to the convent in her will. In 2008 the Prioress, Sister Teresita of Jesus, recalled Pat as 'a very kind, optimistic and loving person. When she was very ill, all she kept saying was that when she was better she wanted to come and see us. Sadly, shortly afterwards she died'. The royalties from George's films and songs had also been bequeathed to her. She in turn willed them to various Lancashire charities, including a hospice and the Lancashire Schools Symphony Orchestra.

At the time of his death George was considered 'uncool'. The times were with Elvis, the Everly Brothers and Billy Fury. A couple of years after George's death the Beatles and the Rolling Stones were creating a new teenage market for pop music. There is no doubt that the disputed will left a nasty taste in some mouths. In 1968 Madame Tussaud's finally removed George's effigy – not really surprising as he had died seven years before. But they chose to explain it to Bill Logan by referring to 'that unpleasantness just before he died and the ensuing wrangle and bother over his will'. But the next decade saw George's memory beginning to evoke a sense of nostalgia for an innocent time past.

In the early 1970s there was still a lot of interest in George's music and films. In *The Ukulele Man* (1973) Eddie Waring reminisced about the Formby career and included fifty minutes of clips from George's films. The show went out in a peak slot on Saturday evening, surprising even the director! The acclaimed Thames TV series *The World at War* (1973) included in its twenty-six episodes one entitled 'Home Fires 1940–44', showing George entertaining 'while Churchill inspires'. On New Year's Eve 1975 Max Bygraves in *I Wanna Tell You a Story*, 'a light-hearted look at 75 years of entertainment', included a film clip of George. In 1987 BBC2 ran a series of his films. *No Limit* has remained to this day a hit with the bike-racing audience and was issued on DVD in 2007 to coincide with the hundredth anniversary of the Isle of Man TT races. *Bell-Bottom George* was shown on BBC as part of their Wartime Films series, and *Let George Do It* was shown in the series of *Music Hall Greats* on BBC2.

By the 1980s Alan Randall, a George Formby impersonator, was heading a Formby revival. In 1983 he had a summer season in the musical *Formby*. But a much more edgy, alternative figure was beginning to speak of his admiration for George about this time. Morrissey, the vocalist and songwriter for the rock band The Smiths, was quoted in an interview for the *New Musical Express* in 1984. 'For me one of the greatest lyricists of all time is George Formby. His more obscure songs are so hilarious, the language was so flat and Lancastrian and always focused on domestic things. Not academically funny, not witty, just morosely humorous, and that really appeals to me.' The following year he spoke of George again. 'His songs were total innuendo. I hate anything that's totally revealed... And I like his blunt, naive Northern element – the clumsy awkward little bugger who found everything enormously difficult. That has tremendous appeal for me...' On their *Queen Is Dead* tour in 1986, The Smiths' intermission music played before gigs included George's song 'Why Don't Women Like Me?'

The Beatle George Harrison was also famously a great fan of Formby, and, like Morrissey, a fellow Lancastrian. He could recall his mother singing Formby songs at home during his childhood and he joined the George

Formby Society. He was very attached to the memory of those songs which 'you just can't sing without smiling'. In October 1991, already suffering from the cancer which was to kill him ten years later, he gave what was to be his last public performance, at a George Formby Society convention, alongside the *Spender* star Jimmy Nail and about forty other ukulele players. He arrived at Blackpool's Winter Gardens from Japan, where he had been performing with Eric Clapton, with his wife Olivia and son Dhani, an accomplished ukulele player.

At first the former Beatle watched from a balcony. But eventually, in the words of one of Formby's films, he was encouraged to 'Come on, George!' and stood modestly at the back while the assembled musicians gave a rendering of 'Leaning on a Lamp Post'. Harrison himself liked to play George's lesser-known songs and favoured 'I Told My Baby with the Ukulele'. At the meeting he was encouraged to play, and with much modesty – 'I'm not really an entertainer... I'm only just learning all this stuff' – he offered one of George's numbers, 'In My Little Snapshot Album' with 'the most chords and the most words' and 'the big solo, for Mr Formby'.

In 1995, in a video documentary series, George played a tribute to Formby at the end of 'Free as a Bird', the last Beatles' song, in a short solo from 'When I'm Cleaning Windows'. John Lennon honoured Formby in the same recording, in a postscript – the words 'turned out nice again' recorded backwards. George Formby had been part of John Lennon's childhood as his mother Julia was a big fan and herself a ukulele player. The 2010 film *Nowhere Boy*, about Lennon's early life, shows his mother teaching the teenager to play the ukulele.

When George died his association with the ukulele was so strong that when the Ukulele Orchestra of Great Britain first formed in 1985 they absolutely refused to perform any numbers by him, to emphasise that the instrument had a greater range than merely his 'daft little songs'. But recently they felt able to include 'Leaning on a Lamp Post', even if they were 'singing one song in the style of another'. Howard Jacobson wrote in *The Independent* in 2004:

Queued the other night to see the Ukulele Orchestra of Great Britain at the 100 Club in Oxford Street. Not something I normally do, queue. But I make an exception for the ukulele. I'd have queued for George Formby, though the Ukulele Orchestra of Great Britain makes a point of not associating itself with him. Nothing prudish, I think. Its argument with George Formby is aesthetic, not moral.

But even when George was being rejected his name was the touchstone of recognition for the ukulele. A *Guardian* editorial in 2008, discussing the Ukulele Orchestra of Great Britain, made the point that: 'The sound of the ukelele is somehow inherently funny – and cheering. George Formby played the (slightly different) banjolele and, along with Churchill's speeches, it was his pizzicato that kept wartime spirits, well, plucky.'

By 2007 the ukulele was taking over from recorders in schools. Children aspiring to play the guitar preferred to strum than to blow. The instruments became so popular they were unobtainable for a while in 2008. Miranda Bryant noted in the *Evening Standard* in October 2010 that even:

> City workers are taking up the ukulele as a way of relieving stress. Experts attribute its surge in popularity in the financial sector to billionaires Bill Gates and Warren Buffett who have taken up the instrument made famous by Forties film star George Formby. Last week accountancy firm PricewaterhouseCoopers held its first ukulele team-building event.

Today Andy Eastwood, a virtuoso player of the ukulele, leads tributes to George in music hall and variety shows all over the UK.

What of George's family? His brother Frank spent much of his adult life trying to carve out a successful stage career for himself. By 1971 he was fifty-seven years old, planning a show business revival by playing the ukulele and singing some of George's lesser-known songs in cabaret. 'Even without an imperson-ation or trying to be like my brother we are really so similar. This has been the terrible part about it.' Presumably he was talking about the contrasting fortunes of George's career and his own. Frank's tragedy was that he *was* undoubtedly a competent performer, better-looking than George and with a voice somewhat similar to his, but he had nothing of the warmth and rapport which his brother had with an audience. Watching him is like watching George with the soul sucked out. He was cool, held back, lacking charisma.

Meanwhile George's mother lived on. She was welcomed at the Windmill Theatre, Great Yarmouth in her ninetieth year for the unveiling of a plaque to George. The press continued to make much of her decline in fortunes. On her 100th birthday, reports claimed she would allow herself only the luxury of 'a simple home-made cake', as she sat in her 'run-down vandalised terrace home'. Eliza died a week after her 102nd birthday, in 1981. Blind for many years and with poor hearing, her mental powers were undiminished and she had insisted on casting her vote in person in a local by-election. But the walk to the polling booth proved too much for her, and she took to her bed, never to leave it again. One newspaper account claimed that her death followed a fall as she tried to get up. At the end she and Louie were eking out a frugal existence in Warrington, totally dependent on their old age pensions and Social Security benefits. Eliza was buried in the family grave.

George's mother Eliza, aged ninety, at the Windmill Theatre. The plaque is behind her.

The last survivor of the children of George Formby senior and Eliza, their youngest son Ted, died in February 2007, aged eighty-eight. After boarding school Ted went off to London at the age of fifteen to become a theatrical booking agent and worked at this until called up for war service. As his funeral Order of Service said, 'he rose through the ranks from Private to RSM, training many tank crews for action. During this conflict he lost many good and close friends whom he never forgot'. After the war he worked for Odeon Cinemas, managing some of the great picture houses of the day. It was in one of them that he met his wife-to-be, Winnie, who was an usherette. Advised to move out of the polluted air of London, he worked on a training farm in a variety of roles – 'a bloody good all rounder' as his family put it. Ted, like George, liked the simple things of life – his touring caravan, a bet on the horses, football and a pint of beer. Without his generous loan of extensive family archives and memorabilia this book could not have been written. Mortified and angry about the depiction of his brother in a previous biography, he asked, in his old age, that the record be put straight. It has been a pleasure to try to do that.

George's possessions have continued to gain value. In 1972 his 'Mr Wu' ukulele came up for sale for the first time. Pat had removed it for sentimental reasons from the Beryldene sale after George's death. But as she herself had died it was for sale as part of her estate. It sold for £310, the buyer considering it a low price. He estimated its worth at £600. It bore the inscription: 'Mr Wu Window Cleaner, George Formby January 20 1952.' The money was given to the hospital where George died, at Pat's request. In December 2007 his Norton International motorbike, desirable in 1947 and today, sold at auction for £30,582. George, in typical restless fashion, had sold it after ten months, in a deal done in his local, for £250. On 18 June 2008 George's Abbott Monarch, which he called his 'Stradivarius', and which he played on 'The Window Cleaner' and in the royal variety performance of 1937, came up for sale at Bonham's, making £72,000. Most recently, in April 2011, George's 1954 Rolls-Royce Silver Dawn, sold by him in May 1955 and still with only 44,000 miles on the clock, was sold, reportedly for £62,000, in Malton, North Yorkshire, where George had worked and lived as a jockey.

The Rolls-Royce sold in 2011

George (and his father) always paid tribute to Wigan, but the town has historically been more reluctant to return the compliment. By the 1990s Wigan council decided at long last that it could acknowledge one of its most famous sons without suffering from the ignominy of being associated with a 'daft gormless comic'. It responded to the George Formby Society's request for a blue wall plaque to mark George's birthplace. By 1998 when it was unveiled Westminster Street had long since been demolished, but it was placed as near as possible to the site, on Central Park Way. In the twenty-first century George's posthumous reputation has continued to grow. After many years of lobbying, mostly by the George Formby Society, a statue of George was commissioned for his native town. Contributions came from a wide-ranging group of people including Ian McKellen (who spent much of his childhood in Wigan), Lord Lloyd-Webber and Richard Howard, one of the present authors. The unveiling, in a shopping mall, the Grand Arcade, took place on 15 September 2007, and in 2009 it was moved to a more prominent position. Shoppers now pass by their famous son on huge hoardings as they leave the car park and meet him as they enter the mall from the Market Square. It is a pity that he is depicted as wearing a fedora rather than his trademark trilby.

George turns up in unexpected places. 'Leaning on a Lamp Post' featured in the 2003 film *Matchstick Men* starring Nicholas Cage. The tune is played as Cage waits to collect his daughter from college. *Coronation Street* writers honoured George by naming a hospital ward in the fictional Weatherfield after him. Alan Bennett, in his highly acclaimed play *The History Boys*, suggests the unconventionality of the teacher by commenting that all his pupils know the words to 'When I'm Cleaning Windows'.

A new generation of fans has discovered George's music and films online on YouTube, which at the time of writing boasts about sixty Formby-related clips, including ukulele tutorials and performances by George on film and television. The comments are for the most part hugely appreciative – 'George is cool!' 'George rocks!' On 4 September 2009 the iconic Robbie Williams appeared on the *Ken Bruce Show*, on BBC Radio 2. 'Brilliant tunes on the box set – very un-PC – brilliant. I love George Formby,' he commented. 'With My Little Stick of Blackpool Rock' was played. 'How beautiful is that?' was Williams' appreciative response. Dennis Taylor of the George Formby Society immediately got in touch and offered to teach Robbie the song.

As the writing of this book reached its final stages one of the authors was contacted by Michael Daly, the elder son of Kevin, a founder member of the George Formby Society. Michael had, just days before, launched a superb website, georgeformby.org, and was interested in finding out about a prospective new biography. When we had talked he offered us access to his transcripts of tape recordings taken by his father and Rex Blaker in the 1960s. The most remarkable of them were of Eliza, recalling in vivid detail events of over sixty years before. A story that began before gramophone cylinders and silent film is now being told through digital technology. The French poet and critic, Paul Valéry, said that 'A poem is never finished, only abandoned', and we look forward to many fruitful discussions as we compare our research and ideas online.

APPENDIX

George's Songs and Songwriters

Geeorge and Beryl bought the performing, publishing and broadcast-ing rights to literally hundreds of songs. Many of them were never recorded but used on radio and on stage, often after additions and alteration. It is impossible to know exactly who wrote many of them as informal collaboration was common. It was also a widespread habit for stars to insist that their name be added to the writing credits before they would buy a song, and that accusation has been made against George. His father was certainly guilty of it. 'Kind Words Never Die', bought from Alfred Rick for a guinea in 1904, appears on the Zonophone record label as composed by Formby, as does his two-guinea investment 'All of a Sudden It Struck Me' by Charles Yorke. There is almost certainly some truth in the same charge against George junior, but it's also fair to say that there were times when his contributions were genuine and important. Original assignment letters and correspondence between the songwriters and Beryl show how George would alter songs to suit circumstances – pantomime performances, for example, when the presence of children ruled out those 'a wee bit too blue' – or even just because he preferred his own version. Sometimes it is clear that the composers were perfectly happy to share the honours even when George had contributed nothing to the composition. Assignment letters for over 300 songs written between 1937 and 1950 show how George changed his preferences in writers, and how much money he was prepared to spend to get good material.

These assignment letters show that he acquired twenty songs in 1937, thirteen of which featured Fred Cliffe. Usually Cliffe collaborated with Harry Gifford, but he also wrote on his own and with George. The three of them claimed four songs and Cliffe and Formby worked together on another. The dominance of the Gifford/Cliffe team continued the following year with sixteen songs of thirty-three penned by them, George assisting with four. In 1939 eight out of fifteen songs bore their names. Usually George paid £10 per song for the sole rights of performance. The war years, though, saw a change. Gifford, who had collaborated with George senior on 'Bertie the Bad Bolshevik' in 1920, was sixty-three in 1941 and nearing the end of his career. The last four songs he and Cliffe wrote together for George were in that year. Fred Cliffe continued to be a favourite writer of the more risqué and punning songs but George began to trawl more widely. Such names as Eddie Latta, Roger MacDougall, and, above all, Fred Godfrey became more prominent.

Latta, real name Bruce Williams, was a Liverpudlian who advertised himself as 'Songwriter to the Stars'. His output for George was small, and he was badly paid in comparison with others, but almost everything he wrote was a winner. When Gifford and Cliffe and Fred Godfrey were earning £10 per song, Latta received only £7. He was also a generous contributor to George's Blitz Fund, donating the song 'Spotting on the Top of Blackpool Tower' in April 1941. However, occasionally the very success of the numbers brought its own reward. In June 1942, shortly after he had received a £10 bonus for 'Mr Wu's an Air Raid Warden Now', he wrote to George and Beryl:

> To say 'Thank you very much' for your letter and the cheque enclosed by you does not really convey all I would like to express. But I feel sure you know me well enough to realise how I appreciate both the kind thought and the generous deed. May 'Mr Wu's an Air Raid Warden Now' be worthy of the confidence you suggest. Have worked on the other numbers but so far cannot see any improvement. Will keep in touch if anything worthwhile comes out of the Grey Matter.

Roger MacDougall was well known as a playwright when George began buying his songs. The Formbys bought 'I'd Do It with a Smile' and 'Swing

Momma' (as it appears in the Assignment Letter) about 1939, splitting the royalties with him 50:50 and Columbia paying him £50 per song for the film rights. They were performed in *South American George*, released in December 1941. But two films earlier that year showed more of the MacDougall influence. Three of the four songs in *Spare a Copper* (April 1941) and three in *Turned Out Nice Again* (August 1941) were written by him, including the brilliant 'Emperor of Lancashire' in the latter. Three years later George acquired 'Please Mr Rees', for which MacDougall retained rights to negotiate with Associated Talking Pictures, but the song was never recorded. His brief moment in the Formby limelight was over.

Harry Parr Davies wrote for some of George's films in the late Thirties and in the Forties. He was a Welsh musician and songwriter, a child prodigy and from the early Thirties accompanist to Gracie Fields. He composed 'Sing as You Go' and 'Wish Me Luck as You Wave Me Goodbye', among other songs, for her. Writing under the name Parr-Davies, his first composition used in a Formby film was 'Your Way Is My Way', for *No Limit* (1936). With Will E. Haines, also a writer for Gracie, and Jimmy Harper he composed 'In My Little Snapshot Album' and with Roma Hunter 'Noughts and Crosses' for *I See Ice* (1938). The title song for *It's in the Air* (1939) was written by him. In collaboration with the lyricist Phil Park he produced the three songs in *Bell-Bottom George* (1944) which caused George so much trouble with the authorities. Apparently he had a phobia about doctors, dying of an untreated perforated ulcer at the early age of forty-one in 1955.

Fred Godfrey (1880–1953), like Harry Gifford, had begun his career writing for music hall stars like Florrie Forde and Dorothy Ward, his earliest-known song being written in 1906. In 1938 George bought from him the rights of 'The Blue-Eyed Blonde Next Door' and so began a professional relationship that profited them both. The following year George bought and recorded Godfrey's 'A Lad from Lancashire' and 'Lancashire Romeo', and in 1941 'Out in the Middle East'. Godfrey was paid £10 for it in return for the 'sole singing, performing, mechanical publishing and all other exclusive rights of the song', but when in 1947 he produced a new comedy version of it he could charge £100. By 1942 Godfrey's usual payment – for such hits as 'Home Guard Blues', 'You Can't Love Two Girls at the Same Time' and

'Oh! You Have No Idea' – was still only £10 a song. He was commissioned to write 'Home Guard Blues' for the film *Get Cracking* (1943). Financially Godfrey's big break in his association with George came in 1947. He was the composer of thirteen of the twenty-three songs George bought that year. He sold two songs for £200 each and 'The Other Side of the World', specially composed for George's Australian tour, for £500. On that tour Beryl commented in an interview that, 'We buy the entire song output of a man named Fred Godfrey. Some are good some are not so good, but the good ones make up for the ones that can't be used. Sometimes we "marry" two songs...' Despite this late success Godfrey left only £202 when he died in 1953, according to his grandson, Barry Norris.

The list of songs bought from Fred Godfrey (in the collection of Assignment Letters) by George and Beryl follows:

1938	The Blue-Eyed Blonde Next Door
1939	The Boys of the Young Brigade
1939	Lancashire Romeo
1939	I'm Hanging My Stocking Up for Xmas
1939	I Kept My Little Flash Light in My Hand
1940	Things Don't Alter Much
1940	You Can't Blame Me for Thinking
1941	Out in the Middle East
1941	Those Were the Days
1942	My Little Bowler in My Hand
1942	Oh! You Have No Idea
1942	Home Guard Blues
1942	You Can't Love Two Girls at the Same Time
1942	It's a Funny World We're Living in Now
1942	Bet You Wouldn't! Bet I Could!
1943	When You're in the Navy
1944	I Was Sitting in a Field All Day
1944	How Are They All at Home?
1944	She Didn't Mean To Do It – But She Did!
1944	The Little Short Shirt That Father Wore
1946	At Grandfather's Wedding

1946	Down on Our Little Farm
1947	A Little Shopping Basket on her Arm
1947	Dreaming of You
1947	Because He was as Simple as could Be
1947	My Pretty Little Dicky Bird
1947	You Can Have Some Fun in Paris
1947	The Other Side of the World
1947	I Think It's Going To Happen Tonight
1947	Waiting Underneath the Clock
1947	If I Had a Magic Carpet
1947	Bless 'Em All (special comedy choruses)
	Out in the Middle East
1947	(new comedy version)
1949	A Little Bit of Home Made Jam
1949	Fishing by the Old Mill Stream
1949	Little Willie's Money Box
1949	Extra couplets for Home Made Jam
1949	In the Middle of the Night
1949	The House with the Little Green Blinds
1949	I Keep Pretty Busy all the Time
1949	Making Up for Lost Time Now
1949	I think I Know the Answer to That
1949	The Runner Beans that Father Grew
1949	Fancy You Remembering That
1949	Fanny Isn't Fickle Any More
1949	Years and Years Ago
1950	Hello Canada!
1950	At the Beauty Competition
1950	Madame Fanella the Fortune Teller

There is an interesting background to 'I Kept My Little Flashlight in My Hand' (1939). The original song was written by a woman, Amy T. Parsons, who wrote a charming letter to George and Beryl accompanying it. The song was a gift. Mrs Parsons, of Lower Walton, told her story to the *Warrington Examiner* in November 1939. Beryl's letter to her was printed. 'George is having a go at it himself', she wrote. Authorship was attributed by now to 'George Formby, Amy Parsons, Fred Godfrey'. Godfrey was clearly given it to work on and work up for performance.

DISCOGRAPHY

78rpm, 10 inch

RECORD. NO./LABEL	TITLE:	MATRIX NO.
1926		
Edison Bell Winner		
4409	John Willie, Come On	9971–N
	I Was Always A Willing Young Lad	9972–H
4418	John Willie's Jazz Band	9966–C
	I Parted My Hair In the Middle	9970–B
4437	The Man Was A Stranger To Me	9964–B
	Rolling Around Piccadilly	9965–C
1929		
Dominion		
A 197	All Going Back	1500–2
	In The Congo	1501–2
C 347	All Going Back	1500–2
	In The Congo	1501–1
1932		
Decca		
F 3079	Do De O Do	4616–2
	Chinese Laundry Blues	4617–2
F 3219	I Told My Baby With My Ukulele	5025–1
	If You Don't Want The Goods, Don't Maul 'Em	5027–1

F 3222	The Baked Potato Man *(Not George Formby)*	5008–1
	The Old Kitchen Kettle	5023–1
F 3259	John Willie At The Licence Office (1)	5040–1
	John Willie At The Licence Office (2)	5041–2
F 3377	I Could Make A Good Living At That	5141–2
	Let's All Go To Reno	5142–3

1933
Rex

| 9878 | Chinese Laundry Blues (1932) | 4617–2 |
| | My Ukulele | 6316–1 |

Decca

F 3458	Sitting On The Ice In the Ice Rink	5532–2
	Levi's Monkey Mike	5533–3
F 3524	Why Don't Women Like Me	5530–2
	Running Round The Fountain In Trafalgar Square	5531–1
F 3615	Sunbathing In The Park	6107–1
	As The Hours, And The Days, And The Weeks,	6018–2
	And The Months, And The Years Roll By	
F 3666	She's Never Been Seen Since Then	6105–1
	Swimmin' With The Wimmin'	6106–1
F 3752	I Went All Hot And Cold	6314–2
	My Ukulele	6316–1
F 3800	The Wedding Of Mr. Wu	6313–2
	Baby	6315–2

Rex

9887	Why Don't Women Like Me?	5530–2
	Sitting On The Ice In The Ice Rink	5532–2
9959	The Wedding Of Mr Wu	6313–2
	I Went All Hot And Cold	6314–2

312

1934
Decca

F 3950	Believe It Or Not	1146-2
	In A Little Wigan Garden	1147-2
F 5183	You Can't Keep A Growing Lad Down	1200-4
	It's No Use Looking At Me	1201-3
F 5232	John Willie's Jazz Band	1542-3
	There's Nothing Proud About Me	1543-5
F 5287	The Best Of Schemes	6723-2
	Madam Moscovitch	6724-4
F 5303	John Willie Goes Carolling (1)	6737-1
	John Willie Goes Carolling (2)	6738-2

1935
Decca

F 5569	Fanlight Fanny	7172-1
	Share And Share Alike	7174-1
F 5669	The Fiddler Kept On Fiddling	7173-1
	I Do Do Things I Do	7175-1

Regal Zonophone

MR 1932	The Isle Of Man	3759-1
	Riding In The TT Races	3761-1
MR 1952	The Pleasure Cruise	3758-1
	The Wash House At The Back	3760-1

1936
Regal Zonophone

MR 2033	A Farmer's Boy	3932-1
	Radio Bungalow Town	3933-1
MR 2060	Gallant Dick Turpin (1)	3930-1
	Gallant Dick Turpin (2)	3931-1
MR 2083	George Formby Medley (1)	4053-1
	George Formby Medley (2)	4054-1
MR 2162	Ring Your Little Bell (Ting Ting)	4146-1
	Quick-Fire Medley	4147-1
MR 2199	When I'm Cleaning Windows	4186-1
	Keep Your Seats Please	4188-1
MR 2232	Sitting On The Sands All Night	4187-1
	Five And Twenty Years	4189-1
MR 2270	I'm A Froggie	4262-1
	The Ghost	4263-1
MR 2295	Dare Devil Dick	4260-2
	Bunkam's Travelling Show	4261-1

1937
Regal Zonophone

| MR 2368 | Hindoo Man | 4444-1 |
| | My Little Goat And Me | 4447-1 |

MR 2399	The Lancashire Toreador	4485-1
	The Window Cleaner (No.2)	4488-1
MR 2430	You're A Li-a-ty	4407-1
	When We Feather Our Nest	4408-1
MR 2431	Oh Dear, Mother	4406-1
	With My Little Stick Of Blackpool Rock	4409-1
MR 2469	Trailing Around In A Trailer	4445-1
	Said The Little Brown Hen	4446-1
MR 2490	Leaning On A Lamp Post	4655-1
	Hi-Tiddly-Hi-Ti-Island	4656-1
MR 2506	Easy Going Chap	4487-1
	Somebody's Wedding Day	4619-1
MR 2570	Keep Fit	4621-1
	Biceps, Muscle And Brawn	4622-1
MR 2571	My Plus Fours	4486-1
	I Don't Like	4620-1
MR 2616	Remember Me	4766-1
	Maybe I'll Find Someone Else *(Not George Formby)*	4767-1
MR 2628	You Can't Stop Me From Dreaming	4764-1
	She Can't Say "No"	4765-1

1938
Regal Zonophone

MR 2684	Does Your Dream Book Tell You That	4847-1
	Like The Big Pots Do	4848-1
MR 2709	Wunga Bunga Boo	4880-1
	Have You Ever Heard This One	4881-1
MR 2735	Springtime's Here Again	4882-1
	The Joo-Jah Tree	4946-1
MR 2752	Noughts And Crosses	4945-1
	Mother, What'll I Do Now	4947-2
MR 2753	I Blew A Little Blast On My Whistle	4879-2
	In My Little Snapshot Album	4948-1
MR 2890	Our Sergeant Major	5068-2
	Rhythm In The Alphabet	5143-1
MR 2891	They Can't Fool Me	5069-1
	It's In The Air	5070-1
MR 2925	Tan-Tany-Tivvy Tally Ho	5140-1
	I Wonder Who's Under Her Balcony Now	5141-1
MR 2947	Sitting Pretty With My Fingers Crossed	5071-1
	Kiss Your Mansy Pansy	5142-1
MR 2969	Frigid Air Fanny	5216-1
	Little Wooden Tool Shed In The Garden	5217-1
DD 444	Our Sergeant Major (Danish issue)	5068-1
	They Can't Fool Me	5069-1

1939
Regal Zonophone

MR 3022	Hill Billy Willie	5346-1
	It's Turned Out Nice Again	5347-1
MR 3039	I Can Tell It By My Horoscope	5348-1
	Hitting The High Spots	5349-2
MR 3081	I'm The Husband Of The Wife Of Mr Wu	5450-1
	It's A Grand And Healthy Life	5451-1
MR 3103	Swing It George (1)	5448-1
	Swing It George (2)	5449-1
MR 3121	Dan, The Dairy Man	5497-1
	The Blue-Eyed Blonde Next Door	5498-1
G 23917	The Low Down Lazy Turk (Australian Issue)	5499-1
	Lancashire Hot Pot Swingers	5500-1
MR 3147	Lancashire Hot Pot Swingers	5500-1
	With My Little Stick Of Blackpool Rock (1937)	4409-1
MR 3160	Goodnight, Little Fellow, Goodnight	5460-1
	Pardon Me	5461-1
MR 3161	I'm Making Headway Now	5462-1
	I Could Not Let The Stable Down	5463-1
MR 3206	Swinging Along	5530-1
	A Lad From Lancashire	5531-1
MR 3233	The Lancashire Romeo	5618-1
	Imagine Me In The Maginot Line	5619-1
MR 3301	Grandad's Flannelette Nightshirt	5620-1
	Mr Wu's A Window Cleaner Now	5621-1

1940
Regal Zonophone

MR 3316	Count Your Blessings And Smile	5797-1
	Ho! Don't The Wind Blow Cold	5798-1
MR 3324	You've Got Something There	5799-1
	I Always Get To Bed By Half Past Nine	5800-1

MR 3325	On The Wigan Boat Express	5843-1
	Down The Old Coal Hole	5844-1
MR 3358	I'm the Ukulele Man	5845-1
	On The Beat	5846-1
MR 3394	Letting The New Year In	5903-1
	Bless 'Em All	5904-1
MR 3411	Guarding The Home Of The Home Guards	5907-1
	I Wish I Was Back On The Farm	5908-1
MR 3425	Our Sergeant Major (1938)	5068-2
	I'm The Husband Of The Wife Of Mr Wu (1939)	5450-1
MR 3432	Hi-Tiddly-Hi-Ti-Island (1937)	4656-1
	Dan, The Dairy Man (1939)	5497-1

1941
Regal Zonophone

MR 3441	Thanks, Mister Roosevelt	5995-1
	Bless 'Em All (No.2)	5996-1
MR 3463	You'll Be Far Better Off In A Home	6029-1
	I did What I Could With My Gas Mask	6042-1
MR 3472	It Might Have Been A Great Deal Worse	6028-1
	Delivering The Morning Milk	6047-1
MR 3482	Formby Favourites For The Forces (1)	5993-1
	Formby Favourites For The Forces (2)	5994-1
MR 3512	The Emperor Of Lancashire	6116-1
	You're Everything To Me	6119-1
MR 3520	You Can't Go Wrong In These	6117-1
	Auntie Maggie's Remedy	6118-1
MR 3521	The Left Hand Side Of Egypt	6133-1
	Who Are You A Shovin' Of?	6134-1
MR 3550	George Formby's Crazy Record (1)	6178-1
	George Formby's Crazy Record (2)	6179-2
MR 3553	I Played On My Spanish Guitar	6176-1
	Swing Mama	6177-1
MR 3567	I'd Do It With A Smile	6132-1
	The Barmaid At The Rose And Crown	6135-1

1942
Regal Zonophone

MR 3599	Formby Film Favourites (1)	6251-1
	Formby Film Favourites (2)	6252-1
MR 3619	Katy Did, Katy Didn't	6309-1
	Frank On His Tank	6310-1
MR 3624	Smile All The Time	6311-1
	Out In The Middle East	6312-1
MR 3640	Got To Get Your Photo In The Press	6344-1
	Mr Wu's An Air Raid Warden Now	6347-1
MR 3645	Talking To The Moon About You	6343-1
	Delivering The Morning Milk (1941)	6047-1
MR 3648	Andy The Handy Man	6341-1
	They Laughed When I Started To Play	6342-1
MR 3654	Thirty Thirsty Sailors	6362-1
	Hold Your Hats On	6363-1
MR 3663	The Cookhouse Serenade	6384-1
	You Can't Love Two Girls At The Same Time	6385-1
MR 3672	When The Waterworks Caught Fire	6406-1
	The Baby Show	6407-1
MR 3689	Get Crackin'	6387-1
	Home Guard Blues	6408-1
MR 3694	Under The Blasted Oak	6386-1
	Oh, You Have No Idea	6409-1

1943
Regal Zonophone

MR 3682	Spotting On Blackpool Tower	6422-1
	Sentimental Lou	6423-1
MR 3705	British Isles Medley	6460-1
	American Medley	6461-1
MR 3710	On The HMS Cowheel	6462-1
	Bunty's A Big Girl Now	6463-1
MR 3720	If I Had A Girl Like You	6483-1
	Bell Bottom George	6485-1

1944
Regal Zonophone

MR 3723	Serves You Right (1943)	6482-1
	Swim, Little Fish	6484-2
MR 3736	The "V" Sign Song	5610-1
	The Old Cane Bottom Chair	5611-1
MR 3745	Our Fanny's Gone All Yankee	6534-2
	Unconditional Surrender	6535-1
MR 3746	Hill Billy Willie (1939)	5346-1
	Got To Get Your Photo In The Press	6344-1

| MR 3750 | Blackpool Prom | 6536-1 |
| | Mr Wu's In The Air Force | 6537-1 |

1945
Regal Zonophone

MR 3760	The Daring Young Man	6557-1
	I'd Like a Dream Like That	6558-1
MR 3761	She's Got Two Of Everything	6599-1
	Up In The Air And Down In The Dumps	6560-1

1946
Columbia

FB 3251	You Don't Need A Licence For That	20019-1
	Mad March Hare	20020-1
FB 3262	It Could Be	20021-1
	We've Been A Long Time Gone	20022-1

1950
Decca

F 9356	Come Hither With Your Zither	14521-1
	Auntie Maggie's Remedy	14518-1
F 9444	Leanin' On A Lampost	14519-1
	When I'm Cleaning Windows	14520-1

1951
His Master's Voice

B 10179	Saving Up For Sally	16093.3
	Pleasure Cruise	16094.2
B 10180	Ordinary People *(With Sarah Gregory)*	16095.3
	Zip Goes A Million. Running Away To Land *(Ward Donovan)*	16096.3
B 10181	It Takes No Time To Fall In Love	16097.2
	(Warde Donovan/Sarah Gregory)	
	Nothing Breaks But The Heart *(Warde Donovan)*	16098.3

All HMV Recordings Are From The Stage Show; "Zip Goes A Million"

78rpm, 10 inch: COMPILATIONS

1934
Regal Zonophone

| MR 1234 | Voice Of The Stars: Volume 1 (Part 1) | 2563-1 |
| MR 1235 | Voice Of The Stars: Volume 1 (Part 2) | 2564-1 |

1935
Jubilee Edition

VS 2	Voice Of The Stars: Volume 2 (Part 1)	1651-2
	Voice Of The Stars: Volume 2 (Part 2)	1652-2
VS 3	Voice Of The Stars: Volume 3 (Part 1)	15670-2
	Voice Of The Stars: Volume 3 (Part 2)	15671-1

1936

Coronation Edition

| VS 4 | Voice Of The Stars: Volume 4 (Part 1) | 16287-2 |
| | Voice Of The Stars: Volume 4 (Part 2) | 16288-1 |

1937

Regal Zonophone

IR 51	Keep Your Seats Please	4448-1
	Trailer For The ATP Picture: Keep Your Seats Please	
IR 52	Keep Fit	4675-1
	Trailer For The ATP Picture: Keep Fit	

1938

MR 2722	Voice Of The Stars: Volume 5	4943-2
	Mother What'll I Do Now (Part 1)	
	Voice Of The Stars: Volume 5	4944-2

78rpm, 12 inch: COMPILATIONS

Decca

| K 714 | The Decca A.B.C. | 6379-2 |

Columbia

| DX 820 | Command Performers | 8121-1 |

1943

Columbia

| DX 1241 | British Film Festival | 9466-3 |

45rpm, 7 inch: SINGLE

1960

Pye Records

| 7N:15269 | Happy Go Lucky Me |
| | Banjo Boy |

45rpm, 7 inch: E/P (Extended play)

1955
Decca

DFE:6144   George Formby And His Ukulele
DFE:6328   George Formby And His Ukulele No.2
DFE:6355   George Formby And His Ukulele No.3
Columbia
SEG 7550   The Ukulele Man No.1

1956
Columbia
SEG: 7661   The Ukulele Man No.2

1959
Columbia

SEG: 7936   Stepping Out With George

SEG: 7964   Stepping Out With George Again

1961
His Master's Voice

7EG: 8644   Tempos Of Time

1972
Columbia

DB.8959   Comedy Recordings (Phoenix Series)

DECEMBER 1934

33¹/₃, 12 inch: L/P (Long Play) ALBUMS

ACL 1062	George Formby Souvenir (Ace Of Clubs)	Decca	1961
ACL 1145	It's Turned Out Nice Again (Ace Of Clubs)	Decca	1963
PA 50	The World Of George Formby	Decca	1969
SPA 446	The World Of George Formby: Vol. 2	Decca	1975

George Formby: The Man With The Ukulele   EMI   1977
(Four Box Album Set)

SM 351	The Window Cleaner (Album 1)
SM 352	Leaning On A Lamp Post (Album 2)
SM 353	The Lancashire Lad (Album 3)
SM 354	The Ukulele Man (Album 4)

RFL.8	George Formby With My Ukulele	Decca	1981
AJA.5003	A Chip Of The Old Block (George Formby Snr/Jnr)	Living Era	1981

(This L/P album also issued on World Record Club WT.4860, New Zealand)

MFP.1182	The Inimitable George Formby	EMI

(This L/P album also issued on Columbia OEX 9482, Australia)

MFP.50335	George Formby (Music For Pleasure: Red Label)	EMI
MFP.1378	It's Turned Out Nice Again	EMI

(This L/P album also issued on MFP A 8189: Music For Pleasure, Australia)

SH 126	The Man With The Ukulele	EMI
SDH 151	Presenting George Formby And His Ukulele	EMI
OU 2072	The Best Of George Formby	EMI

(This L/P album also issued on SOXLP.7596: EMI His Master's Voice, Australia)

MFP.1032	Leaning On A Lamp Post (Double Album)	EMI	1983
RECDL.4	Leaning On A Lamp Post (Recollections: Double album)	Decca	1986
CMS 003	Easy Going Chap (Movie Star Series)	Conifer	1989
AJA 5079	When I'm Cleaning Windows	Living Era	1991

33¹/₃, 12 inch: L/P (Long Play) ALBUMS: COMPILATIONS

ACL 1170	Stars Who Made The Music Hall (Ace Of Clubs) *(Side 2: John Willie; Come On)*	Decca	1968
TPSM 2001	Colditz (Purple Records Ltd) *(Bless 'Em All)*	EMI	1973

(Previously released on the title 'The Shadow Of Colditz: AXIS 6273)

SH 213	Britain Can Take It (World Record Club) *(Side 1: Imagine Me In The Maginot Line)* *(Side 2: Mr Wu's An Air Raid Warden Now; I Did What I Could With My Gas Mask)*	EMI	1974
XTRA 1161	Sounds Of All Our Yesterdays *(Side 1: With My Little Stick Of Blackpool Rock)* *(Side 2: When I'm Cleaning Windows; Imagine Me In The Magniot Line)*	Transatlantic	1976
DPA 3029/ DPA 3030	This England (Double Album) *(Record 1, Side 2: Leaning On A Lamp Post)*	Decca	1976

SPA-R 502	The World Of; Your Family Favourites: Vol. 2	Decca	1976
	(Side 2: Leaning On A Lamp Post)		
NTS 222	Nostalgic Memories: Vol. 2	EMI	1981
	(Side 2: Leaning On A Lamp Post)		
DUO 126	32 Slices Of Showbiz (Double Album)	EMI	1982
	(Record 1, Side 1: Leaning On A Lamp Post)		
RFLD 30	They Played The Palladium (Double Album)	Decca	1983
	(Record 1, Side 2: Fanlight Fanny)		
JOY D 274	A Little Of This…A Little Of That	President	1983
	(Side 1: Chinese Laundry Blues)		
	(Side 2: Do De O Do)		
EG 26 0293 1	Songs And Stars Of The Forties	EMI	1984
	(Side 1: The Left-Hand Side Of Egypt)		
AJA 5030	Listen To The…BANNED	Living Era	1984
	(Side 1: With My Little Ukulele In My Hand)		
OLD 2	Comic Cuts	Old Bean	1985
	(Side 2: Chinese Laundry Blues)		
GX 4125321	Keep Smiling Through	EMI	1985
	(Side 1: Imagine Me In The Maginot Line)		
	(Side 2: Mr Wu's An Air Raid Warden Now;		
	I Did What I Could With My Gas Mask)		

(Previously released as 'Britain Can Take It'; EMI: World Record Club, 1974: SH213)

JOY D 289	Radio Personalities Of The Thirties	President	1987
	(Side 1: Ring Your Little Bell (Ting Ting))		
	(Side 2: Quick Fire Medley: It Ain't Nobody's Business What I Do; Coody		
	Goody; I Like Bananas)		
OLD 13	Comic Cuts: Volume 2	Old Bean	1987
	(Side 2: Fanlight Fanny)		
RECDL 11	They Played The Hippodrome (Double Album)	Decca	1987
	(Record 1, Side 1: Leaning On A Lamp Post)		
DL 1155	Stars Of Variety (Double Album)	EMI	1989
	(Record 1, Side 1: The Barmaid At The Rose And Crown)		
EM 1341	The Day War Broke Out (Double Album)	EMI	1989
	(Record 1, Side 1: Imagine Me In The Maginot Line)		
	(Record 1, Side 2: I Did What I Could With My Gas Mask)		
CHD 163	Radio Days (Happy Days Series)	Conifer	1989
	(Side 2: Keep Fit(Commercial trailer to the feature film))		
REB 728	Saucy Songs	BBC Records	1989
	(Side 1: When I'm Cleaning Windows)		
DL 1182	Keep Smiling Through (Double Album)	EMI	1990
	(Record 1, Side 1: Bless 'Em All)		
	(Record 2, Side 1: Serves You Right)		
	(Record 2, Side 2: Mr Wu's An Air Raid Warden Now)		
EM 1366	Britain At War (Double Album)	EMI	1990
	(Record 1, Side 2: Out In The Middle East: Mr Wu's An Air Raid Warden Now)		

CANADIAN L/P ISSUES

ACL 7903	George Formby Collection	Ace Of Clubs	
ACL 7927	It's Turned Out Nice Again	Ace Of Clubs	
ACL 7906	George Formby Souvenir	Ace Of Clubs	
SPA 142	The World Of George Formby	London	1973
T 6002	When I'm Cleaning Windows	Capital	

NEW ZEALAND L/P ISSUES

WT 4860	A Chip Off The Old Block	World Record Club

AUSTRALIAN L/P ISSUES

CMS 003	Easy Going Chap (Movie Star Series)	Conifer	1989
AJA 5079	When I'm Cleaning Windows	Living Era	1991
OEX 9482	The Inimitable George Formby	EMI Columbia	
SPA 50	The World Of George Formby	Decca	
MFP A8189	It's Turned Out Nice Again	EMI	
SOXLP 7596	The Best Of George Formby	EMI	

MUSIC CASSETTES

KCSP 50	The World Of George Formby	Decca	1969
TC-EXE 145	The Best Of George Formby	EMI	1980s
DTO 10204	All The Hits Of: George Formby (Double Cassette)	Ditto	1985
KGRS 1224	Formby At War	Grosvenor	1989
ECC 20	Turned Out Nice Again (Double Cassette)	EMI	1991
MSR CLP 139	Formby's Farewell	Mastersound	1993

MSR 141 CP	The George Formby Library: Volume 1	Mastersound	1993
MSR 142 CP	The George Formby Library: Volume 2	Mastersound	1993
MSR 143 CP	The George Formby Library: Volume 3	Mastersound	1993
MSR 144 CP	The George Formby Library: Volume 4	Mastersound	1993
MSR 145 CP	The George Formby Library: Volume 5	Mastersound	1993
MSR 146 CP	The George Formby Library: Volume 6	Mastersound	1993
MSR 147 CP	The George Formby Library: Volume 7	Mastersound	1993
MSR 148 CP	The George Formby Library: Volume 8	Mastersound	1993
MSR 149 CP	The George Formby Library: Volume 9	Mastersound	1993
MSR 1150 CP	The George Formby Library: Volume 10	Mastersound	1993
RAJMC 801	I'm The Ukulele Man	Empress	1994
RKC 23	"V" For Victory	Redrock	1995

COMPACT DISC: COMPILATIONS

CD–SDL 350	The Wibbly Wobbly Walk	Saydisc	1985
	(I Parted My Hair In The Middle)		
CC 207	Great Singers Of Yesteryear	EMI	1988
	(Mr Wu's An Air Raid Warden Now)		
DOLD 2	Comic Cuts	Old Bean	1989
	(Chinese Laundry Blues)		
CDHD 163	Radio Days	Conifer	1989
	(Keep Fit – Film Commercial*)*		
CD AJA 5020	Film Star Parade	Living Era	1991
	(I Could Make A Good Living At That!)		
KGHCD 157	A Golden Hour Of Comedy	Knight	1991
	(Happy Go Lucky Me)		
CD–DL 1131	The Sounds Of England (Double CD)	EMI	1992
	(Disc 1: The Lancashire Toreador)		
	(Dis 2: With My Little Stick Of Blackpool Rock)		
CD AJA 5030	Listen To The Banned	Living Era	1993
	(With My Little Ukulele In My Hand)		

CD HD 208	Radio Fun (*Chinese Laundry Blues*)	Conifer	1993
YULE 300	Christmas Time With The Stars (*Sitting On The Ice In The Ice Rink*)	Conifer	1994
PPCD 78100	The Great Sounds Of The 20's, 30's & 40's (*Home Guard Blues*)	Past Perfect	1994
75605 52281 2	Classic Children's Favourites (*Rhythm In The Alphabet*)	Conifer	1996
PPCD 78128	Perfect Nostalgia (*Leaning On A Lamp Post*)	Past Perfect	1997
PPCD 78130	The Sampler (*On The Wigan Boat Express*)	Past Perfect	1997
RAJDD 8002	Songs From The Shows (Double CD) (*Disc 1: Zip Goes A Million; Ordinary People; I'm Saving Up For Sally*)	Empress	2002

COMPACT DISC COLLECTION

DBCD 29	George Formby And His Ukulele "The Ukulele Man" (Australian Import)	Tempo	1988
CMS CD 003	Easy Going Chap	Conifer	1989
SDC 8083	Stagedoor	Stage Door	1989
PLAT CD 28	"The Very Best Of" George Formby	Prism Leisure	1990
CDP 7 97725 2	Turned Out Nice Again	EMI	1991
CD AJA 5079	When I'm Cleaning Windows	Living Era	1991
ENBO-CD 5/92	Americans In London 1947-1951	Box Office	1992
7243 8 27481 2 0	The Legendary George Formby	EMI	1993
RAJCD 801	I'm The Ukulele Man	Empress	1993
PAST CD 7001	His Greatest Favourites	Flapper	1993
MU3006 CD	The Best Of George Formby	Muskateer	1994
PPCD 78105	It's Turned Out Nice Again	Past Perfect	1994
CDGRS 1224	Formby At War	Grosvenor	1994
820 609-2	Formby Favourites	Eclipse	1994
PAST CD 7043	Bell Bottom George	Flapper	1994
300282	That Ukulele Man	Hallmark	1995
PLATCD 176	24 Family Favourites	Prism Leisure	1995
RKD 23 P.P.L.	'V' For Victory	Redrock	1995
PLCD 538	When I'm Cleaning Windows	President	1995
PLCD 554	At The Flics	President	1996
RAJCD 878	It's Turned Out Nice Again	Empress	1996
CD 6019	The Best Of George Formby	Music Digital	1996
EMPRCD 777	The Emperor Of Lancashire	Emporio	1997
7243 8 59087 2 9	Mr Ukulele	Sovereign	1997
PDS CD 547	The Ultimate Collection (Double CD)	Pulse	1997

PLCD 565	The Great Stars Entertain The Forces	President Records	1997
SWNCD 017	The Very Best Of George Formby	Sound Waves	1997
SUMCD 4208	The Very Best Of George Formby	Summit	1998
PLATCD 28	The Very Best Of George Formby (Reissue)	Prism Leisure	1999
544 281-2	Formby Favourites	Spectrum	2000
PGN CD 817	When I'm Cleaning Windows	Pegasus	2000
300282	That Ukulele Man (Re-issue: see 1995 issue)	Hallmark	2000
7243 5 27409 2 5	The George Formby Collection	HMV Easy	2000
NAXOS 8 12054	Let George Do It	Nostalgia	2001
MS CD 352	George's Top 20	Mastersound	2001
HALMCD 1096	When I'm Cleaning Windows	Hallmark	2001
APW CD 1198	George Formby	Musicbank	2001
MP 905068	Golden Greats (3 CD set)	Disky	2002
PLS CD 597	Turned Out Nice Again	Castle Records	2002
701812	When I'm Cleaning Windows (Import)	Hallmark	2002
PAST CD 7857	Count Your Blessings	Flapper	2002
GO 3804	The Window Cleaner	Golden Options	2002
C51	George Formby	Evergreen Melodies	2002
MP 905068	Golden Greats (3 CD set)	Disky	2002
SUN 2129	It's Turned Out Nice Again	Sunflower	2003
	Formby Goes To War	Alan Randall	2004
	V For Victory	Alan Randall	2004
	The George Formby Centenary Celebration	Alan Randall	2004
SIGNCD2476	Vintage George Formby	Signature	2004
JSP 1901 A	England's Famed Clown Price Of Song (5 CD set)	JSP Records	2004
JSP 1901 B	England's Famed Clown Price Of Song	JSP Records	2004
JSP 1901 C	England's Famed Clown Price Of Song	JSP Records	2004
JSP 1901 D	England's Famed Clown Price Of Song	JSP Records	2004
JSP 1901 E	England's Famed Clown Price Of Song	JSP Records	2004
JSP 1902 A	The War And Postwar Years (5 CD set)	JSP	2005
JSP 1902 B	The War And Postwar Years	JSP	2005
JSP 1902 C	The War And Postwar Years	JSP	2005
JSP 1902 D	The War And Postwar Years	JSP	2005
JSP 1902 E	The War And Postwar Years	JSP	2005

PDSDD 112	It's Turned Out Nice Again (2 CD set)	Sanctuary	2005
REXX 111	I'm The Ukulele Man	Rex Label	2006
CD AJS 2018	Leaning On A Lamp-Post	Living Era	2007
NAXOS 8 120837	It's Turned Out Nice Again: Vol. 2	Nostalgia	2007

SONGS RECORDED BY OTHER ARTISTS

ILP 1015	Eee! What A Whopper! (Diz Disley: Sings George Formby's Greatest Songs)	Surprise	1965
MS 3	Blackpool's Golden Mile (Eli Bickerstaffe: His Tribute To George Formby)	Miracle	1968

VHS VIDEO

Let George Do It	EMI (Thorn)	1980s
Come On George	Warner Home Video	1991

DVD

Come On George	Warner Home Video	1991
The George Formby Show	BBC	2004
The Life & Wartimes of George Formby	Mastersound	2004
George Formby: Ukulele Man	Mastersound	2004
George Formby: Formby's Farewell	Mastersound	2004

Feature Films Digitally Restored

Boots! Boots! (1934)	DD Home Entertainment	2006
Off The Dole (1935)	DD Home Entertainment	2007
No Limit (1935)	Studio Canal	2007

South American George (1941)	Columbia Pictures
Much Too Shy (1942)	Columbia Pictures
Get Cracking (1943)	Columbia Pictures
Bell Bottom George (1944)	Columbia Pictures
He Snoops To Conquer (1945)	Columbia Pictures
I Didn't Do It (1945)	Columbia Pictures
George In Civvy Street (1946)	Columbia Pictures
Comic Icons (Box set of 7 DVDs)	Studio Canal

> No Limit (1936)
> I See Ice (1938)
> It's In The Air (1939)
> Come On George (1940)
> Let George Do It (1940)
> Spare A Copper (1941)
> Turned Out Nice Again (1941)

Keep Your Seats Please (1936)	Ealing Studios Collection
Trouble Brewing (1939)	Ealing Studios Collection

OTHER DVD RELEASES OF 'GEORGE FORMBY'

The George Formby Show	BBC 1960	2004
The Life & Wartimes of George Formby	Mastersound	2004
George Formby: Ukulele Man	Mastersound	2004
George Formby: Formby's Farewel	Mastersound	2004

Van Klomph